First World War
and Army of Occupation
War Diary
France, Belgium and Germany

48 DIVISION
Headquarters, Branches and Services
Commander Royal Artillery
1 March 1915 - 31 October 1917

WO95/2747/2

The Naval & Military Press Ltd
www.nmarchive.com
Published in association with The National Archives

Published by

The Naval & Military Press Ltd

Unit 10 Ridgewood Industrial Park,

Uckfield, East Sussex,

TN22 5QE England

Tel: +44 (0) 1825 749494

www.naval-military-press.com

www.nmarchive.com

This diary has been reprinted in facsimile from the original. Any imperfections are inevitably reproduced and the quality may fall short of modern type and cartographic standards.

© Crown Copyright
Images reproduced by permission of The National Archives, London, England, 2015.

Contents

Document type	Place/Title	Date From	Date To
Heading	WO95/2747-2 48 Div HQ-CRA Apr 1915-Oct 1917		
Heading	48th Division CRA Mar 1915 Oct 1917		
Heading	Hdqrs R.A 1/1 South Midland Division Vol I 1-31.3.15 Mar 19		
Heading	War Diary R.A. Hd Qrs 1/1st S Mid Divn From 1/3/15 To 31/3/15 Vol VIII		
War Diary	Chelmsford	01/03/1915	29/03/1915
War Diary	France	30/03/1915	31/03/1915
Heading	Hd Qrs RA South Midland Div Vol II 1-30.4.15		
War Diary	France Caestre	01/04/1915	04/04/1915
War Diary	N Of France Caestre	05/04/1915	09/04/1915
War Diary	Merris	10/04/1915	14/04/1915
War Diary	Merris-Nieppe	15/04/1915	16/04/1915
War Diary	Nieppe	16/04/1915	30/04/1915
Heading	Hd Qrs RA 48th Division Vol III 1-30.5.15		
War Diary	Nieppe N. France	01/05/1915	11/05/1915
War Diary	Nieppe	11/05/1915	22/05/1915
War Diary	Nieppe N. France	23/05/1915	30/05/1915
Miscellaneous	Appendix A War Diary	07/05/1915	07/05/1915
Miscellaneous	C.R.A	14/05/1915	14/05/1915
Miscellaneous	C Form (Duplicate) Messages And Signals		
Miscellaneous	C Form (Original) Messages And Signals		
Miscellaneous	C Form (Duplicate) Messages And Signals		
Miscellaneous	H.Q 48 (SM) Div	23/05/1915	23/05/1915
Miscellaneous	O.C. 1.2.3.4 (5) 29. 2mb	07/05/1915	07/05/1915
Miscellaneous	C Form (Original) Messages And Signals		
Miscellaneous	H. Q 48 Divn.	23/05/1915	23/05/1915
Heading	48th Division Hd Qrs R.A. 48th Division Vol IV 1-30.6.15		
War Diary	Nieppe N France	01/06/1915	17/06/1915
War Diary	Nieppe	18/06/1915	27/06/1915
War Diary	Busnes	28/06/1915	30/06/1915
Heading	48th Division Hd Qrs R.A. 48th Division Vol V 1-310715		
Heading	War Diary Of R.A.H.Q 48 Division From /1/7/15 To 31/7/15 Vol XII		
War Diary	Lillers	01/07/1915	18/07/1915
War Diary	Terramesnil	19/07/1915	20/07/1915
War Diary	Authie	21/07/1915	29/07/1915
War Diary	Bus	30/07/1915	31/07/1915
Miscellaneous	Relief Of French Artillery	29/07/1915	29/07/1915
Heading	Hd Qrs R.A 48th Division Vol VI		
War Diary	Bus En Artois	01/08/1915	26/08/1915
War Diary	Bus	27/08/1915	31/08/1915
Miscellaneous	48th Div Arty. B.M. Circular No.61	27/08/1915	27/08/1915
Miscellaneous	48th Div Arty. B.M. Circular No.62	28/08/1915	28/08/1915
Miscellaneous	48th Div Arty. B.M. Circular No.64	30/08/1915	30/08/1915
Heading	Hd Qrs R.A 48th Division Vol VII Sept 15		
Heading	War Diary Of 48th Divisional Artillery Vol XIV From Sep 1st To Sep 30th 1915		

War Diary	Bus	01/09/1915	22/09/1915
War Diary	Bus (En Artois)	23/09/1915	30/09/1915
Miscellaneous	Bombardment	23/09/1915	23/09/1915
Miscellaneous	Bombardment	24/09/1915	24/09/1915
Miscellaneous	Bombardment	25/09/1915	25/09/1915
Miscellaneous	Operation Orders		
Heading	War Diary Of H.Q 48th Divl. Artillery From 1.10.15 To 31.10.15 Volume 8		
War Diary	Bus (En Artois)	01/10/1915	23/10/1915
War Diary	Bus	24/10/1915	31/10/1915
Miscellaneous	48th Div Arty. B.M Circular No. 84	11/10/1915	11/10/1915
Miscellaneous	48th Div Arty. B.M Circular No. 86	17/10/1915	17/10/1915
Miscellaneous	Bombardment A	19/10/1915	19/10/1915
Miscellaneous	Bombardment B	25/10/1915	25/10/1915
Heading	H.Q R.A 48th Division Nov 1915 Vol IX		
Heading	War Diary Of 48th Divisional Artillery Vol XVI November 1st To 30th 1915		
War Diary	Bus (Les Artois)	01/11/1915	15/11/1915
War Diary	Bus En-Artois	16/11/1915	30/11/1915
Miscellaneous	Bombardment C	03/11/1915	03/11/1915
Miscellaneous	Bombardment D	19/11/1915	19/11/1915
Miscellaneous	Enterprise For Thursday	24/11/1915	24/11/1915
Miscellaneous	Rough Report Of Action Of 3rd Sm F.A. Bde	26/11/1915	26/11/1915
Miscellaneous	Plan For Enterprise	23/11/1915	23/11/1915
Diagram etc	Diagram		
Heading	War Diary Of 48th Divisional Artillery Vol 10 Dec 1st To Dec 31st 1915		
War Diary	Bus (En Artois)	01/12/1915	31/12/1915
Miscellaneous	Bombardment E For Friday	03/12/1915	03/12/1915
Miscellaneous	48th Div Arty	09/12/1915	09/12/1915
Miscellaneous	Report On Wire Cutting By 1st S.M.F.A Brigade 10th Dec.1915	10/12/1915	10/12/1915
Miscellaneous	Bombardment F. For Thursday	16/12/1915	16/12/1915
Miscellaneous	Bombardment G. For Tuesday	21/12/1915	21/12/1915
Miscellaneous	Bombardment J For Friday	31/12/1915	31/12/1915
Heading	War Diary Of 48th Divisional Artillery Vol II January 1st To January 31st 1916		
War Diary	Bus En Artois	01/01/1916	31/01/1916
Miscellaneous	48th Div Arty. B.M Circular No.129	03/01/1916	03/01/1916
Miscellaneous	48th Div Arty. B.M Circular No.134	05/01/1916	05/01/1916
Miscellaneous	Corps Bombardment Friday	07/01/1916	07/01/1916
Miscellaneous	48th Div Arty B.M. Circular No 140	12/01/1916	12/01/1916
Miscellaneous	Corps Bombardment Thursday	13/01/1916	13/01/1916
Miscellaneous	Bombardment K Saturday	22/01/1916	22/01/1916
Miscellaneous	48th Div Arty B.M Circular No.145	20/01/1916	20/01/1916
Miscellaneous	3rd S.M.F.A Brigade Report Of Artillery Action	30/01/1916	30/01/1916
Heading	War Diary Of Head Qrs 48th Divisional Artillery Vol 12 1st February To 29th February 1916		
War Diary	Bus	01/02/1916	19/02/1916
War Diary	Bus Les Artois	20/02/1916	29/02/1916
Miscellaneous	1st. Warwick Bty. 3rd S.M.F.A Brigade	01/02/1916	01/02/1916
Miscellaneous	48th Div. Arty. B.M Circular No.150	03/02/1916	03/02/1916
Miscellaneous	Bombardment L. Friday	04/02/1916	04/02/1916
Miscellaneous	Headquarters, R.A. 7th Corps	19/02/1916	19/02/1916
Miscellaneous	Front Of The 143rd Infantry Brigade	18/02/1916	18/02/1916
Miscellaneous	Front Of The 144th Infantry Brigade	19/02/1916	19/02/1916

Type	Description	Start	End
Miscellaneous	Headquarters 48th. Div. Artillery	20/02/1916	20/02/1916
Miscellaneous	Report On Hostile Raid Carried Out By The Enemy On The Evening Of 19th. February 1916 Against Part Of The Line Held By The 2nd. Bn. Lancashire Fusiliers	20/02/1916	20/02/1916
Heading	War Diary Of Head Qrs 48th Divisional Artillery Vol 1st-31st March 1916		
War Diary	Bus	01/03/1916	26/03/1916
War Diary	Couin	27/03/1916	31/03/1916
Miscellaneous	Bombardment	15/03/1916	15/03/1916
Miscellaneous	Report On Action Of Artillery-Night 18th/19th March 1916		
Miscellaneous	48th. Div.Arty B.M 267/2	20/03/1916	20/03/1916
Miscellaneous	1st Phase Infantry Leaving Trenches And Crossing Open		
Miscellaneous	2nd. Phase Cutting Enemy's Wire And Entering Trenches		
Miscellaneous	3rd Phase Crossing Open After Leaving Enemy's Trenches		
Miscellaneous	1st. 2nd. & 3rd. Phases-Corps Artillery		
Heading	HQ RA 48 Div Vol XIV		
War Diary	Couin	01/04/1916	30/04/1916
Heading	War Diary Of Headquarters 48th Divisional Artillery 1st To 31st May 1916		
War Diary		01/05/1916	31/05/1916
Miscellaneous	Headquarters, R.A. 8th Corps	16/05/1916	16/05/1916
Heading	War Diary Of Headquarters 48th Divisional Artillery Volume XXIII 1st To 30th June 1916		
War Diary	Couin	01/06/1916	30/06/1916
Heading	War Diary C.R.A. 48th Division July 1916		
Heading	War Diary Of Headquarters 48th Divisional Artillery Volume XXIV 1st To 31st July 1916		
War Diary	Couin	01/07/1916	31/07/1916
Operation(al) Order(s)	48th Divisional Artillery Operation Order No. 1	21/07/1916	21/07/1916
Heading	48th Divisional Artillery C.R.A. 48th Division August 1916 Artillery Operation Orders Attached		
Heading	War Diary of Headquarters 48th Divisional Artillery Volume 1st to 31st August 1916 Vol 18		
War Diary		01/08/1916	31/08/1916
Operation(al) Order(s)	48th. Div Arty Operation Order No. 3	18/08/1916	18/08/1916
Miscellaneous	Table A-Relief Of 12th Div Arty By 48th Div.Arty	10/08/1916	10/08/1916
Operation(al) Order(s)	48th. Div Arty Operation Order No. 5	15/08/1916	15/08/1916
Miscellaneous	Bombardment Table	15/08/1916	15/08/1916
Operation(al) Order(s)	48th Div Arty Operation Order No. 6	17/08/1916	17/08/1916
Operation(al) Order(s)	48th Div Arty Operation Order No. 7	21/08/1916	21/08/1916
Miscellaneous	48th. Divisional Artillery Bombardment Table		
Miscellaneous	II Corps R.A		
Miscellaneous	Proposed Barrage For Attack Of Line	25/08/1916	25/08/1916
Map	Map		
Operation(al) Order(s)	48th Divisional Artillery Operation Order No. 9	26/08/1916	26/08/1916
Miscellaneous	48th Divisional Artillery-Bombardment Table		
Operation(al) Order(s)	48th Divisional Artillery Operation Order No. 10	27/08/1916	27/08/1916
Miscellaneous	48th Divisional Artillery-Bombardment Table		
Heading	48th Divisional Artillery C.R.A. 48th Divisional Artillery September 1916		
War Diary		01/09/1916	30/09/1916
Operation(al) Order(s)	48th. Divisional Artillery-Operation Order No. 11	13/09/1916	13/09/1916

Type	Description	Start	End
Miscellaneous	48th. Divisional Artillery-Bombardment Table 18 Pounders		
Operation(al) Order(s)	48th. Divisional Artillery-Operation Order No. 12	14/09/1916	14/09/1916
Operation(al) Order(s)	48th. Divisional Artillery Operation Order No. 14	19/09/1916	19/09/1916
Miscellaneous	48th Div. Arty-Bombardment Table-18 Pounders		
Miscellaneous	Bombardment Table-4.5" Howitzers		
Operation(al) Order(s)	48th. Div Arty Operation Order No. 15	25/09/1916	25/09/1916
Miscellaneous	Amendment	25/09/1916	25/09/1916
Miscellaneous	48th Div. Arty.-Bombardment Table-18-Pounders		
Miscellaneous	4.5" Howitzers		
Operation(al) Order(s)	48th. Divisional Artillery Operation Order No. 16	29/09/1916	29/09/1916
Miscellaneous	Relief Of 48th Div. Arty By 25th Div. Arty.		
Heading	War Diary Of Headquarters 48th Divisional Artillery From 1st To 31st October 1916 Volume		
War Diary		01/10/1916	31/10/1916
Heading	War Diary Of Headquarters 48th Divisional Artillery From 1st To 30th November 1916 Volume		
War Diary		01/11/1916	30/11/1916
Heading	War Diary Of 48th Divisional Artillery Headquarters From 1st To 31st December 1916		
War Diary		01/12/1916	31/12/1916
Heading	War Diary Of 48th Divisional Artillery Headquarters From 1st To 31st January 1917		
War Diary	Lavieville	01/01/1917	31/01/1917
Heading	War Diary Of 48th Divisional Artillery Headquarters From 1st To 28th February 1917 Volume XXXI		
War Diary		01/02/1917	28/02/1917
Operation(al) Order(s)	48th Div & Arty. Order No. 43	31/01/1917	31/01/1917
Miscellaneous	Relief Of Artillery Of 152 French Division By 48th Div Artillery		
Heading	War Diary Of 48th Divisional Artillery Headquarters From 1st To 31st March 1917 Volume XXII		
War Diary		01/03/1917	31/03/1917
Heading	War Diary Of 48th Divisional Artillery Headquarters From 1st To 30th April 1917 Volume XXXIII		
War Diary		01/04/1917	30/04/1917
Heading	War Diary Of 48th Divisional Artillery Headquarters From 1st To 31st May 1917 Volume XXXIV		
War Diary		01/05/1917	31/05/1917
Heading	War Diary Of 48th Divisional Artillery Headquarters From 1st To 30th June 1917 Volume XXXV		
War Diary		01/06/1917	30/06/1917
Heading	War Diary Of 48th Divisional Arty Headquarters From 1st To 31st July 1917 Volume XXXVI		
War Diary		01/07/1917	31/07/1917
Heading	War Diary Of 48th Divisional Arty Headquarters From 1st To 31st August 1917 Volume XXXVII		
War Diary		01/08/1917	31/08/1917
War Diary		07/08/1917	10/08/1917
Heading	48th Divisional Artillery War Diary From 1st September 1917 To 30th September 1917		
War Diary		01/09/1917	30/09/1917
Heading	48th Divisional Artillery War Diary From 1st October 1917 To 31st October 1917 Volume XXXIX		
War Diary		01/10/1917	31/10/1917

Heading	War Diary 48th Divisional Artillery From 1st October 1917 To 31st October 1917		
War Diary		01/10/1917	31/10/1917

WO95/2742 - 2

48 Div HQ — CRA

Apr 1915 – Oct 1917

48TH DIVISION

BEF

C. R. A.

MAR 1915 – ~~MAR 1915~~ – Oct 1917

To ITALY

137/4890

H⁴ Qrs RA. 1/1 South Midland Division

Vol II. 1 – 31. 3. 15
          1
         March '15

CONFIDENTIAL.

WAR DIARY
of
R.A. Hd Qrs 1/1st S. Mid Divn

from 1/3/15 to 31/3/15.

Vol viii

H.H.Butler
Brig Gen. CRA
1/1 S M Divn

April 3/15.

2.

Forwarded direct to A.G's Office at the Base in
accordance with S.M Divn Orders 5 of 4.4.14
(vf. S Reg. II §140 (2))

HQ PSM Div Art?
March 1915
Vol viii

WAR DIARY
or
INTELLIGENCE SUMMARY
(Erase heading not required.)

Army Form C. 2118.

Instructions regarding War Diaries and Intelligence Summaries are contained in F.S. Regs., Part II. and the Staff Manual respectively. Title pages will be prepared in manuscript.

Hour, Date, Place	Summary of Events and Information	Remarks and references to Appendices
Chelmsford.		
1 March 1915	C.R.A. & B.M. to Galliwood to see 1/1st Warwick Battery. Brigade manoeuvres 1/4 Sm Howrs	And
2 March Tuesday.	do do to West Hanningfield: Brigade manoeuvres 1/2 SMFA Bde	And
3 March Wednesday.	do do to Ingatestone: Horse Inspection 1/2 SMFA Bde with the A.D.V.S.	And
	7pm to night brigade parade of 1/1st SMBde near Broomfield }	And
	9pm to do do do do for SMSE at Galliwood }	
4 March Thursday	C.R.A. & B.M. to GT WALTHAM. Entrenchment 1/1st SM Bde & Ranbury. Telephones 1/4th Shropshire. Bivouac & E.Hanningfield. (1/1st Warr.Heavy Bty) on to	And
5 March Friday	CRA & Bm to Baddow, 1/1st Warwick Heavy Battery: or to GOOD EASTER & MASHBURY; 1/2" (Lutley) SmFA Bde on tactical operation with 1/1st Sm. Inf. Bde. C.R.A. on 3 days leave.	And
	B.M. to Boreham Range. MUSKETRY 1/1st SMFA Bde	And
8 March Monday.	C.R.A. returned from leave.	
9 March Tuesday.	CRA, SL to PURLEIGH & E.HANNINGFIELD. Firing of 1/1st Sm.FA Bde & 1/1st Warwickshire Heavy Battery. 7pm to MASHBURY night firing of 1/3rd SM.FA Bde.	And
10 March Wednesday.	C.R.A. & B.M. on BOREHAM RANGE all morning. Musketry of 1/1st & 1/2 w SMFA Bdes. B.M. tonight operation 1/1st 9pm LITTLEY GREEN.	And
11 March Thursday.	C.R.A. & B.M. to Baddow, C.R.A. interviews Capt Sutherland 1/3rd SMFABde on Boreham Range. Musketry 1/4th R.G.A. 1/3rd Bde. Lt lecture at Broomfield by Major Todd on Experience in recent front. to night operation 1/4th Bde Grace's Walk	And

H.Q. R.A.   Vol viii   p 2.

WAR DIARY
or
INTELLIGENCE SUMMARY
(Erase heading not required.)

Army Form C. 2118.

Hour, Date, Place	Summary of Events and Information	Remarks and references to Appendices
Friday, 12 March	CRA + Bde to LITTLEY GREEN (1st Bde Tactical Scheme) & to BOREHAM Range (nth R.G.A.) CRA app to INGATESTONE. (1/2 nth RCS) lecture by Capt Dixey returns from front	Appd.
Sat. 13 March	CRA to BOREHAM RANGES 1/3rd Murphy	Appd
Mon 15 March	CRA to BARROW, inspected R.S. Drivers at 6/1/4th Bde. CRA to Ingatestone. 1/5th Bde	And.
Tues 16 March	CRA + 3 nth + 1st Warwick Heavy Battery Field Major Richards from Gen French R. arsenal Rifle signals of 4 7th sec.	Appd
Wedne. 17 March	CRA to BARROW 1/3rd Bde. BM. & W. HANNINGFIELD 1/2nd Bde. Notice Cen + Driver McCulloch left with DARMG for FRANCE.	Appd ""
Thurs. 18 March	CRA + DM to Ingalestone + Horse list for Remount Officer	Appd.
Fri. 19 March	CRA. with D.A.D.R. to Bromfield, Ingatestone, Barlow etc to arrange to D.Am Col. to inspect their horses	Appd April
Sat. 20 March	do	Appd
Mon 22 March	Staff Captain, Divisr + Can to FOLKESTONE as billeting officer RA	Appd
Tues 23 March	Capt Priday 1/3rd Bde Capt Davis 1/2 Bde, Capt d'Eney R.F.A. to Southampton	Appd
Wed. 24 March to Thurs 25 to	to HAVRE: in standing + Entraining duties Officers on all day	Appd

Army Form C. 2118.

WAR DIARY
or
INTELLIGENCE SUMMARY.
(Erase heading not required.)

Vol viii / p.3

Instructions regarding War Diaries and Intelligence Summaries are contained in F. S. Regs., Part II. and the Staff Manual respectively. Title pages will be prepared in manuscript.

Hour, Date, Place	Summary of Events and Information	Remarks and references to Appendices
Chelmsford		
Friday 26 March 15	Office work all day	fine
Sat'y 27 March 15	do.	fine
Sunday 28 March 15	CRA & Staff & see Entraining of 1/1 SM FA Bde for abroad 2pm	fine
	6 pm 28th (to 10.40 am 29th)	fine
Monday 29 March 15	ADC horses, men & wagons (12) left Chelmsford 10 am for abroad	
FRANCE	CRA + BM Major left Chelmsford 7.5 pm for abroad	
Tuesday 30 March 15	CRA + BM arrive BOULOGNE with H.Q. Staff S. Mid. Divn 1 am	fine	weather Very fine
	CRA + BM, left ADMS, DADVS, ADVS, left by train from PONT de	
	BRIQUES Station 4 arrived CASSEL at about 5 pm. Met by Staff	fine
	Capt'n motored to Billet at CAESTRE arrived 6 pm.	
We Thursday 31 March 15	CRA, BM, SC to CASSEL HAZEBROUCK etc, interviews with officers	fine
	9, 9½ S/h Bde RFA + ADC with HQ Staff RA, arrived between	Rain
	3 pm + 10 pm + proceeded to billets near ROUGECROIX + in	
	CAESTRE respectively	

48.

121/5195

H.Q. Ord: R.A. South Midland Div"

Vol II 1 — 30.4.15

Army Form C. 2118.

Vol ix (P)

WAR DIARY
or
INTELLIGENCE SUMMARY.   H'qr R.A. 4th Smid Div'n
(Erase heading not required.)

Instructions regarding War Diaries and Intelligence Summaries are contained in F.S. Regs., Part II. and the Staff Manual respectively. Title pages will be prepared in manuscript.

Hour, Date, Place.	Summary of Events and Information	Remarks and references to Appendices
France CAESTRE April 15.	CRA. & BM to CASSEL to D.H.Q. & also ordered certain officers of B.A. & By Staff & 19th M.Bde to proceed to NIEPPE to be attached to 27th R.F.A. Bde. Visit from Brig Phipps-Hornby VC III Corps CRA. & S.C. to HAZEBROUCK to meet 2nd Sm.F.A.Bde. who arrived during the night 31/1 & visited to meet Caestre Visit from Major for Heads Cap SM Div.	Weather very fine And.
2 April (Good Friday)	Church parade 9.30 a.m. 12.30 a.m. 10 officers & others 3 horses 1 M. & Signal C.Y.R.E. joined Ain. Staff, & communication established with H.Q. S.M. Div. CRA. & Staff Capt. at HAZEBROUCK meeting R.G.A. & 3rd S.M.F.A Bde which arrived between 10pm and 10.7pm & went into Billets S.W. of CAESTRE & near LA KREULE & 4th How Bde proceeded direct to 3rd Bde & STEENWERCK to join 4th Division Divisional Amm. Col. arrived at CASSEL between 5pm and 3 pm – proceeded to billets during morning S. of LE BRÉARDE CRA went on official to call on G.O.C. II Corps BAILLEUL.	Weather hot & clear And
3 April Sat 3		And
4th April Easter day	Church parade 9.30 a.m. for R.A. H.Q. Staff. 2nd Brigade & R.G.A. to rendezvous near L'EPINETTE by 6.30 pm. 2nd M Bde to rendezvous S. of NEUVE EGLISE by 4 pm. 3rd Brigade proceeded after noon to arrive in billeting area SE of METEREN by 4 pm. CRA & BM to Epinette to call on G.O.C. V Div'n & to Art Position E of NEUVE EGLISE with CRA. 4th Div'n.	And. Weather dull & misty

WAR DIARY
INTELLIGENCE SUMMARY.
(Erase heading not required.)

Army Form C. 2118.

Vol IX p.2

Hour, Date, Place	Summary of Events and Information	Remarks and references to Appendices
N. of France 1915		
CAESTRE. 5 April Monday	1st & 3rd Bde of 1st Brigade left to rendezvous S.W. of NEUVE EGLISE by 6pm to join 4th Division. CRA to CASSEL Div. H.Q. & on to new billetting area S.W. of BAILLEUL. Ordered to move H.Q. & MERRIS tomorrow but cancelled this pm. forward accommodation there. Chaplain McNulty joined R.A.H.Q. Staff.	Weather wet & cold. Fine
" 6 April Tuesday	Div. Ammn Column moved to billetting area S. of MERRIS. C.R.A. & B.M. to Div. J.H.Q. at M., to call on H.Q.R.A. N. Mid. Div., to O.C. 3 W.S.M.F.A. Bde, on to Bn. Paget C.R.A. to H.Q. of VI Division, interview with Br. Gen Paget C.R.A. on to position of S.M. Warwickshire R.G.A, where up 4 det. one gun was in action & back to CAESTRE.	Weather fairly fine. Fine.
" 7 Apr. Wednesday	Ammn Col. 15t SM.FA Bde to join Bde. with 4th Division. Br. major to YPRES to hqs of 3rd C.R.A. 27 & 28 Divn. C.R.A & A.D.C. to 1st Bde R.F.A.(SM) at NEUVE EGLISE	Fine.
" 8 Apr Thursday.	C.R.A. & B.M. to billetting area S. of MERRIS to visit of famrs. on to CROISDANBAC. saw GO.C.R. 6th Div & also B.O.C. 6th Division in action N. of FLEURBAIX. on to 2 W S M. FARM to S.M. R.G.A. in action. near L'ARMEE. Back through ARMENTIERES.	Fine - colder Fine
" 9 Apr Friday.	Moved Div. H.Q. (Inf.) to MERRIS. C.R.A. & B.M. to HAZEBROUCK & See Ad. Admin II Army	Fine

WAR DIARY
or
INTELLIGENCE SUMMARY.

(Erase heading not required.)

Army Form C. 2118.

Vol IX p. 3

Hour, Date, Place	Summary of Events and Information	Remarks and references to Appendices
MERRIS. 10 April Sat?	CRA & B.M. to see O.C. 2nd, 3rd SM Bdes FA. & O.C. SM Dist. Amm? Col". 2nd SM. FA. Bde returned from 6th Div? park, arr. 3rd SM. FA. Bde moved to join 6th Divn. Arm. CRA & B.M. to PLOEGSTEERT - Shell marks caught car. Saw positions of Hows. of 4th SM FA Bde attached to 4th Div? Report that Br. Hickman 4th Warwick Bde had been killed on 9th April by a shell.	Weather fine. Fine.
11 April Sunday	CRA & B.M. m.t. see O.C. 1/1st SM FA Bde at NEUVE EGLISE. Celebration of Holy Communion 9 a.m. for all of Hd. QA Staff. CRA & Bon to HAZEBROUCK & see Art? Ad. viser II Army, & Major Burke of Flying Corps. Lecture on F. & C. M. at 3 p.m. by R.T.A.I. II Army at Dist. H.Q. SM Warwickshire Heavy Battery moved into our area from the 6th Division.	Fine. Weather fine.
12 April Monday	No 234 N.C.O. took 1/4 SM FA Bde shot himself about 5 a.m. Cant. of injury hid. & Opinion that he died of self inflicted rifle wound whilst of unsound mind. Proceedings to H.Q. S.A. Divn. CRA & Bm. to 4th Divn HQ. & to ARMENTIERES but failed to find O.C. 3rd Bde.	Fine. Weather fine.
13 April Tuesday.	Funeral of D? Took. CRA & Bm. to find parade ground for M.C. to area ? BM gave lecture to C. Os. Adj?s & 5.o.s on "F.G.C.M." CRA. to visit Batteries of 3rd SM FA Bde at ARMENTIERES.	Fine. Weather fine.
14 April Wednesday	CRA & B.M. to H.Q. 4th Div? (C.R.A.) & on to ARMENTIERES to 3rd SM FA Bde. Visited 1st Battery at HOUPLINES. Football match SM Div? v beat IV Division	Fine. A C.B.E. & some rain.

(9 29 6) W 4141—463 100,000 9/14 HWV Forms/C. 2118/10

Vol IX / 1 / 4   Army Form C. 2118.

WAR DIARY
of
INTELLIGENCE SUMMARY.
(Erase heading not required.)

Hour, Date, Place	Summary of Events and Information	Remarks and references to Appendices
MERRIS-NIEPPE 1915.		
Thursday 15th April Friday 16 April	CRA & S.C. to NEUVE EGLISE 1st S.M.F.A.Bde. Moved Head Qrs to NIEPPE. CRA & BM went round with OC 3rd SMFABde; also met OC & officers 2nd SMFABde at H.Q of 32nd FA Bde.	Very fine still do. fine, do
NIEPPE Night 16-17 April	2nd SMFA Bde moved into positions vacated by 27th + 134th Bde Batteries 1 Kr 32nd Bde	fine
Saturday 17 April	CRA & BM to visit 2nd Bde. 5th How Bty, 4th Bde H.Q, 29th	do
M.N 17 18 April Sunday 18 April	Brigadier RFA H.Q 1st Bde N.Q. CRA SMR: Early command of portion of defence RA allotted to SMR Shot Fianers Esternation from CRA to ARMENTIERES to 3rd SMBde	fine
	Early A.M. SM Warwick RGA moved from MERRIS area to position near ARMENTIERES ASYLUM, & came under orders of G.O.C. 4th Division. P.M 3rd SM FA Bde went to relieve 135th/32nd 13th RFA + 127/29th Bde RFA near PLOEGSTEERT.	
Monday 19 April	CRA & BM to 5th Warwick Bty, 1st + 2nd + 3rd SMFA Bdes. OC to POPERINGHE & see GOC 5th Corps & on to YPRES & POTIJE & see GOC 27th Div + CRA 27th Div.	fine. do
Tuesday 20 April	CRA to 5th How Bty & 2nd + 3rd Bdes (morning) BM & 29th Bde & 1st Bde afternoon night 20-21, 3rd Bde, 1st Bde moved to T17.a. from T15.d.	fine. do

Army Form C. 2118.

Vol IX p 5

WAR DIARY
or
INTELLIGENCE SUMMARY.
(Erase heading not required.)

Hour, Date, Place	Summary of Events and Information	Remarks and references to Appendices
NIEPPE 1915		
Wed 21 April	CRA to 3rd & 2nd S'Staff Bdes (morning) BM to see shortly of 1st Bde, 1st Bde aftn	weather fine
Thurs 22 April	CRA. BM. & 3 o'other offrs visit R.A. & AERODROME, BAILLEUL, for instruction in aircraft coop'n with Arty. S.O. to arrange for D.A. Col & Major F.L.O.T.R. 2nd Bde aftn.	fine
Fri. 23 April	BM, RA & others from BARREL HOUSE. CRA to 2nd Bde Eagln -	fine
Sat. 24 April	in afternoon. CRA & BM. to Observation Post 1/3rd Brigade - Major Ward - on through	fine
Sun. 25 April	PLOEGSTEERT WOOD to 2/3rd Brigade - Major Daniel.	"
Mon. 26 April	CRA to visit D.A.M. Col & Bde Ammn Cols.	"
Tues. 27 April	CRA visits 1/3rd & 3rd Bde. Ob. post at St. Yvon.	"
Wed. 28 April	BM met Adjutants to discuss items of fire & other matters.	" v.hot
Thurs 29 April	BM to 2nd Bty & examine CO's F.A. to various matters. CRA offrs to conference of inspection at HQ S'maj Brig 13 Bde. CRA visits to west section of HQ 2 Mr PH4 in PLOEGSTEERT WOOD & hill B' Gen Phillpotts V.C. to h'shoes, 2nd line position	" v.hot
Friday 30 April	to Artillery HQ War at Lascelles RFC & Lt Col Lucas, coords Heavy Artillery to reconnaissance Tomorrow. BM visit Col 1, 2, 3 Bdes and Divine Artillery positions & with S.O. Regts Group to R.F.C. 4th Squadron to arrange for aeroplane observation.	fine

121/5573

Hd Qrs R.A. 48th Division

Volume 1 — 30.5.15

Army Form C. 2118.

Vol X.
p. 1.

WAR DIARY
or
INTELLIGENCE SUMMARY.
(Erase heading not required.)

R.A. H.Q. S.M. Div.

Instructions regarding War Diaries and Intelligence Summaries are contained in F.S. Regs., Part II. and the Staff Manual respectively. Title pages will be prepared in manuscript.

Hour, Date, Place NIEPPE, N. France	Summary of Events and Information	Remarks and references to Appendices
1. May. 15	CRA to see practice 114th Bde (H.7) in conjunction with aeroplanes. RM to Warwickshire Heavy Bty. Obs. room.	Fine {cloudy {cooler
2. May. 15. Sun.	Church parade at PORT de NIEPPE for Bishop of PRETORIA. Good too! BM with O's Cdrs after service at HQ of BSA Ede & discussed Ammon. supply etc.	Fine warm — wet
3. May. 15. Mon. 4. May. Tuesday. 5. May. Wednsd.	CRA & BM reconnoitred roads for Ammunition Supply. Office work all day. CRA to Conference of O's. C.B. de R.F.A. at Hd. 3rd Staffers &c. BMK HQ 29th Bde (Retaliation at request of SM Inf Bde on Press. sent to Appetits Douve. Fine v. hot	Fine Fine
6 May Thursday 7 May Friday.	CRA & BM to PLOEGSTEERT wood from her/vailed the ledin No 2 NB. CRA & BM to Conference of C.O's (R.A.) at 7.23. 2 Candles on subject of Demonstration. Col. R.P. Benson (Siege) called to arrange re comm. unication with R.F.C. BM.	Fine Fine do.
8 May Saturday	CRA & to reconnoitre positions for defence (R.A.) in G.H.Q. line. BM visits positions of 29th FAB with Col MacLaren Canadian Art. "A" Gr Brock 29th FAB.	Fine do.
9 May Sunday	From 4.30 am. to 7pm SM D Artillery & 29th Bde R.A. & 27th Bde F.A. assisted by slow bombardment of Germans line in accordance with other attack.	Fine — do — See Appendix "A"
10 May Monday	CRA to reconnoitre positions for R.A. in connection with G.H.Q line. Orders received for Br Gen. Ross Johnson to relieve Br Gen Butler, 125, 116, 107 Battns 4 29th.	Fine — do —
11 May Tuesday 1.30 am	7, 8, 11th Canadian Batteries relieved. Rate R.F.A. 14 Talbot proceeded North.	Fine — do —

Army Form C. 2118.

Vol X. p.2

WAR DIARY
or
INTELLIGENCE SUMMARY.   H.Q. D'Art. S.M.D.

(Erase heading not required.)

Instructions regarding War Diaries and Intelligence Summaries are contained in F.S. Regs., Part II. and the Staff Manual respectively. Title pages will be prepared in manuscript.

Hour, Date, Place	Summary of Events and Information	Remarks and references to Appendices
NIEPPE Tues. 11 May 15.	Brig. Gen. C.M. Ross Johnson took over command of R.A. S.Mid. Div'n from Brig. Gen. H. Butler, the latter proceeded en route to England. CRA & BM & 1st SM Bde FA HR & an O.S. also to 2nd Canadian Bde HQ at PLOEGSTEERT 4 p.m.	V.Fine. fine
Wed. 12 May 15.	CRA & BM & HQ. 3rd SM FA Bde & 1st & 1st Bd4 Obs. Station. Saw O.C. 5th Warwick Bd4. & 2, & 3rd Bdg's O.S.'s at St Yvon aftn.	fine
Thurs. 13 May 15.	4.30 a.m. about 2nd Canadian Bd. RFA. retaliated a German minor explosion C.U.C. 9, 10, & fired 8 rounds S.S. at request of Infantry. In support, at 5.15 a.m. activity reported as practically ceased. Notification received that S.M. D'n is in the 48th Div'n in (IInd). CRA & BM & HQ. of 2nd SM FA Bde, & KBARREL Hd. Quart'rs. Did not fire. CRA. N Mid. (46th Div) knee CRA. talked to H.Q. 3rd Corps.	fine (see Appendix B) some rain much colder
Friday. 14 May 15.	BM Ernest all O.'s C. F. A. Bdes & Captain GOCRA' wished to defence & Salutary of HQ & tunes. CRA to see GOC 6th Division. Retaliation 9 a.m. received at by 5th How By & 2nd SM FA Bde in conj'n with Warwick 1/5th on La PETITE DOUVE Fme. light way to end.	fine.
Sat' 15 May 15.	CRA, & BM, & HQ of 27th Battery (32" Bde FA), & G.H.Q. 1st SM FA Bde, 1st, K H.Q Bn Canadian Bde FA GSO'n of IIIrd Corps to see C.R.A.	Fine. Am.5.
Sun'e 16 May 15.	11 0 a.m. 1st Battery 2nd SM Bde & Lt & 5th How Bty cooperated with Infantry German Station in shelling Remauchench S. end of AVENUES O.15.a.38.} Good effect. 6.30 p.m. 2nd Canadian FA Bde shelled BIRDCAGE U.21.70. 11.30 – 11.45 p.m. 3rd SM FA Bde shelled in reprisals to a.n.S. of Bois CHASSEUR CABARET U.16. b. & cross roads at LATRUIE U.17. a.	Fine Am 5

Army Form C. 2118.

Vol X.
p.3

WAR DIARY
or
INTELLIGENCE SUMMARY.
(Erase heading not required.)

Instructions regarding War Diaries and Intelligence Summaries are contained in F.S. Regs, Part II. and the Staff Manual respectively. Title pages will be prepared in manuscript.

Hour, Date, Place	Summary of Events and Information	Remarks and references to Appendices
NIEPPE May 1915. 17 May Mon.	Arrangements made for relief of 7.8.10.11 Canadian Batteries by the 50th Bde FA. 9th Div. & 27th RFA Battery by C.D. batteries of 1/5? 1300 9th Div. to take place night of 18-19 just. G.O.C. 9th Div. & CRA 9th Div. called. Brig. Major 15am to meet Capt. HANNAN RFC, at H.Q. of 5th Warwick How. Bde & discuss arrangements for cooperation in registering ranges. CRA & 5th M.(Am.) to see free replacements of 2/3rd Battery.	Lost. Arud. hello ent. Arud.
18 May Tues.	General The following relief took place 7.8.10.11th Batteries Canadian Arty relieved by A,B,C,D. Batteries 3 50th FA Bde. 9th Div. 27th Battery (32 FAB) relieved by C.D. batteries 57th FA Bde. 9th Div.	cheese int. Arud.
19 May Wed.	CRA v B.N. & H.Q. 50th FAB + on to Shaw's S? LE GHEER. CRA v G.O.C. 9th Div. to hasten arrival of 50th FAB in posn. Authorise heads for a more extensive ? promise officer to relieve maj. A. Murray Smith v B.M. major (B.M. C/53.)	Erie Arud.
20 May Thurs.	CRA & BM vAd? C. & observing stations of 57th FA.B at. or near LE GHEER 63 (Am). (P.M.) CRA v S.C. re A B C D Batteries of 50th FA Bde & 50th FA.B de LE GHEER A,B, Batteries 57th FA.B relieved 1st + 3rd Batteries.	Arud.
21 May Friday.	9am. A,B. S.M FA.B. SCRA, B.M. & H.Q. 50th FA.B. + on to 'A' Battery some place: CRA to near LOCRE to meet CRA. 46th (N.Midn) Div. B.M. & H.Q. of 2nd & 4th S.M F.A.B's & 50 L FAB.	v. finis Arud.
22 May Saturday.	CRA. to observing stations on Hill 63.	V. finis Arud.

Army Form C. 2118.

Vol X / (p4)

WAR DIARY
or
INTELLIGENCE SUMMARY.
(Erase heading not required.)

Instructions regarding War Diaries and Intelligence Summaries are contained in F.S. Regs., Part II. and the Staff Manual respectively. Title pages will be prepared in manuscript.

Hour, Date, Place	Summary of Events and Information	Remarks and references to Appendices
NIEPPE, N. FRANCE		
23 May Sunday.	3am & 12 noon 50th & 51st F.A. Bdes (9th Div: alt 7 & 8 Bdes (5th Div) fired on enemy's trenches as set forth in Appendix 'C'. CRA & S.C. 16 Reserve Station (RA) on Hill 63. O.C. 4 Squadron RFC. per 6pm to arrange for Cooperation work tomorrow.	see App.'C'. Vrai fine And
24 May Monday.	CRA to Hill 63. B.M. with O.C. 4 Sq. RFC. to meet all Adjutants at H.Q. 3rd S.M. F.A. Bde. to explain "J.Q.J.J." Scheme of cooperation with Airaeft. 3rd S.M. Bde & 5th How. Bty. Carried out firing with Aeroplane. results: 9.	V. fine And
25 May Tuesday.	CRA. & B.M. to H.Q. 9 & 4th Sm Hwy Bde, 9 & 5th Bty H.Q. met O.C. 4th Squadron RFC, & H.Q. 50th F.A.B. 3rd S.M. Bde & 2nd How. Falling cooperation expl. Col Du Boulay & Branch IIIrd (Corps) over 6.25 pm. to review as to Shelling of Amm'n.	V. fine And
26th May Wednesday.	3rd S.M.F.A. Bde & 5th How. Battery carried out firing with aid of aeroplane. 9pm orders received to Major T & V.B. order R.A. V. B. relieve Major Murray-Smith on 18th May in R.A. 48 Div.	V. fine And hot
27th May Thursday.	3rd S.M.F.A. Bde & 5th How Bty carried out firing (6pm) with aid of aeroplane.	V. fine Artil
28 May Friday.	Orders received for Major Murray-Smith to join 3rd Div in view of being to command D.W. Am Col. Major J. & V. Bindes RFA joined the Staff as B.M. Major R.A. 48 Div. Division established at H.Q. R.A. 48th for Aeroplane work with 3rd S.M.F.A. Bde & 5th How Bty.	And hotter
29. May Saturday	Major Murray-Smith left this Division to join 3rd Div if reqd. Ammunition Column, D Battery 51 Bde Shells & not fit to Blanchisserie. N.M. Frelingham which was used as a store by Germans.	V. fine And Showers
30 May Sunday.	Nil.	V. Fine And

SECRET Copy No 8

U.C. 1234(s) 29.2 MB.

Bn C
23.

APPENDIX A
(War Diary)

Please note that since writing the attached order, 3rd Corps have notified us that the Demonstration is postponed 24 hrs. Accordingly 4.30 a.m. means 4.30 a.m. SUNDAY morning 9th inst. NOT tomorrow morning

R Murray Smith
Major
A/Adjt. RWSRo

I.S.O.
7.30 pm

Appendix "B"

C.R.A.

Returned with thanks in case you may require them for your diary

A Girtwood Capt
G. Staff

14/5/15

"C" Form (Duplicate). Army Form C. 2123.
MESSAGES AND SIGNALS.

| Service Instructions. | Charges to Pay. £ s. d. | Office Stamp. |

Handed in at _____ Office ____ m. Received ____ m.

TO: 5th Can Div Arty 7.50

| Sender's Number | Day of Month | In reply to Number | AAA |
| DA 8 | 13 | | |

At 4/40 am foo 7 battery reports enemy shelling house 25 yds right of our observing station with small HE one shell every 30 seconds

FROM PLACE & TIME: 2nd Can Arty Bde
Ploegsteert

"C" Form (Duplicate).   Army Form C. 2123.

MESSAGES AND SIGNALS.   No. of Message_____

	Charges to Pay. £ s. d.	Office Stamp. 13. V. 15 DH
Service Instructions.		

Handed in at _____ Office _____ m. Received _____ m.

TO   5th Cnd Div Arty   8 a.m

Sender's Number	Day of Month	In reply to Number	AAA
Aa 9	13		

At 4.45 am F.O.O. 7th
Battery reports enemy shells our
Observing Station with small
H.E. and heavy rifle fire
on our front
                       (B.M 145a)
To S.O. S.M.D
    Forwarded in connection with
previous message of this morning
13.5.15.   R. Johns   A.A. S.M.D   Lt. ADC

FROM PLACE & TIME	2nd Can Arty Bde Ploegsteert 6.15 am

"C" Form (Original). Army Form C. 2123.
MESSAGES AND SIGNALS.   No. of Message

Prefix	Code	Words	Received From	Sent, or sent out At	Office Stamp
Charges to collect £ s. d.			By	To	Y 13.V.15
Service Instructions				By	

Handed in at .... Office .... m. Received .... m.

TO South Md Div Arty

*Sender's Number	Day of Month	In reply to Number	A A A

At 4:50 am FOO 7th Battery reports that Capt Coyne A Co Gloucester asks for artillery support

FROM PLACE & TIME 2nd Lan Arty Bde
Ploegsteert 6:20 am

"C" Form (Original).   Army Form C. 2123.

MESSAGES AND SIGNALS.

Prefix	Code	Words	Received From	Sent, or sent out At	Office Stamp
Charges to collect	£ s. d.		By	To	13.V.15 DH
Service Instructions.				By	

Handed in at .... Office 6.45 a.m. Received .... m.

TO 5th Ind Div Arty

*Sender's Number	Day of Month	In reply to Number	AAA
DA 11	13		

At 4.50 am FDO 11th Battery reports that a small mine was exploded near Monmouth House between 4.30 am and 4.45 am

FROM PLACE & TIME   2nd Lan Arty Bde Ploegsteert 6.45 am

*This line should be erased if not required.

"C" Form (Duplicate). Army Form C. 2123.

MESSAGES AND SIGNALS.

No. of Message_____

| Service Instructions. | Charges to Pay. £ s. d. | Office Stamp. Y 13.V.15 TELEGRAM |

Handed in at _____ Office 6.50 m. Received ____ m.

TO 5th Ind Div Arty B.a.m

Sender's Number	Day of Month	In reply to Number	AAA
aa 12	13		

At 5.15 am 7th Battery FOO reports artillery and rifle fire practically ceased

HQ SM 2
Forwarded

13.5.15

HEADQUARTERS, 1.1st SOUTH MIDLAND
No. _____
Date 13.5.15
DIVISIONAL ARTILLERY

FROM PLACE & TIME 2nd Can Arty Bde
Ploegsteert 6.50 am

"C" Form (Duplicate).   Army Form C.2123.

MESSAGES AND SIGNALS.

No. of Messages

Charges to Pay. £ s. d.

Office Stamp: Y 13.V.15 TELEGRAPH

Service Instructions.

Handed in at _____ Office 7 a.m. Received 7 a.m.

TO: 11th Ind Div Arty   8 a.m.

Sender's Number	Day of Month	In reply to Number	AAA
No 13	13		
At	5.35	am	500 11th
Battery	reports	that	at 4.30
am	the	Germans	opened fire
with	their	light	field guns
sweeping	the	reserve	trenches and
the	fields	around	infantry HQ
at	about	10	seconds interval
aaa	In	the	trenches there
was	rapid	rifle	fire they
also	used	rifle	grenades and
trench	mortars	this	lasted for
about	half	an	hour We
opened	fire	at	request of
Infantry at		4.45	am and
fired	8	rounds	shrapnel on
our	right	lines	

FROM PLACE & TIME: 2nd Can Arty Bde Ploegsteert 7 am

Appendix C. 39

SECRET
Form 762

H.Q. 48 (SM) Divn

Report on Artillery action between
3 A.M and 10 a.m. 23/5/15.
Batteries firing 18 pr Q.F.

a) 50th F.A.Bde (near PLOEGSTEERT)
(i) One battery fired 105 rounds S.S. on
enemy's trench U.28.A.44 to U.28.A.8.10
between 3.30 am and 4 am. 20% burst
on graze most of which were direct hits
on parapet.
(ii) One battery fired 145 rounds S.S. into the
BIRDCAGE U.21.C.7.6. The whole of it was
searched practically all rounds going
into it, about 30% being on "graze".
Firing from 3.30 am to 3.55 am.

b) 57st F.A.Bde (SE of NEUVE EGLISE)
4 batteries fired 119 rounds on to enemy's
trenches between LA PETITE DOUVE Farm U.8.A
to U.1.B: effect appeared to be good
Firing commenced at 3 A.M. & ended at
3.45 a.m.

A Murray-Smith
Bde Major RA 48 Divn Major
for GOCRA 48 Divn

23/5/15
11. am

SECRET   Copy No 8   58

O.C. 1.2.3.4.(5) 29. 2 M.B.   BMC/23

With reference to the Secret instructions given you by the CCRA today for tomorrow's demonstration. The following is the Time Table just received from S.M.A. H.Q. You will note that the actual hours, or periods, are slightly altered; but the allotment of Ammunition will remain as ordered by the SOCRA.

4.30 am - 5.30 am (1 hour). Artillery "Cutting wire" in areas (A) & (B), i.e. in front of our trenches 14.15.16 & 4D.6.
(126 Batt, 1/2"d & 2/2"d Batts.)

6.0 am - 6.30 am (½ hour).
5" How* & Mountain Battery (H.E.) to shell German trenches in areas (A) & (B).

7.0 am - 7.30 am (½ hour) Inf. & M.G. fire on the trenches areas (A) & (B).

8.0 am - 10 am (2 hours) Inf. Mortar & Rifle Grenades, supported by Artillery fire as already ordered.

2 rds per { 125. 127 Batts
gun. { 1/3"d Battery
{ Section No 2. M.B. (Shrapnel)
{ 2/2"d & 3/2"d Batteries
                           over

2.

10.30 am: 1 Round Battery Fire
        20 Secs. from last mentioned Battery
11.30 am - 12.30 pm: (One hour instead of 2 as previously ordered) Artillery fire all along the lines - on night lines (except 5" Howitzers). 18pr 20 [?] bty. 15br 12 [?] bty
1 pm - 2 pm (1 hour) M/M Pan Fire
2.30 pm - 3 pm (½ hour) 5" Howitzers fire 12 rounds at selected points as ordered by S.O.C.R.A.
3.30 pm - 5.30 pm (2 hours) Infantry Mortar & rifle grenade fire
6 pm - 7 pm (1 hour) Infantry fire combined with Artillery Fire, as already ordered, all along the line, directed our points about 200 x in rear of "night line" points. Battery of [?]

N.B. Infantry go on firing thro' the night
12. This programme will be carried out whatever the weather.
13. Set your watches by signal time
14. Acknowledge receipt of this

P Murray Smith
    Major
Bde Major R.A.S.M.D

7 pm.
7/5/15.

"C" Form (Original).   Army Form C. 2123.

MESSAGES AND SIGNALS.

| Prefix SM | Code Ca | Words | Received From ... By Parr | Sent, or sent out At ... To ... By | Office Stamp Y.13.V.15 |

Service Instructions: 7B9

Handed in at .... Office 5.5 a.m. Received 5.11 a.m.

TO   S.M.D. Arty 7.5 a.m.

| Sender's Number | Day of Month | In reply to Number | AAA |
| DA7 | 13 | | |

Capt. Cayne Gloster asks for artillery support at 4.50 am from 7th Batty too 11th Batty reports enemy exploded a mine in front of our lines and that infantry asks for support have fired a few rounds and awaiting further information

HQ S M D
Forwarded
A Murray Smith
Major

5.35 am 13/5/15

FROM   2 Can Arty Bde
PLACE & TIME   Ploegsteert 5 am

This line should be erased if not required.

Bm G/E 2(2)

H.Q. 48 Divⁿ

Report on Artillery Action at
12 noon 23.5.15.

(a) 50th Bde F.A. engaged enemy's trench
U.20.a.4.4. to U.28.a.8.10. and obtained
21 direct hits. Trench knocked about
a good deal.

(b) 5th Howitzer Bty:
Fired 6 rounds at DRESDEN F^m (S. of
LA DOUVE) U.9638. 3 fell just beyond
the house; 1 fell in German trenches just
in front of the house; 2 were slightly off
the line.

(c) 51st Bde F.A:
(i) Fired on DRESDEN F^t U.9638 - effect
reported good.
(ii) Also on German trench, S. end of
PETIT BOIS (I.15.a.4.8) result satisfactory
(iii) Also on German trenches
where they cross MESSINES-WULVERGHEM
Rd, about U.1.6. General effect good.

S Murray-Smith
Major
Bde Major RA 48 Div
23/5/15
5.40 pm

121/5870

48th Division

Hd Qrs R.A. 48th Division

Vol IV 1 — 30.6.15

Army Form C. 2118.

WAR DIARY
or
INTELLIGENCE SUMMARY.
(Erase heading not required.) R.A. H.Q. 48. DIV. ARTY.

VOL XI

Instructions regarding War Diaries and Intelligence Summaries are contained in F. S. Regs., Part II. and the Staff Manual respectively. Title pages will be prepared in manuscript.

Place	Date	Hour	Summary of Events and Information	Remarks and references to Appendices
NIEPPE Nr FRANCE	June 1	5¹	German Anti Aircraft Gun located near LA POTTERIE. FME. & WARWICK How. Battery in conjunction with 1/3 Batty 2 SMRMB engaged the gun and once silenced—	Very fine & Lightning
	2.		Nil	"
	3.		Enemy's working parties shelled	"
	4.		A section of No 2 M.T. Coy confusion amongst french infantry parallel to the AVENUE CoL infantry operated with machine gun fire. No movement was seen enemy did not retaliate. Shooting appeared well directed—	"
	5.		Nil	"
	6.		Two mines were exploded under German trenches near PLOEGSTREET WOOD known as the Bird cage at 10.21 am. The NW corner of the BIRD CAGE Broom parapet was completely destroyed. The 5th WARWICK How Battery fired 20 rounds into the BIRDCAGE getting 6 direct hits on the parapet. C & D Batteries 50 FA/B fired shrapnel in conjunction with 3/3 Battery into the Bird cage & parapet & communication trenches behind. During the afternoon about 30 German wire piercing mortar shells. The 5th How. dropped a by death spits into the Gantry who were not again seen. Intermittent fire was kept up all day by friend & German mortar until 4.0.	
	7.		64. F.A.B. of 12 Div. started to Division. At 10 pm A/64 replaced 1/3 Battery and B/64 the 2/3 Battery in action. C/64 went into action at LE PETIT MUNIQUE FME D/64 dismount. The 1st and 2nd Batteries. 3 SM FA.B. went into Reserve at LA PACHIE.	Very hot
	8.		63. R.F.A. of 12 Div. attached to Division. A/63 on D/63 took up a position at LE BIZET. Thunderstorm B/63 relieved B/60 the latter going into Reserve at LE PT MORTIER.	
	9.		C Battery 53 relieved C Battery 50 F.A.B. the latter going into reserve.	Very hot.

WAR DIARY VOL XI
or
INTELLIGENCE SUMMARY.
(Erase heading not required.)   R.A. H.Q. 48. DIV ARTY.

Army Form C. 2118.

Instructions regarding War Diaries and Intelligence Summaries are contained in F. S. Regs., Part II. and the Staff Manual respectively. Title pages will be prepared in manuscript.

Place	Date	Hour	Summary of Events and Information	Remarks and references to Appendices
NIEPPE FRANCE	June 10"		The Germans exploded a mine in front of PLOEGSTREET WOOD. It was short of our trenches and did no damage. They followed it up with sharp rifle fire and Artillery fire the only damage being done was caused. C. Battery 63 F.A.B opened out on on BERNAN TRENCHES. A Battery 63 F.A.B relieved D Battery 50 F.A.B. The infantry into division at 12 pm Norton	Rain
	11.		5 How Battery and 112 F.A.B at 6.4.5 pm shelled Le PUTOIRE FME. 3 repeated hits were obtained by the Howitzers. The field battery shelled the approaches to the Fme & communication trenches. Our bombardment of the enemy was invisible, although it was assisted by Colonel SHORT relieved lt Col STRAUDENZIE in command of arty. Comprising the 10th gps of defence.	Very hot for morning
	12.		A Battery 50 F.A.B 10th Div arty	Very hot for Thunder Storm light rain
	13.			
	14.		The Germans exploded a mine and shelled PLOEGSTREET WOOD at 2.30 am. No damage was done. 2 H D Batteries 63 F.A.B fired on German trenches. The 5 MAXWELL HOW 13* and 12 & 2 Batteries 10 S.H F.A.B engaged a house where Germans were seen to enter. The Howitzers got 2 direct hits.	fine
	15.		Heavy artillery shelled FRELINGHEIN, LE BASSE/VILLE, and Battery close to BLANCHISSERIE and shelled artillery shelled PLOEGSTREET asia. The hostile guns were silenced.	Very fine light gun
	16.		5 How Battery and 2 F.A.B shelled BRUHEIM FME which the Germans have been hutting in a state of defense. Several direct hits were obtained.	fine Cool
	17.		2nd. Lt. 28 French Munitips Battery under command of 2 Lt. C. CHADWORTH MUSTERS. joined the Divisional Artillery	fine

Army Form C. 2118.

WAR DIARY
or
INTELLIGENCE SUMMARY.

(Erase heading not required.) Div Arty H.Q. 48 Division.

Instructions regarding War Diaries and Intelligence Summaries are contained in F.S. Regs., Part II. and the Staff Manual respectively. Title pages will be prepared in manuscript.

Place	Date	Hour	Summary of Events and Information	Remarks and references to Appendices
NIEPPE	18.		Nil	
	19.		C/1 F.A.B. shelled hostile trenches 5 S.W. Hon Bty shelled BIRD CAGE. 28 Trench Hon Battery came into action and shelled German Trenches opposite PLOEGSTREET with good effect.	Fine & still good
	20.		4.5 Howitzer How Bty opened fire attached 27th Division. One section replaced the right sect. of 5th How Bty in action the 5th Battery section going into action beside its left section. The remaining section 4.5 Battery remained in Billets.	Fine Hot
	21.		2/2 Battery to billets in LA CRECHE from action. 9/64 replaced 2/2. 1/3 relieved 9/64 in action. Experimental test with incendiary shell carried out by 19 pm D/64 and one 18 pr gun 7.09 against a house in 63. Several rounds of petroleum shell used but they then burst without setting fire to it.	Fine
	22.		3/2 Battery to billets in LA CRECHE from action. 8/64 replaced 3/2. and 2/3 1/64 replaced D/64 in action. Very quiet day.	Fine
	23.		1/2 Battery to billets in LA CRECHE from action. C/64 replaced 1/2. 3/3 replaced C/64 in action.	Fine
	24.		At 6 p.m. 3/3 Battery fired 16 rounds with Heavy Artillery at LA BASSE VILLE in retaliation for Germans shelling PLOEGSTREET. 3 S.M. A.19.B. with aircraft to La CRECHE and replaced by 3 Batty's 62 Bde 12 Div in action. 2 F.A.B. Horse Group(s) under orders 146 Inf. Bde to BAILLEUL. Annie BAILLEUL night 24/25.	Fine

Army Form C. 2118.

WAR DIARY
or
INTELLIGENCE SUMMARY.

(Erase heading not required.) D.A. H.Q. 48. Division

Vol XI

Instructions regarding War Diaries and Intelligence Summaries are contained in F.S. Regs., Part II. and the Staff Manual respectively. Title pages will be prepared in manuscript.

Place	Date	Hour	Summary of Events and Information	Remarks and references to Appendices
NIEPPE	25.		3. S.M.F.A.B from LA CRECHE march under the orders GROUP B to BAILLEUL. (GROUP B = 148 Hy Bde, 3.S.M. F.A.B.) An withdrawal of 143 Hy Bde, 12 Division took over responsibility for defences of 48. Div. line.	Fine
	26.		1. S.M. F.A.B withdrawn from action and replaced in action by 5th 7th and 8th Batteries 2.1.G. CANADIAN ARTY. 4. S.M. F.A.B from action replaced by 458, 459, CANADIAN Howitzer By's. B2 Major CANADIAN Arty arranged for 12 Div Arty to take everything over from 48. Div Arty and inspected 48 Div Arcs. 1st and 4th S.M. F.A.B. joined GROUP.C. 144 Inf 13th and marched to BO 144 MCL GROUP.A march to BONNEHEM AREA. GROUP.B " " VIEUX BERQUIN	Fair Cool
	27"		48 Division from IV Corps. Head Quarters moved to BOSNES. 48 Div Arty handed over to 12 Div Arty. Divisional Head Quarters GROUP including D.A.C. marched from NIEPPE under E.O.C.R.A. to VIEUX BERQUIN at 6 am. attaining 10 am E.O.C III Corps inspection the Column marching through BAILLEUL. At 8 p.m H.Q Group marched to BOSNES arriving 12.30 p.m and went into BILLETS. GROUP.A march to ALLOUAGNE from BONNEHEM AREA GROUP B march to HAM. EN. ARTOIS from VIEUX BERQUIN area GROUP C march to VIEUX BERQUIN from BAILLEUL	Showery

Army Form C. 2118.

WAR DIARY
or
INTELLIGENCE SUMMARY.
(Erase heading not required.)

Instructions regarding War Diaries and Intelligence Summaries are contained in F. S. Regs., Part II. and the Staff Manual respectively. Title pages will be prepared in manuscript.

Place	Date	Hour	Summary of Events and Information	Remarks and references to Appendices
BUSNES	28.		HQ in Billets BUSNES. GROUP B moved to LOZINGHEM from MAM EN ARTOIS. GROUP C " " ROBECQ from VIEUX BERQUIN.	Sperier
	29.		Divisional H.Q. moved to PHILOMEL from BUSNES. GROUP C including D.A.C. moved to BURBURE from ROBECQ.	
	30.		Conference IV Corps attended by G.O.C. R.A. HQ 48 Div RA moved from BUSNES to LILLERS.	

J Ainsworth Major
B.M.
48 P. Div Arty
30/6/15.

48th Division

121/6292

HdQrs R.A. 48th Division

Vol I

1-31-7-15

CONFIDENTIAL.

WAR DIARY
of
R.A. H.Q. 48° Division.
from 1/7/15 - to 31/7/15.

Vol XII

2nd Aug: 1915.   J.M Bowler Major
                      B.tu. 48° D.A.

Army Form C. 2118.

WAR DIARY
or
INTELLIGENCE SUMMARY.
(Erase heading not required.) H.Q. R.A. 48 Division Vol XII

Instructions regarding War Diaries and Intelligence Summaries are contained in F.S. Regs. Part II. and the Staff Manual respectively. Title pages will be prepared in manuscript.

Place	Date	Hour	Summary of Events and Information	Remarks and references to Appendices
LILLERS	July 1.		1 S.M.F.A.B. 4 S.M.F.A.B. and Divisional Ammn Column billeted at FERFAY with the 144 Inf Bde Troops whose H.Q. was at BURBURE.	
			2 S.M. F.A.B. billeted at LE MONT EVENIE with the 145 Inf Bde Troops. H.Q at ALLOUAGNE.	
	2.		3 S.M. F.A.B billeted at AUCHEL with the 143 Inf Bde H.A at LOZINGHEM.	
	3		Divisional Artillery overhauling cleaning up.	
	4.		" Drills under Bde arrangements.	
	5.		Reconnaissances of 1st and 47th Div Area by G.O.C. R.A. and Bde Majors forwarded by General Fauchois and Brig. Gen. RAT. VERMELLES Railway Station visited and reported on was MAZINGARBE. 6" Trench Mor Battery billeted at ALLOUAGNE attached to 48 Div Arty. Divisional Artillery drills under Bde arrangements. Road reconnaissances.	
	6.		Brig. Gen. RAT. Wilson C.M.G CSO. 7 days leave. Divisional Training.	
	6a.		The 144 Inf Bde carried out night operations in The BOIS DE REVEILLON cooperation by 1st S.M. F.A.B and 4 S.M.F.A.B.	145 Inf Bde 2 F.A.G
	7.		Staff Ride arranged by 48 Division.	
	8.		"	144 Inf Bde. 3 F.A.B
	9.		"	
	10		The 8 Trench Mortar Battery works 2nd Lt Young attached 47 Division. Staff Ride 144 Inf Bde and 1 and 4 S.M. F.A.Bs. 143 Inf Bde Night operations attended by B. S.M F.A.B.	

Army Form C. 2118.

WAR DIARY
OF
INTELLIGENCE SUMMARY. Vol XII
(Erase heading not required.)   R A 118 48 Div ATY

Instructions regarding War Diaries and Intelligence Summaries are contained in F. S. Regs., Part II. and the Staff Manual respectively. Title pages will be prepared in manuscript.

Place	Date	Hour	Summary of Events and Information	Remarks and references to Appendices
LILLERS	11		IV Corps conference at CHATEAU HINGES. Attended by B.M. Major and G.S.O.1. Reconnaissance by Bgd. Commander of 1st Division and of 47 Division sectors scheduled and second times. Positions selected to cover our left on that front.	
	12		Reconnaissance by 73rd Army order as above cancelled. Instructions received that 47 Division would relieve 47 Division in line on night 14/15. Info. Conference of B.G. Commanders Road Zones allotted to 3.F.A.B. and Info. Battery 2.F.A.B. half Trench W, W2, W3 Zone allotted to 1½ S.M.F.H.B Trenches X, X1. Orders issued See Appendix I. How in order considered and Batteries about to execute relief ordered also to proceed. Batteries had marched 15 miles into action with a left of 4 hours to billets. Battalion relation & order the instructions of 47 Div Arty.	
	13		IV Corps conference at CHATEAU HINGES attended by B.M. Major & G.S.O.1.	
	14		Batteries training under brigade arrangements. Brigade Major leave for England 7 days. Cond.	
	15		Received notification from Divl H.Q. that 18 pdr A.T. equipment to be issued to field batteries 48 Div. instead of 15 pdr B.L.C. 2nd & 3rd Pr. T.A. Prs. move from MONT EVENIC to AUCHEL. (Pendym collect)	
	16		Adjutant 15th M.T.A.Pr. relieved to HQ temporarily in reference to proceed South to be billetting for Headquarter group 48 to Div. Batteries training under Brigade arrangements.	

Army Form C. 2118.

WAR DIARY
or
INTELLIGENCE SUMMARY.

(Erase heading not required.) H.Q. H.B. Div. Artillery

Vol XII

Instructions regarding War Diaries and Intelligence Summaries are contained in F. S. Regs., Part II. and the Staff Manual respectively. Title pages will be prepared in manuscript.

Place	Date	Hour	Summary of Events and Information	Remarks and references to Appendices
LILLERS	17		Battery Training with Brigade arrangements. Orders received for move by Bus from LILLERS and BERGUETTE.	
LILLERS	18		SOCRA left for new area at 10 am by car, accompanied by CRE. H.Q. Div. Arty left LILLERS for DOULLENS at 11.1 p.m. and proceeded to TERRAMESNIL.	
TERRAMESNIL	19		4th S.m.7.A.Bde, H.Q. & 1st Bty, 1st S.m.7.A.Bde, H.Q. & 1st & 2nd Btys, 2nd 5 m 7 A Bde left LILLERS & BERGUETTE for MONDICOURT & DOULLENS by train, detraining at the last 2 places, and proceeded to bivouac at THIEVRES.	
"	20		The remainder of the Div. Artillery less 3rd & 4th Sect. Div. Amm Col and 3rd & 4th Sect Div Amm Col left by train during the day from LILLERS & BERGUETTE to DOULLENS & MONDICOURT. H.Q. Div. Arty moved from TERRAMESNIL to AUTHIE. Div. Amm. Col billeted at AUTHIE, remainder at THIEVRES.	
AUTHIE	21		SOCRA went to see French General. 2nd & 3rd S.m.7.A.Bdes moved from THIEVRES to AUTHIE leaving 1st S.m.7.A.Bde. equipment at THIEVRES. 1st Bde remained.	

Army Form C. 2118.

WAR DIARY
or
INTELLIGENCE SUMMARY.

(Erase heading not required.)

Vol. XII
R.A.H.Q.
4th Div Arty

Instructions regarding War Diaries and Intelligence Summaries are contained in F.S. Regs., Part II. and the Staff Manual respectively. Title pages will be prepared in manuscript.

Place	Date	Hour	Summary of Events and Information	Remarks and references to Appendices
AUTHIE	21		at THIEVRES. 36.15 pdr Q.F. guns & 105 Brit. Amm. wagons arrived at POUKENS and brought along & taken over by the 1st 2nd & 3rd 5th 7a Bdes in place of 15pdr 15CP equipment. 4th S.m. 7a Bde moved from THIEVRES to just West of AUTHIE. Battalion practicing gun drill with new guns.	
"	22			
"	23		Battalion gun drill. Notification received of attachment of the 2S Siege Battery (RA, 18th) & officer of 4th Sm 7a Bde reconnoitring positions for howitzers. Ammunition received for 18 pdrs.	
"	24		Batteries gun drill. Reconnaissance by C.O.C.R.A. & B.M. Mar R. restaurants with O.C. 21 Batteries RA, (RH, 13, 23, 28) & Capt. Lewis joined Division from Boulogne. French Div Gen & at AUTHIE.	
"	25		German Rct Offr visited AUTHIE & reported 500 Boches killed by Auck two light guns. Batteries gun drill. Reconnaissance by Major RA & B.M. Major.	Showery
"	26		11 Sept. 04. 2nd Siege Battery (6" hows.) under the Major S.O. AE Pelley joined the Division & coming & strength Battery 1 Col 5.5 Howitzer Battery came into action under the name of S.of. AE Pelley. A.D.S.S./Forms/C. 2118.	

HEADQTRS 2/3 on a 3/1 Battalion came into action in rue of replacements / positions R. of SOUTH/ MARITIME under Colonel MORIZET at Farm at AUTHIE.

WAR DIARY
or
INTELLIGENCE SUMMARY.
(Erase heading not required.)

Army Form C. 2118.

Vol XII

48 Div Arty

Place	Date	Hour	Summary of Events and Information	Remarks and references to Appendices
	27.		19 Siege Bty 8th & 6th E.C. Buckle commanding joined for attachment. Reconnaissance of positions for 1st Battery 2nd Bde and 16 Siege Bty. G.O.C R.A and B.C. Major visited 38 French Divison HQ and reconnoitred country N of SAILLY AU BOIS.	
	28.		Reconnaissance by G.O.C R.A & Bde Major. The 21 French Division wants staff at Div to confirm Div instead 48 Howitzer Battery Commander taken over S of HEBUTERNE.	
	29		Nil	
	30		R.A. Headquarters moved to BUS 1st Battery 3rd Bde relieved 9th French Bty in section — See Appendix A	
BUS.	31		1st Bde / S.M.F.A.B relieved 4 B. French Bty in section 2nd Bde 1 " 3rd Bde 3 S.M.F.A.B 9 B G.O.C R.A assumed responsibility for defence of their [sector].	

A

SECRET

RELIEF OF FRENCH ARTILLERY

Unit Order of March	Night of Relief	Route to Action	Starting Point	Time	Relieve French Battery in Action at	Zone	Remarks
One Battery 3rd S.M.F.A.Bde.	30/31st	ST. LEGER COIGNEUX SAILLY	X of COIGNEUX	9 pm.	9th French Battery (position D.)	Pt. 301 to Pt. 508 inclusive	
One Battery 3rd S.M.F.A.Bde.	31/1st	do.	do.	9 pm.	5th French Battery (position C)	Pt. 861 road inclusive to Pt. 863 road exclusive	
One Battery 1st S.M.F.A.Bde.	31/1st	do.	do.	9.3 pm	6th French Battery (position B)	Pt. 308 to 314 inclusive	
One Battery 1st S.M.F.A.Bde.	31/1st	do.	do.	9.6 pm	4th French Battery (position A)	Pt. 503 road inclusive to Pt. 508	

29/7/15.

J. de V. BOWLES, Major,
Bde. Major, 48th Div. RA

48th K Dracon

12/6539

A/A

A/d Ord R.A. of 5th Division

Army Form C. 2118.

WAR DIARY
Vol. XIII
or
INTELLIGENCE SUMMARY.
(Erase heading not required)

Hd. Arty. 48 Div Arty.

Instructions regarding War Diaries and Intelligence Summaries are contained in F.S. Regs., Part II. and the Staff Manual respectively. Title pages will be prepared in manuscript.

Place	Date	Hour	Summary of Events and Information	Remarks and references to Appendices
BUS en ARTOIS	1		Registration of Zones by 1/1 2/1 and 3/3 Batteries.	Fine
	2		At 12 noon next Zone taken over and front of 48 Division covered by 8 Batteries. 48 Division and one French Battery. One Battery 48 Div in reserve at AUTHIE.	
	3		Registration by Batteries	Heavy Rain.
	4		do	
	5		do	
	6		2/3 Battery withdrawn to Billets at COIGNEUX. R.O.C.A.R. selected positions for 2 Line of defence.	Fine
	7		1/3 Battery withdrawn to wagon line billets.	Showers V. Hot
	8		2/1 Battery replaces 3/2 Battery by sections, the latter returning to Billets. Battery positions severely shelled.	" "
	9		The above completed. Our Battery positions shelled no casualties. 3 direct hits on gun casemates	Thunder Storm
	10		Battery COLINCAMPS shelled.	
	11		2/2 & 1/3 relieve with a return next position at Souilly 16 B'ty & 6" How 5th How B'ty and 3/3 Battery successfully bombarded German Trenches South of GOMMECOURT.	

1577 Wt.W10791/1773 500,000 1/15 D.D.&L. A.D.S.S./Forms/C 2118.

Army Form C. 2118.

WAR DIARY
or
INTELLIGENCE SUMMARY.
(Erase heading not required.)

Vol XIII

H.Q. 48 Div Arty.

Instructions regarding War Diaries and Intelligence Summaries are contained in F.S. Regs., Part II. and the Staff Manual respectively. Title pages will be prepared in manuscript.

Place	Date	Hour	Summary of Events and Information	Remarks and references to Appendices
BUS en ARTOIS.	12		Conference at RAMCHEVAL, Army Arty General; attended by C.O.R.A. and O.C. Army.	fine
	13.		Nil. 4th How. How. fired successfully at a German French mortar.	
	14.		2 Rockets Battery went into action east of COINSCAMP	
	15.		Registration Very little Artillery fire	
	16.		" "	
	17.		Enemy's Sap shelled by 8.4 How Battery. Fine	Snowing
	18.		Enemy's Trenches shelled by 5 How " " Nil	Bright
	19.		Nil	Bad light
	20.		Nil	Bad light
	21.		Nil	
	22.		SOYER and COLINCAMP shelled by German Arty. Retaliation on POISIEUX and	Fine
	23.		COMMÉCOURT by German Arty. Several German hostile parties shelled Nil.	fine
	24.		2 Howitzer Battery fired successfully at machine gun emplacement	fine
	25.		Very misty observation difficult	
	26.		"	

Army Form C. 2118.

WAR DIARY
or
INTELLIGENCE SUMMARY. 3rd XIII H.Q. 48 Div Arty
(Erase heading not required.)

Instructions regarding War Diaries and Intelligence Summaries are contained in F. S. Regs., Part II. and the Staff Manual respectively. Title pages will be prepared in manuscript.

Place	Date	Hour	Summary of Events and Information	Remarks and references to Appendices
Bus	27.		Morning Batteries outside. Registration.	Misty
	28.		1/1 Battery moved to position D. Fresh allotment of 3 am. see Appendix I	fine
	"		Relief of Field Artillery commenced see Appendix II attached	fine Zepp raid
	29.		Registration of new zones.	fine
	30.		Relief continued. see appendix III attached.	
	31.		Registration	

J. Marshall Major
BM 48 Div Arty

Appendix I

HEBUTERNE
Ref: 1/10,000

48th DIV. ARTY.

B.M. CIRCULAR NO. 61.

Re-allotment of zones to take effect at 12 noon tomorrow.

The 1st Brigade will be responsible for the line from Communication Trench C.29.b.8.7, 200 yards N. of Point 863, to Point 504 inclusive.

The 1/1st Battery will move tonight at 8.30pm. to D. position and take over its new zone from Communication Trench C.29.b.8.7 inclusive to Point 871 exclusive.

3/1st Battery zone from Point 871 inclusive to Point 301 inclusive.

2/1st Battery zone Point 301 exclusive to Point 504 inclusive.

The 3rd Brigade will be responsible for line from Communication Trench C.29.b.8.7 exclusive to Point 855 inclusive.

The 3/3rd Battery from C.29.b.8.7 inclusive to Point 861 exclusive.

The 2/3rd Battery from Point 861 inclusive to Road at 855 exclusive.

The 1/3rd Battery will cover zone C.29.b.8.7 to Point 871 until 1/1st Battery has registered this zone.

The 1/2nd Battery will cover Point 349 inclusive to Road 855 inclusive.

The French Artillery covering zone Point 349 to Point 861 will not move till registration is completed.

27/8/15.

J. de V. BOWLES, Major,
Bde. Major, 48th Div. R.A.

Appendix II

48th. Div Arty.

Ref: 1/20,000.
18th. July 1915.

B&M. Circular. No. 62.

1. The line now occupied by 58th. French Division will be taken over by the 37th. and 48th. Divisions commencing the relief on the 2nd. Sept. 1915.

    The extreme left of the Infantry of the 48th. Division will rest at Point C.10.d.6.8 – 100 yards N.E. of second L in FONQUEVILLERS.

2. 2nd.F.A.Bde. will be responsible for Line from Point 164 C.16.b.2.9 to Point 855 road inclusive.

    2/2nd and 3/2nd Batteries will send one gun each to French positions at C.13.d.3.5 and C.25.a.10.7 to be in action at 9pm tonight and register zones as follows :-

    2/2nd Battery from Communication Trench Point 346 exclusive to 100 yards N. of Point 348 inclusive.

    3/2nd Battery from 100 yards N. of Point 348 exclusive to Point 349 exclusive.

3rd F.A.BRIGADE

2/3rd Battery will send one gun to position C.8.d.2.0 and register zone Point 855 exclusive to Point 860 inclusive.

1/3rd Battery will send one gun to C.20.d.2.3 and register zone from Point 346 inclusive to a point on German Trench opposite U of HAE des SAUTES. Guns to be in action by 9 pm. tonight.

3. Brigades will make necessary arrangements to ensure their telephone communications being completed by September 5th.

28/8/15.

J. de V. BOWLES, Major,
Bde. Major, 48th Div. R.A.

Appendix 75

48th. Div. Arty.

D.M. Circular No. 64.

Ref: 1/20,000.
July 13th. 1915.

The following moves will take place in continuation of relief of French Artillery. -

Two more guns 2/2nd. Battery on night 30/31st. to position G.13.A.5.5. The remaining gun of this Battery to come into action at 9pm. on night of 4/5th.

Two guns 1/3rd. Battery on night 30/31st. to position G.H9.A.5.5. The remaining gun of this Battery to be withdrawn to Wagon Line after 9pm.

30/8/15.

J.deV.Bowlen, Major,
Bde. Major., 48th. Div. Arty.

121/6983

48th Division

H.d Qtr R.A. 48th Division

Sept 15

CONFIDENTIAL

WAR DIARY

of

48th Divisional Artillery

Vol XIV.

from Sep 1st to Sep 30th 1915

October 3rd 15.

J de V Bowles Major — B.M.
for B.G. 48th Div Arty

WAR DIARY VOL. XIV
INTELLIGENCE SUMMARY
(Erase heading not required.)

Army Form C. 21.

Instructions regarding War Diaries and Intelligence Summaries are contained in F. S. Regs., Part II. and the Staff Manual respectively. Title pages will be prepared in manuscript.

Place: B.n.S
HQ 48 Divisional Arty

Date	Hour	Summary of Events and Information	Remarks and references to Appendices
1		La LOUVIERE FME, GOMMECOURT, and BRAYELLE WOOD shelled by our Arty.	Fine
2		Registration	Fine
3		"	Showers
4		3/2 Battery relieved the 26th French Battery in action. 2/2 Battery taken off Fire at 9am then composing their Battery in action. H.E. Bursters L.F.A 15 rounds from ROTHE to BAVENCOURT.	Cloudy
5		The 26th French Battery withdrew from our area. the last unit of French Artillery to leave the Area.	fine
6		Registration. Eng. Liffe. Shorthelp, steering of German Trenches by 10p. 1530. a 6" Howitzer Battery Breaking Factory engaged by 10p. 1530.	Very fine
7		"	"
8		"	"
9		"	"
10		1/2 Battery and 3/3 Battery changed positions.	
11		German First and Second Positions with our Trenches. 3/2 Batterys and 3/3 large Battery which on German Trenches in front of GOMMECOURT WOOD. few opposition.	

Army Form C. 2118.

WAR DIARY
or
INTELLIGENCE SUMMARY.
(Erase heading not required.)

Instructions regarding War Diaries and Intelligence Summaries are contained in F. S. Regs., Part II. and the Staff Manual respectively. Title pages will be prepared in manuscript.

Hour, Date, Place	Summary of Events and Information	Remarks and references to Appendices
Bus. 12. Sept.	Battery fired successfully on working party. Germans firing some kind of incendiary or star shell. HEBUTERNE shelled.	very fine.
13. Sept.	Battery experimented at new cutting. Enemy's artillery not active. 2nd G.v.C.R.A. reconnoitred positions for new cutting 13½'.	"
14. Sept	Naval shelling by Batteries of working parties.	"
15. Sept	Hebuterne shelled by Germans. Nearly every day some shells are fired into or about the village.	"
16. "	SAILLY shelled. H.S.M.F.A.B. retaliated on CONNEUX. SAILLY shelled. H.S.M.F.A.B. HEBUTERNE again shelled the 1st F.A.B. on PUISIEUX. 3.F.A.B. shelled enemy's 12 gun Howitzer in the enemy No Man's Land.	Weather beautiful very hot.
17.		"
18.	Enemy aeroplane came over all B½oo in working by wireless with aeroplane. Our Battery from 1st to 18th engaged by Aeroplane. Successful so far as communication was concerned from a Recovery point of view. Useless ~~bombardment from~~ though took it ammunition	"

Army Form C. 2118.

WAR DIARY
or
INTELLIGENCE SUMMARY.
(Erase heading not required.)

Instructions regarding War Diaries and Intelligence Summaries are contained in F.S. Regs., Part II. and the Staff Manual respectively. Title pages will be prepared in manuscript.

Hour, Date, Place	Summary of Events and Information	Remarks and references to Appendices
Bus 19 Sept 1915	2nd. 1.F.A.B. fired a few shell into PUISIEUX in retaliation for Germans shelling HEBUTERNE.	Very fine
20 "	1.F.A.B. fired 2 rds per fire at 3pm into PUISIEUX.	
21.	2 F.A.B. Rode recony East from COMMECOURT.	
	3 F.A.B. 3pm Shelled BITTENCOURT and our own trenches ESSYMECOURT.	
	4 F.A.B.	
	At 3.30 am further round of Gun fire was given. Germans retaliated on our Front trenches and HEBUTERNE and SAILY no serious damage done. At 8.45 pm our guns again retaliated on German trenches.	
22.	HEBUTERNE. SAILY and COLINCAMP shelled by Germans no damage done. Retaliation by our Batteries on PUISIEUX BOMMECOURT and ROTENOY FME	

Army Form C. 2118.

WAR DIARY Vol XIV
or
INTELLIGENCE SUMMARY.   H.Q. 48 Div. Arty.
(Erase heading not required.)

Instructions regarding War Diaries and Intelligence Summaries are contained in F.S. Regs., Part II. and the Staff Manual respectively. Title pages will be prepared in manuscript.

Hour, Date, Place	Summary of Events and Information	Remarks and references to Appendices
Bus. (En Artois) 23 Sept 15.	See Appendices A and B.	Rain. Light bay East
24. Sept 15.	Bombardment of German line and wire cutting. See Appendix C.	
25. Sept 15	Bombardment continued see Appendix D	Light fair clouds low
26. Sept 15	" " E	Light 13cc clouds low rain.
27. Sept 15.	Our Artillery did not shoot. German Artillery also inactive.	Rain. Cloudy cold.
28 Sept 15	Our Artillery did not shoot. German Artillery also inactive.	Dust light 13 n d.
29 Sept 15	Artillery inactive	Rain
30 Sept 15	Germans started on front line trenches in about 180 shells. No damage done. Our heavies shelled position. Germans retaliated with 8 shells on Souchez.	Cold fine Night

J. Humbers Major B M 118 Bo

Appendix A & B

Ref. 1/20,000.

BOMBARDMENT – THURSDAY 23rd SEPTEMBER, 1915.

UNIT	TASK	AMMUNITION ALLOWED PER BRIGADE			RESULTS
		18-pr.S.	18-pr.H.E.	5"HOW.	
4th HOW.BRIGADE	(a) Redoubt S.W.GOMMECOURT. (b) GOMMECOURT VILLAGE (c) Pt.862 Pt.863. (d) Machine Gun Pt.871.			100 rds.	(a) Direct hits badly damaged. Sweetspot (b) Bricks & dust seen flying about. 2 F.A.B Strongpoints lit up with shrapnel (c) Parapet not badly damaged, but Trenches knocked about especially at Pt 862 (d) Direct hits with 18 lbr H.E.
1st F.A.BRIGADE	(a) Comm.Trenches Pt.869 Pt.877 (b) (Pt.863 LA LOUVIERE FME.with HE) (c) 2 rds.Gun-fire into PUISIEUX at 5.pm.	275	100		(a) Fire apparently effective (b) Direct hits – A big farm probably little damaged, but always occupied. (c) Always disliked by the Germans
2nd F.A.BRIGADE	(a) Bombardment Pt.349 (b) & GOMMECOURT	50	50		(a) Badly damaged. (b) Impossible to say.
3rd F.A.BRIGADE	(a) Bombardment Pt.862 Pt.866 (b) Comm. Trenches running East. (c) Cut Wire Pt.862.	125 50	100		(a) Trenches very numerous here, much damage done (b) Effective fire – no visible damage done (c) A lane from 8 to 10 yards wide cut. (During night Germans have thrown some loose entanglement wire over their parapet)
	TOTAL	500	250	100	

GERMAN RETALIATION

Very feeble. The Germans fired 120 shells about our Batteries at C.33.D. F 3 A & B. Shellfire for 2 hours. 1 man wounded, no damage done. 100 shell fired into our Trenches at C.29.B. C & D.

J. de V. BOYLES, Major,
Bde. Major, 48th Div. R.A.

Ref.1/20,000.

Appendix C

BOMBARDMENT – FRIDAY 24th SEPTEMBER, 1915.

UNIT	TIME	TASK	18-pr.S.	18-pr.H.E.	5"HOW.	RESULTS
1st F.A.BDE.	2.30pm	(a) Bombard Trenches in C.30.d. C.30.b. Pt.869 Pt.868	150	100		(a) Satisfactory co-operated with Hows.
	5.30pm	(b) LA LOUVIERE FME.				(b) " " " "
	In afternoon when light permits, but must be completed before dark.	(c) Wire cutting at Pts. 301, 873 & 863.	600			(c) Wire at point 301 not all demolished. Some new German wire close to trench standing. Wire at point 873 a clearing of 20 yds cut. Wire at point 863 a clearing of 20 yds cut. At Point 301 Parapet of German trench knocked down.
2nd F.A.BDE.	5.30pm	(a) GOMMECOURT				(a) Successful co-operation with Hows(?)
	2.30 & 5.30pm	(b) Pt.349, C.22.a.7.9 Pt.356, 358, 357, in	100	50		(b) 5 or 6 direct hits. a direct hit on machine gun emplacement and roof blown in
	2.30pm	(c) Comm.Trenches C.17.c. & d.				c. Satisfactory
3rd F.A.BDE.	2.30pm	(a) Bombard enemys 3rd Line in any 2 or 3 of the following places selected by O.C.Bde. Pts selected Pt.359,360,361,362, 366,367,865.	150	100		(a) Fire generally effective impossible to say damage done.
	In afternoon when light permits, must be completed before dark.	(b) Wire cutting at Pt. 862.	200			(b) A front of 30 yds of German wire cut through and clear for inf. to pass. ....
4th HOW.BDE.	2.30pm	(a) Pt.862. Pt.863.				(a) Considerable damage 8 yds of Parapet demolished
	5.30pm	(b) LA LOUVIERE FME.				(b) 5 Direct Hits 10 rounds fell into trenches
		(c) RETTEMOY FME.				(c) " "
		(d) GOMMECOURT VILLAGE & Pt.349.			110 rds	(d) 6 How.to hit .... 6 How shell through roof and 5 yds of parapet knocked down
						(E) Redoubt at 349 had shell through roof and 5 yds of parapet knocked down

GERMAN RETALIATION

A direct hit on gun emplacement in C.33 D.i.i. No mm injured as gun was Southern Redoubt hit twice. Cable damage done.
Some very very out. not firing at the time gun buried in debris. ... one 85 of
Infantry Trenches shelled all along front South of GOMMECOURT WOOD mostly by Falk guns and 5.9 How.
Pt.48 Div lit? By Wood Row Bth?

Appendix D

Ref. 1/20,000

BOMBARDMENT - SATURDAY 25th SEPTEMBER, 1915.

UNIT	TIME	TASK	AMMUNITION ALLOWED			RESULTS
			18-pr.S.	18-pr.H.E.	5"HOW.	
1st F.A.BDE.	2.pm.	(a) Keep lanes in wire open (b) Shell Comm.Trenches Pt.371 to 368. Pt.501 & 869.	150	125		(a) Wire cutting at about 301 quite satisfactory. Lanes already cut at others. (b) Satisfactory, a machine gun silenced.
	6.12pm.	(c) Shell LA LOUVIERE FME. PUISIEUX				(c) Satisfactory
2nd F.A.BDE.	2.pm.	(a) Shell Comm. Trenches Pt.352 & Pt.356 to Pt.359 inclusive. (b) Shell redoubts S.W.corner GOMMECOURT WOOD & Pt.546.	100	50		(a) Shooting appeared good. (b) Very effective iron shooting knocked about. One shell through doorway of Redoubt at Point 394
	6.12pm.	GOMMECOURT				(c) Satisfactory
3rd F.A.BDE.	2.pm.	(a) Keep lanes in wire open. (b) Trenches 360-362 Wood at Pt.448 H.E.	150	125.		(a) Satisfactory (b) Many direct hits (c) Apparently effective
	6.12pm.	(c) Shell Pt.365. Pt.387. (d) RETTEMOY FME.				(D) Effective
4th HOW.BDE.	2.pm.	(a) Redoubts S.W.of GOMMECOURT Pt.862,863,864,877,374.			150	(a) Very effective 16 7ers fell into Trenches 301. 874. (B) 17 others effective on wire and parapet.
	6.12pm	(b) GOMMECOURT (c) LA LOUVIERE FME. (d) RETTEMOY FME.				Bombs seen flying about. (C) Satisfactory (D)

GERMAN RETALIATION

The German artillery were singularly inactive.

J. de V. BOWLES, Major,
Bde. Major, 49th Div. R.A.

Ref.1/20,000.

Appendix E

OPERATION ORDER No. 4

UNIT	TIME		AMMUNITION			RESULTS
			18-pr.S.	18-pr.H.E.	5"HOW.	
1st F.A.BDE.	during day	(a) Usual working parties any signs of work or movement. A few rounds to keep wire gaps clear if required.	36	10		(a) No working parties visible.
	6.a.m.	(b) Trenches & approaches to LA LOUVIERE FME.				(b) Satisfactory
	6.a.m.	(c) PUISIEUX				(c) — " —
2nd F.A.BDE.	during day	(a) Shell trenches pt.852,358, 347, 346. A few shell into S.W. corner GOMMECOURT.	36	10		(a) Satisfactory - light b.a.a.
3rd F.A.BDE.	during day	(a) Usual working parties, any signs of work or movement.	36	10		(a) No working parties visible 862 & 863 shelled
		(b) Trenches 366 & North of BOIS ROSSIGNOL.				(b) light not good enough
	6.a.m.	(c) RETTEMOY FME.				(c) No ammunition available
4th BRIGADE	6.a.m.	(a) Bombard Pt.852,877,373.				(a) Point 301. 862. 864 shelled, 50 yards of hampet destroyed. 2 Nests complete with own platter demolished which were put up during night. 1 still Remains.
	6.a.m.	(b) RETTEMOY FME. LA LOUVIERE FME				(b) 5 MGs on LA LOUVIERE FME
	during day	(c) Be prepared to co-operate with aeroplane by wireless			100	(c) Not Satisfactory

GERMAN RETALIATION

Nil

J. de V. BOWES, Major,
Bde. Major, 40th Div. R.A.

48th Division

121/733

Confidential

War Diary

of

H.Q. 48th Divl. Artillery

from 1.10.15. to 31.10.15.

VOLUME 8.

Confidential

Army Form C. 2118.

WAR DIARY From Oct 1st 1915
or to Oct 31st 1915.
INTELLIGENCE SUMMARY.
(Erase heading not required.) Vol XV Headquarters 48 Div Arty.

Hour, Date, Place		Summary of Events and Information	Remarks and references to Appendices
BUS EN ARTOIS October 1915.	1.	Enemy very quiet. Our guns did not shoot.	Weather fine & clear.
	2.	Captain C.E. BOYS Adjutant 1.S.M.F.A.B posted to 15 Division and posted accordingly. Captain G.E. KIDD adjutant to S.M.F.A.B. posted to 15 Division and posted accordingly. Enemy very quiet. Our guns did not shoot.	Fine cold.
	3.	A.S.M.F.A.B shelled enemy trenches at Pt 862. 80.5 and Pt.3. Captain G.R. BARON posted as adjutant to 1.F.A.B vice Boyce from 48 Div Amm Column.	"
	4.	Germans shelled FONQUEVILLERS on epecial by railway. GOMMECOURT & ROTOYNOY. FAB with 4.3"+3" F.B & 4.5 Germans then fired a few shells into HEBUTERNE.	"
	5.	A quiet day.	Twenty rain.
	6.	Germans shelled ENNOIS at Heavy rifle & m.g. barrels from fire on J. section of our trenches at intervals from 5.30 pm to 8.30 pm. 2 German field batteries fired about 60 gas into J section trenches. Our Infantry supposed that this. 3. F.A.B opened fire on German trenches and contained at	Light fine.

Forms/C. 2118/10

(9 29 6) W 4141—463 100,000 9/14 H W V

Instructions regarding War Diaries and Intelligence Summaries are contained in F. S. Regs., Part II. and the Staff Manual respectively. Title pages will be prepared in manuscript.

Army Form C. 2118.

WAR DIARY
or
INTELLIGENCE SUMMARY. Vol XV Headquarters of Div Artillery
(Erase heading not required.)

Instructions regarding War Diaries and Intelligence Summaries are contained in F. S. Regs., Part II. and the Staff Manual respectively. Title pages will be prepared in manuscript.

Hour, Date, Place	Summary of Events and Information	Remarks and references to Appendices
October 7.	A quiet day. 2/3 Battery negatived from our position.	Four light hits
8.	La BASSÉE FME appeared to be on fire. Several aerial torpedoes fired into our trenches to aft COMMECOURT. H.I.A.O shells seen on trenches in outskirts of COMMECOURT. H.I.A.O shells shelled POISIEUX.	Very misty
9.	A quiet day. One heavy battery shelled POISIEUX. 1/2 London Bde RFA arrived at THOSY RES. under Lt Colonel TURNER. Officers and 50 Col. S. reconnoitred gun positions.	Good.
10.	2nd Battle Batteries came into action at 8 p.m.	build
11.	H.S.M.I.O.B. shelled some machine gun emplacements S of COMMECOURT WOOD. 1/2 London Bde reported four batteries arrived. New communications. Enemy's battery quiet.	Dusty build glass upon light gun
12.	See appearance of German retreat on FONCQUEVILLERS. 1/2 London Bde commenced registration.	Morning misty
13.	Enemy sent a few shells into SAILLY to LONDON Bde re position to trenches.	Left corner
14.	A quiet day	Fair

(9 29 6) W 4141—463 100,000 9/14 H W V   Forms/C. 2118/10

Army Form C. 2118.

WAR DIARY
or
INTELLIGENCE SUMMARY.
(Erase heading not required.) Vol XV Headquarters 48 Division Arty —

Instructions regarding War Diaries and Intelligence Summaries are contained in F. S. Regs., Part II. and the Staff Manual respectively. Title pages will be prepared in manuscript.

Hour, Date, Place	Summary of Events and Information	Remarks and references to Appendices
Bus (EN ARTOIS) October 15.	1/2 London 18th continue Firing.	Very misty.
16.	Registration by 1/2 London B.A.C.	" "
17.	Quiet except from Formecourt wood and from the Infantry — 2.F.A.B. and 4th Mon Battery shell machine gun emplacement at B.28.C.8.1. and Grenier Trenches S.E. West of CONNECOURT WOOD. 3.F.A.B. shelled Trenches S.E. of CONNECOURT WOOD. At 11.30 am German bombardo of FONQUILLERS, SAILLY ou HEBUTERNE — also Enemy Artillery active on PUISIEUX and BUCQUOY — the German are of gun shell l sniper wheel was replied to by our 1.F.D.B. shelling PUISIEUX. 1/2 London 18th put 8 men wounded. 250 shells in all fell about Bihef.	" "
18	Enemy's Artillery very active they shelled area finished East of HEBUTERNE from 2.45 pm till 3.35 pm also our Trenches N.E. of TOUVENT FARM. At 3.30 one shell struck German Trenches see opposite Wid. B. the 4/3 Battery casualties returned a Bombardier. The 3 F.A.B. & 1 F.A.B. Batteries enjoyed German Trenches.	

Forms/C. 2118/10

Army Form C. 2118.

WAR DIARY
or
INTELLIGENCE SUMMARY.
(Erase heading not required.)

Vol XV Headquarters n.8 Corps Arty

Instructions regarding War Diaries and Intelligence Summaries are contained in F. S. Regs., Part II. and the Staff Manual respectively. Title pages will be prepared in manuscript.

Hour, Date, Place	Summary of Events and Information	Remarks and references to Appendices
BUS (EN ARTOIS) October 19.	Enemy's artillery quiet — German fusiliers in front of SCARPE shelled by 4th Division — 2nd Hour A.P. Solon 6.0 & Ammunition. The London B.Bs having completed its attachment and equipment from reserve & reinforce at THIEVRES on night 19/20th	Windy
20	1/2 London B.B. opened 5B. Division — 1/3 London B.B. fired for attachment & relieved at THIEVRES night 20/21. — Hostile Artillery quiet	Windy
21	1/2 London 70" went into action 7.2.d.1.6. 10.8.c. in front of SAILLY 9r 10.59 on ALBION 1st Direction. Hostile Arty quiet	Windy
22	1/2 London 108 fired out telephone lines at 0 stations & tank out town lines of firm Germans saw about 30 guns shell into one trunks. E.t.f. Maintained	Clear
23	73. 8" + 73 Howitzer Commenced registration, but enemy Bombarded Quinn in trenches SE of Commeccont. The Bombardment was very Sandbagmont due 6.0.5 of HARTSHNG and S.W. of Commeccout. See appendix C. The Bombardment was very assumpt & was considered dangerous	

FMC See appendix C. 2118/10

Army Form C. 2118.

Confidential

WAR DIARY
or
INTELLIGENCE SUMMARY.

(Erase heading not required.) Vol. XV Headquarters 48 Div Artly

Instructions regarding War Diaries and Intelligence Summaries are contained in F. S. Regs., Part II. and the Staff Manual respectively. Title pages will be prepared in manuscript.

Place	Date	Hour	Summary of Events and Information	Remarks and references to Appendices
Bus Douve	24		Registration by 1 London By	fine
	25		Hostile artillery very quiet and prevented shooting	quiet
	26		Hostile Artillery inactive. 3rd London R.G.A continued practice	mist
	27		A few shots fired in HEMOTENNE. Our heavy Artillery engaged in wire cutting party. 3rd London R.G.A registered.	mist
	28		Light enemy shells. Bombardment arranged had to be postponed.	very much rain
	29		Bombardment. See Appendix D	rain
	30		One Bgde to CALAIS - Lt Col QW Balfour 1st Inst Bde RFA temp. in command.	fine
Apr	30		Quiet day. 3rd London R.A. withdrawn to THIEVRES. 3 killed. Three night 30/31 CRA returned.	fair
	31		Quiet day. 3rd London R.A. left divisional area. 17 Bde R.G.A. H.Q & 48 Hvy Bty R.G.A arrived & bivouaced in WARNIMONT wood. Attached for administration.	rain

[signature] Capt for
BRIGADE MAJOR, 48th DIV. ARTY.

Appendix A

48th DIV. ARTY.

B.M. CIRCULAR NO. 84.

ENTERPRISE FOR TUESDAY, 12th OCTOBER.

At 4.pm.
    The 6" Howitzers will bombard German work K.3.d.7.8 (Pt.349) also Machine Gun North of Barricade E.28.c.7.5.

    2nd F.A. Brigade will enfilade with 2 roving guns the German Trenches West of GOMMECOURT and cooperate with the 6" Howitzers in shelling ...... Pt. 349 - K.3.d.7.7
    5"   do   do   ...... Pt. 346 - E.28.d.2.9

    Ammunition allowed 18-pr. Shrapnel .... 40 rds.
                          18-pr. H.E.   .... 10 rds.

    3rd F.A. Brigade will shell Machine Guns and trenches in and about K.4.d.2.6.

    Ammunition allowed 18-pr. Shrapnel .... 24 rds.

4th F.A. BRIGADE

1. Select a portion of trench West of GOMMECOURT you can best enfilade - creep up it with 10 rounds.

2. Work at Pt. 346.
   Machine Guns at E.28.d.2.7
                  E.28.c.7.2
   Machine Guns at E.28.b.3.3
                  K.4.d.2.5

    Ammunition only what is required to do the work in no case to exceed 40 rounds.

    All Forward Observing Officers to keep a specially keen look-out to pick up Flashes of Hostile Artillery.

    The Heavy Artillery have been asked to deal with any Counter Batteries.

    Our Infantry will co-operate with rifle and Machine Gun fire.

    Reports of FLASHES of Hostile Artillery to be sent at once to this Office.

    An aeroplane will look out for Counter Batteries and may call up a Brigade to shoot.

    This Ammunition is all part of Weekly Allowance.

11th Oct. 1915.   J. de V. BOWLES, Major,
                                    Bde. Major, 48th Div. R.A.

Appendix B

48th DIV. ARTY.

B.M. CIRCULAR NO. 96.

ENTERPRISE FOR MONDAY, 18th OCTOBER.

Ammunition from Weekly Allowance.

At 3.30pm. the 6" HOWITZERS will shell Pt.301 - K.23.b.2.9.

At 3.25pm. the 1st F.A.BRIGADE will shell Front Line Trenches from Pt. K.17.b.2.10. to K.23.b.8.5. Ammunition .. 36 rds.

At 3.25pm. the 3rd F.A.BRIGADE roving gun at K.9.c. enfilade German Trench from K.23.b.2.9. to K.23.b.10.3. Ammunition 30 rds.

At 3.25pm. the 2nd LONDON BRIGADE ......

    4th London Bty.,
    5th London Bty.   Shell BOIS ROSSIGNOL.

    6th London Bty.   Shell Comm. Trench from K.17.d.5.2. to K.18.d.1.7 and from K.24.a.6.7 to K.24.b. 5.10. Ammunition allowed - all that remains of your allowance (under no circumstances will this be exceeded).

At 3.30pm. the 4th F.A.BRIGADE shell Pt. 363 - K.17.b.1.8
                                                   K.17.d.2.6
                                                   K.17.d.4.1½

Ammunition ... 30 rds.

2.   Our Infantry will co-operate with rifle and machine gun fire.

    The Heavy Artillery will deal with Hostile Guns.

    The 8th Squadron Royal Flying Corps will co-operate.

17th October, 1915.

J. de V. BOWLES, Major,
Bde. Major, 48th Div. R.A.

Ref: 1/20,000.

BOMBARDMENT A.

TIME	UNIT	TASK	AMMUNITION ALLOWED		
			18-pr.S.	18-pr.HE.	5"HOW.
	1st F.A. BRIGADE	K.17.b.3½.2½ to K.23.b.5.8 inclusive		80	
		On K.17.b.2.9 to K.17.b.0.6		20	
	4th HOW. BRIGADE	K.17.d.5.6 to K.23.b.4.8			40
	6" HOWITZERS	Pt.863.			

BOMBARDMENT A.

ALL ARRANGEMENTS TO BE MADE FOR ABOVE BOMBARDMENT TO TAKE PLACE WITHIN 5 MINUTES NOTICE FROM THIS OFFICE.

J. de V. BOWLES, Major,
Bde. Major, 48th Div. R.A.

19th October, 1915.

Appendix D

BOMBARDMENT B. for THURSDAY 28th October, 1915.

Bombardment will commence by 18-pr. guns opening on trenches at 3.8.pm. followed by Howitzers & 18-pr.H.E. at 3.10.pm.

UNIT	TIME	TASK	AMMUNITION		
			18-pr.S.	18-pr.H.E.	5"HOW.
1st F.A.BRIGADE	(3.8.pm.	Trenches K.17.b.3½.2½ – K.24.a.0.8	36	30	
	(3.10.pm	K.17.b.2.9 – K.17.b.0.3	18	20	
3rd F.A.BRIGADE	(3.8.pm.	Trenches K.4.d.2.7 to K.11.a.3.8	36	30	
	(3.10.pm.				
	3.30pm......	Communication Trenches to be searched with a few quick bursts of gun fire.	36		
3rd LONDON BRIGADE 7th & 8th Btys.	(3.8.pm.	Trenches K.5.a.0.5 to K.5.b.5.2 B.2.5 K.6.D.1.4.	36	5	
9th Battery	(3.8.pm	K.18.a.0.7 to K.18.c.5.5	36	30	
	(3.10.pm				
	3.30pm......	Communication trenches to LA LOUVIERE FME & BOIS ROSSIGNOL to be searched with a few quick bursts of gun fire.	36		
4th F.A.BRIGADE	3.10pm	K.17.d.5.6 – K.23.b.4.8			60
	3.10pm	K.4.d.2.5 – K.4.d.9.0			30
		Pt 321			12
6" HOWITZERS	3.10.pm.	Pt. K.17.b.0.7 Pt. K.4.d.2.5.			

25th Oct.1915.

J. de V. BOWLES, Major,
Bde. Major, 48th Div. R.A.

121/7637

H.O. B.A. 485 Sind.

Novr 1915

Vol. IX

Confidential

War Diary

of

48th Divisional Artillery

VOL XVI

November 1st to 30th 1915.

J W Bowles Major R.A.
Bde Maj. 48th Div Arty

CONFIDENTIAL.

Army Form C. 2118.

WAR DIARY
or
INTELLIGENCE SUMMARY.

from Nov. 1st 1915
to Nov. 30th 1915.

(Erase heading not required.) VOLUME XVI. H.Q. 48th Bde. C. in C. (R. Artillery)

Instructions regarding War Diaries and Intelligence Summaries are contained in F. S. Regs., Part II. and the Staff Manual respectively. Title pages will be prepared in manuscript.

Place	Date	Hour	Summary of Events and Information	Remarks and references to Appendices
BUS-LES-ARTOIS				
do.	1.11.15		Light rain. Observation difficult. Enemy shelling as usual.	rain
do.	2.11.15		Enemy fired aerial torpedoes into FONQUEVILLERS. 9 S.A.A.(brass) pm Wiehled on BOMMECOURT —	rain
do.	3.11.15		Hostile artillery fairly quiet.	fair
do.	4.11.15		A few 5.9 into HEBUTERNE	misty
do.	5.11.15		Bombardment 'C' (see Appendix A) postponed from 8 am to 11 am owing to misty weather. Weather clear & observation good at 11 am. & bombardment successful. many direct hits on enemy trenches & dug outs being made. Retaliation feeble.	misty to fine
do.	6.11.15		Very misty, observation very difficult. Hostile artillery quiet. Battery located thro 3rd Bde.	misty

CONFIDENTIAL.

Army Form C. 2118.

WAR DIARY
H.Q. 118th Bde Artillery

INTELLIGENCE SUMMARY.
(Erase heading not required.)

Vol XVI

Place	Date	Hour	Summary of Events and Information	Remarks and references to Appendices
BUS-LES-ARTOIS				
	7/11/15		Quiet day. Misty morning, clear afternoon	Fine
	8/11/15		Misty morning. Clear afternoon. 2nd Yorks Bty shelled with 4.2" howitzers	Fine
	9/11/15		Germans shelled HEBUTERNE and SAILLY	Rain
	10/11/15		Very wet and misty	Fine. Showers
	11/11/15		Light frost. German wiring were offensive opposite GOMMECOURT WOOD. 2 F.A.B. silenced them	
	12/11/15		Revived day. Light rain. Rain & storms	
	13/11/15		1 F.A.B. shelled German working parties amongst intelligent guess	High wind Showers
	14/11/15		Heavy activity in conjunction with 2. F.A.B. shell houses at WEST end of GOMMECOURT VILLAGE close to Barricade on road - 1. F.A.B and 4 F.A.B. successfully shelled German Trenches WEST of LA LOUVIERE FM. 3 F.A.B. ranged with aeroplane observation on hostile trenches difficult to observe owing to enemy at high altitude	Bright light
	15/11/15		3. F.A.B. ranged by aeroplane on German Trenches not successful owing to useless on aeroplane failing. Working parties dispersed by our Artillery.	Slight frost. Snow night 14/15

CONFIDENTIAL.

Army Form C. 2118.

WAR DIARY
INTELLIGENCE SUMMARY.
HEADQUARTERS.
48 DIVISIONAL Arty.

(Erase heading not required.)

Instructions regarding War Diaries and Intelligence Summaries are contained in F. S. Regs., Part II. and the Staff Manual respectively. Title pages will be prepared in manuscript.

Place	Date	Hour	Summary of Events and Information	Remarks and references to Appendices
BUS en ARTOIS	16/11/15		Germans sent some aerial Torpedoes from N edge of GOMMECOURT WOOD into our trenches — 2 F.A.B. 4 F.R.B and 1 Section 16 siege Bty searched for Torpedo gun and shewn front line trenches — the Torpedoes were quickly silenced	Slight [illeg] But snow storm 2night 18/16
	17/11/15.		Too thick for observation	3" on ground very misty Grey misty
	18/11/15.		Hostile artillery inactive. A few aeroplanes were fired from GOMMECOURT who our trenches but were quickly silenced by 5" How Bty —	Light hrs
	19/11/15		Enemy sent a few shells into our communication trenches 2 F.R.B shelled hostile trenches N of GOMMECOURT in reply to German 77 m.m. Enemy nothing to report.	
	20/11/15			Very frosty & cold
	21/11/15		H.E Division Trenches German trenches at 10.30 am. One battery at 3 pm Sax Appendix B attached. Several machine gun emplacements & wires were removed about.	Light wd
	22/11/15		Impossible to see owing to fog. All quiet	fog

Army Form C. 2118.

WAR DIARY
INTELLIGENCE SUMMARY.
(Erase heading not required.)

Vol XVI Headquarters 48 Div Inf y

Instructions regarding War Diaries and Intelligence Summaries are contained in F. S. Regs., Part II. and the Staff Manual respectively. Title pages will be prepared in manuscript.

Place	Date	Hour	Summary of Events and Information	Remarks and references to Appendices
BUS (en ARTOIS)	23/11/15		Hostile artillery by shelling 10 LONDON BAY (MINOR BRIDGES) 38 Division worked into our area & trenches at THIEVRES.	Foggy light rain
	24.		Germans bombarded trenches of HT Dot on right of our line - Retaliated by the 10 & 6 London B.G. (R.G) much entanced to Repairs at ARCHEVES.	fine light air
	25.		Bombardment at 2.45 on SOUTH EAST CORNER of FONNECOURT WOOD to break up wire & destroy German wopen. At 12 midnight our infantry entered a barrage the position of German Trenches (5th Gloucesters and entered into 8 wounded. SEE APPENDIX. (C) (D) made by 3 F.M.10 counter bat.	foggy Afternoon light gust
			1 BKt practice ranging by machine with Shrapnel 10 LONDON B69 registrated. Germans shelled SAILLY and COLINCAMPS about 7 p.m	Cold Somer Showers
	26		Our guns inactive. Germans shelled PUISIEUX and SERRE at 9 am and again at 8 am also HEBUTERNE no damage done - Henry Arty shelled PUISIEUX into SAILLY 10 LONDON B Continued registration Germans had a few shell into SAILLY about 300 shell falling in	hard frost
	27		at 1 am Germans shelled our trenches East of HEBUTERNE. a hostile aeroplane dropped the area. Our guns and the shelling ceased. two bombs on SAILLY.	hard frost quite bright
	28			

Army Form C. 2118.

WAR DIARY
of
INTELLIGENCE SUMMARY. Vol XVII Headquarters 48 Div Arty

(Erase heading not required.)

Instructions regarding War Diaries and Intelligence Summaries are contained in F. S. Regs., Part II. and the Staff Manual respectively. Title pages will be prepared in manuscript.

Place	Date	Hour	Summary of Events and Information	Remarks and references to Appendices
ARRAS	29/11/15		Staffor & Xmas battalion joined	
	30/11/15		Artillery in action	France
				[signature] Major R.A.
				Comdg 48 Div Arty

"SECRET"

BOMBARDMENT O. for FRIDAY, 5th November, 1915.

Bombardment to commence at 3. pm.
8 am.

UNIT	TIME	TASK	AMMUNITION		
			18-pr.S.	18-pr.HE.	5"HOW.
1st F.A.BRIGADE	8 am / 3. pm.	Trenches K.11.d.4.0 to K.24.a.0.9 " K.11.d.2.0 to K.17.b.0.3	48 20	30 20	
3rd F.A.BRIGADE	8 am / 3. pm.	Trenches K.11.c.9.6 to K.11.d.2.0 " K.11.d.3.6 to K.11.d.4.0	24 36	20 30	
4th HOW.BRIGADE	8 am / 3. pm.	Trenches K.17.b.5½.2½ to K.23.b.5.3 K.11.d.0.4 to K.17.b.0.5 Pt.301			40 30 10
6"HOWITZERS	8 am / 3. pm.	Points K.11.c.9.5 and K.17.b.0.6½			

A.L.CHANDLER, Capt.,
for Major,
Bde. Major, 48th Div.R.A.

3rd Nov.1915.

Appendix B

BOMBARDMENT D. for Sunday 21st Nov.1915.

Ammunition to be taken from this week's allowance but will be shown as fired before 12 noon Sunday.

UNIT	TIME	TASK	AMMUNITION ALLOWED		
			18-pr.S.	18-pr.HE.	6"HOW.
2nd F.A.BRIGADE	3.pm.	K.3.d.6.8 to K.4.c.1.6	20	25	
3rd F.A.BRIGADE	3.pm.	All trenches in K.4.c. & d. K.5.c.	80	60	
6" HOWITZERS	3.5pm.	K.4.d.0.4 - K.5.c.0.0 1st & 2nd Lines Particular attention to be paid to works at S.E. corner of GOMMECOURT WOOD and Cemetery.			50

J. de.V. BOWLES, Major,
Bde. Major, 48th Div. R.A..

19th Nov.1915.

SECRET
Appendix L

ENTERPRISE for THURSDAY November 25th.

UNIT	TIME	TASK	AMMUNITION ALLOWED			
			18-pr.S.	18-pr.HE.	6"How.	60-pr.
1st F.A.BRIGADE	2.40.pm.	K.17.b.	50	30		
60-pr. B.L.	2.45.pm.	3 Mounds beside CHEMIN CREUX				Barrage 4.70.S
3rd F.A.BRIGADE	2.40.pm.	K.4.c.8.6 to K.4.d.5.2½ Particular attention to Works at S.E. corner of WOOD	50	30		
6" HOWITZER	2.45.pm.	Wire and Works at S.E. corner of WOOD			HE AP 40 20	

J. de V. BOWLES, Major,
Bde. Major, 48th Div. R. A.

24th Nov.1915.

Rough report of action of 3rd S.M.F.A. Bde in support of 6th Bn. Gloucester Regt. on night of 25/26 Nov: 1915

Appendix D

An Arti: Officer with a signaller accompanied the Company Comdr. to the Z Hedge & was in touch with Arti: Bde Comdr. throughout the operation. (A scheme for lamp signalling had also been arranged for in case telephone broke down.)

The order "Ready" was received & fire on lines of first barrage opened at rate of Section fire 5" at 1.3 A.m. At request of Inf: Compy. Comdr. at Z hedge this quick rate was kept up till 1.10 A.m. then slowed down to X.F. 20" at 1.11 A.m. & then to 30" at 1.12 A.m. At 1.13 A.m. "Stop" was received from F.O.O. & barrage ceased.

At 1.14 A.m. the 2nd barrage was asked for by Arti: F.O.O. who took his orders from Compy. Comdr. This message was received through

2.

both Art: & Inf: telephones & orders were at once issued to the battery concerned but almost immediately "Stop" was received from F.O.O. & acted on by me.

At 1.20 a.m. 1st barrage was again asked for & opened. This was kept up till 1.29 a.m. when "stop" was received.

Artillery then stood by ready to open 2nd barrage but this was not asked for & at 2.0 a.m. the Infantry were reported all in.

The barrage seemed to be well maintained & effective.

Telephone communication between F.O.O. & Art Bde Comdr. & through B.C.s to Batteries worked without a hitch.

The number of rounds fired throughout the operation by the three batteries was 340 shrapnel.

Retaliation by enemy's Artillery was

3.

slight and dilatory & was mostly directed at our front trenches. About 50 to 60 rounds from Field Guns & Howitzers were fired into Sector "K" between 1.30 Pm & 2 Pm - Bearings taken to the 3 enemy batteries firing have been reported in my "Z" report of today's date.

A.R.B.Bessard ?Col?RA
Comdg 8th ?n?FA Bde

26/11/15.

Plan for Enterprise

First Phase

An Art: Officer & signaller will accompany the Inf: Co. Comdr to the "Z" hedge and be in communication with Art: Bde Comdr.

As soon as Inf: send back word that the two parties are ready to push in the Artillery will open fire forming the barrage of the First Phase.

A quick rate of fire will be maintained for the first 30" after which a slower rate will be kept up for same time till information is received that the Infantry have got back to the Z hedge.

Second Phase

The barrage of the Second Phase will be formed if & when the Infantry require it.

J.R. Blossant Lt Col R.A.
Comdg 3rd South Af Bde

23/11/15

Sketch to illustrate barrage of First Phase

2nd Bty (4 guns)

1st Bty (2 guns)

3rd Bty (8 guns)

Telephone

British Front

BC3 BC2
Bde Comdr BC1

Line trenches faites

X Infantry objective

open with
2 Rds X.F. 10" (12 guns)
continues with
X.F. 30" (7 guns)
unless otherwise
ordered.

22/11/15

Barrage of Second Phase on front line German trenches

1st Bty
(4 guns)

Line of retirement

OPF
Bttn Comdr.   OPC

X Fire 15" unless otherwise ordered

MBC
23/11/15

121/7930

Confidential War Diary

of

48th Divisional Artillery

VOL ~~XVII~~ ~~IX~~ 10

Dec 1st to Dec 31st 1915.

Jan 1st 1916

J. du Boulay, MAJOR,
BRIGADE MAJOR, 48th DIVL. ARTILLERY.

WAR DIARY
or
INTELLIGENCE SUMMARY. VOL XVII

(Erase heading not required.)

HEADQUARTERS 48 DIV. ARTY.

December 1 – 31st

Army Form C. 2118.

Place	Date	Hour	Summary of Events and Information	Remarks and references to Appendices
BUS (LEN ARTOIS)	1/12/15		Our Artillery active during the day shelling hostile working parties. Enemies artillery inactive.	
	2.		Enemy fired a few shells into SPIVEY. Our Artillery busy on usual enemy parties and machine guns. 2.O.C.R.A. inspected 2. How. Bty at ARCHEVES.	
	3.		1st 3rd 10th LONDON Bty and HEAVY ARTY. bombarded German trenches NORTH of the Bois ROSIGNOL and at CHENIN CREUX. The effect on trenches was considerable. (See Appendix A attached). GERMAN retaliation on our trenches E of HEBUTERNE very slight.	
	4.		Artillery mistake. 10" LONDON Bty shelled GERMAN Trenches and withdrew from action at 6 P.M. Dickens night M/S at THEIVRES.	
	5.		10" LONDON Bty (MAJOR BRIDGES) left 48 Div area and marched to BEAUVAL. 4" How Bty from Builds at ARCHEVES to action in their old positions S of HEBUTERNE. 2nd Bty 1 FAB cut a lane in German wire 10yds wide at K 17 D. 2. 2. – Germans sent some minenwerfer into our Trenches EAST of FONQUEVILLERS, 2 FAB retaliated on GOMMECOURT Village GERMANS then shelled HEBUTERNE, 1 FAB shelled PUISIEUX. Germans again shelled SAILLY and 1 FAB PUISIEUX.	
	6.		149 Bde (Lt Col Hon E Stanley 13th Staff A & B Offs) billeted at THEIVRES. BOCRA inspected D.A.C.	
	7.		149 Bde went into action at SAILLY. GERMAN Arty active on our trenches. Minenwerfer from GOMMECOURT silenced by one 2 FAB.	

Army Form C. 2118.

WAR DIARY
or
INTELLIGENCE SUMMARY. Vol XVII
(Erase heading not required.)

HEADQUARTERS. 48 Div Arty

Instructions regarding War Diaries and Intelligence Summaries are contained in F. S. Regs, Part II. and the Staff Manual respectively. Title pages will be prepared in manuscript.

Place	Date	Hour	Summary of Events and Information	Remarks and references to Appendices
BUS EN ARTOIS	8/12/15		German Artillery active on our billages. Total damage done about 4 houses relia and 2 men wounded. SEE Appendix B.	Heavy rain & misty
	9/12/15		Continuation of above Bombardment. Nuisance Artillery machine 149 Bde Batteries commenced registration. G.O.C.R.A. inspected Batteries shooting.	Rather clear after misty misty
	10/12/15		1. F.A.B. Wire cutting on German Trench very successfully carried out. Two wire troughs to hire on the opening made throughout the night. See (Appendix C. attached) Light guns. The 1/2 Battery co-operated with a Bombardment of 37th Div Arty on GERMAN Trenches and completed from GERMAN Trenches N & W of COMMECOURT WOOD with a very gun.	Heavy rain
	11/12/15		A quiet day	Rain misty
	12/12/15		Bienenwerfer action from COMMECOURT WOOD dealt with by 2.F.A.B. and 4.F.A.B. Howitzers also shell'd & kept out K5 A.9.1.	Rain misty
	13/12/15		Artillery inactive.	Rain
	14/12/15		2 F.A.B. & F.A B. retaliated and silenced GERMAN Bienenwerfer firing from CommeCourt	Frost clear

Army Form C. 2118.

WAR DIARY
or
INTELLIGENCE SUMMARY. Vol XVII

(Erase heading not required.) HEADQUARTERS 48 Div Arty.

December 1 — 31st

Place	Date	Hour	Summary of Events and Information	Remarks and references to Appendices
Bus(en Artois)	15/12/15		4 Div Bombarded GERMAN Trenches on our right in K.29.3 at 10.30. Our heavy Arty opened on a GERMAN Battery on outskirts of PUISIEUX hitting a house, the cause the Germans to retaliate on the Eastern entrance of SAILLY. Our 1 FAB immediately fired 50 shell into S. PUISIEUX and communication trench leading from GERMAN Trenches to LA LOUVIÈRE FME. At 3.30 our heavy Arty (17.5) R.G.A opened on PUISIEUX with two Bys of 60 pr. the Germans retaliated heavily on SAILLY COINCAMP & COURCELLES firing in all about 100 shell into SAILLY (4.2 and 5".9. Howitzers) Our heavy Artillery quickly stopped response on PUISIEUX. The cannonade at SAILLY during the entire bombardment amounted to 1 man killed & wounded.	
	16/12/15		Too misty to see. Our Artillery silenced some fire amongst plans in German Trenches. He 149 Bde Bombarded the S.E. corner of BOMMECOURT WOOD. (He emitting German mouseripes was active it. A & B) during the day. 2 FAB and HFAB failed to silence it. Bys. 149 B.de withdrawn from action in conclusion of attachment ordered 9night 16/17 at THEIVRES return to 30 Div. Area on morning 17th Dec.	

WAR DIARY
or
INTELLIGENCE SUMMARY. Vol XVII

(Erase heading not required.)

HEADQUARTERS. 48 Div Arty.

Army Form C. 2118.

Instructions regarding War Diaries and Intelligence Summaries are contained in F. S. Regs., Part II. and the Staff Manual respectively. Title pages will be prepared in manuscript.

Place	Date	Hour	Summary of Events and Information	Remarks and references to Appendices
BUS (EN ARTOIS)	17/12/15		German minenwerfer active from COMMECOURT WOOD. At 12.55 p.m. Bombardment F was successfully carried out, much damage was done to GERMAN TRENCHES and their wire was cut. see Appendix C attacks, owing to insufficient light the 37 Div Arty were unable to cooperate. The Germans retaliated by sending about 100 shell into FONQUEVILLERS - C and D Batteries 149 Bde arrived at THEIVRES from PERNOIS & billeted there night 17/1/8.	Brit C.b. Appendix C
	18/12/15		C and D Batteries 149 Bde from THEIVRES went into action at SOUIX. Usual fire on German working parties and Snipers. 2 FAB kept a continual fire on portion of wire and during previous day.	quiet
	19/12/15		Germans shelled LA CARRIER and trenches S.E. of HEBUTERNE with 77 mm 1 FAB retaliated on German trenches. One enemy anti-aircraft gun fired 3 German aeroplanes were reconnoitring our lines, of whom stopped counter bombs over our Batty positions between HEBUTERNE and COIGNEUX'S.	light good
	20/12/15		C & D Batteries attempted to register Lot light was so bad it was impossible to begin up. Ran at shelling of working parties. Our Batteries through unable to see owing to mist fired at Hyphens, places throughout the day in the hopes of hitting a few Germans moving over the [...]	very quiet
	21/12/15		Div Arty sent a good number of shell at various times into German trenches & search grade in the fog. A successful bombardment was carried out by the 3 F.A.B. and 4 F.A.B. and 15 Seige Battery against enemy trenches S.E. of BOMMECOURT. Neither see Appendices C Div activity was abandoned owing to fog. German reply very feeble. 149 Bde Batty registered. Very feeble.	Quiet a fog

1577 Wt. W10791/1773 50,000 1/15 D. D. D. & L.   A.D.S.S./Forms/C. 2118.

WAR DIARY
or
INTELLIGENCE SUMMARY. Vol XVII

(Erase heading not required.) HEADQUARTERS 48 Div. Arty.

December 1 – 31.

Army Form C. 2118.

Instructions regarding War Diaries and Intelligence Summaries are contained in F. S. Regs., Part II. and the Staff Manual respectively. Title pages will be prepared in manuscript.

Place	Date	Hour	Summary of Events and Information	Remarks and references to Appendices
BUS (EN ARTOIS)	22/12/15.		Dense mist and rain all day. Artillery inactive.	
	23/12/15.		German Coni Bombardment on west edge of GOMMECOURT WOOD and also at CHEMIN CREUX. Wire cut at K.8.B.5.0 successfully by a section of 3/2 Battery. See appx. on div. F. Germans retaliated by shelling our trenches East of HÉBUTERNE.	Light fogs.
	24/12/15.		German minenwerfer silenced by 5th How Arty. Artillery inactive. Light good.	Rain.
	25/12/15.		Xmas Day. 4th & 5th Battery of Howitzers bombarded enemy trenches at a point S.W. of LA LOUVIERE FME (P.8.c) and SOUTH of FME SANS NOM doing considerable damage. All our guns were busy during the day at about H.30p, the Germans bombarded SPECK the 1/1 R/A retaliated with 40, and the 4/8 Battery with 30 shots on PUISIEUX. The Germans cut into R/R fire & 2 salvoes each into BAYEUX, the Germans sent & 1/4 Battery R&R fire 2 salvoes into SAILLY mostly S.O.S. They however sent up the a few more shots into suffered. No casualties.	Rain. Storms.
	26/12/15.		Minenwerfer action from GOMMECOURT WOOD. We replied by shelling German trenches W of GOMMECOURT.	Mist Showers.
	27/12/15.		German artillery fairly active particularly against our trenches East of HÉBUTERNE. Our Artillery retaliated.	

Army Form C. 2118.

WAR DIARY
or
INTELLIGENCE SUMMARY.   VOL XVII

(Erase heading not required.)

HEADQUARTERS 48 DIV ARTY.

December 1 – 31st

Instructions regarding War Diaries and Intelligence Summaries are contained in F. S. Regs., Part II. and the Staff Manual respectively. Title pages will be prepared in manuscript.

Place	Date	Hour	Summary of Events and Information	Remarks and references to Appendices
BUS (Can ARTOIS)	28/12/15		Hostile trenches S.W. of LA LOUVIERE FME. Shelled by Lt. How. Battery. 5" How. Battery and 2 F.A.B. searched for hostile maxim-guns return from COMMECOURT WOOD. Four German aeroplanes crossed our lines making for 2o.E. R.F.C. at MARIEUX. They were fired on by our anti air craft guns & one of them were hit but the others dropped a few bombs – one or two on some of our villages but no damage was done.	Bright Starry morning Light frost
	29/12/15		The German Artillery was active and shelled on all our roads and shelled the trenches opposite to HEBUTERNE and the village. A few shrapnel also fell about SAILLY. Our Artillery replied by bombarding SERRE and COMMECOURT.	Great frost
	30/12/15		Maxim-guns active from COMMECOURT WOOD. Silence by Lt. How. Bty. 5" How. and 2 F.A.B.	Great frost
	31/12/15		Bombardment J (see appendix G attached) successfully carried out. Commencing at the close of Phase 1 a German artillery sent some 60 4.2 shells in reply to what twenty of ours, fired off from two or three batteries against our retaliating trenches between HEBUTERNE & COMMECOURT. Their attention was to knock-out point movement the Butterne. They turned their attention to our trenches E of HEBUTERNE. It was however the Germans did not keep what was taking place as they sent an aeroplane out to reconnoitre, although the sky was very hazy for aircraft our anti-aircraft guns fired at the plane apparently located 3 German Batteries.	Story left front

1577 Wt.W10791/1773 500,000 1/15 D. D. & L.   A.D.S.S./Forms/C. 2118.

SECRET

Appendix A

BOMBARDMENT E. for FRIDAY 3rd DECEMBER, 1915.

UNIT	TIME	TASK	AMMUNITION ALLOWED					
			18-pr.S.	18-pr.HE.	4.5"	6"How.	5" gun
1st F.A.BRIGADE	10.40.am.	(A). 1st, 2nd & 3rd Line Trenches K.17.b.2.10 K.17.b.4.10 K.17.b.9.10 on the North, and as far South as the HEBUTERNE-PUISIEUX Road (inclusive).	100	24			
3rd F.A.BRIGADE	10.40.am.	(B). Trenches in K.6.c. extending South as far as the HEBUTERNE-BUCQUOY Road	150	44			
		Roving Gun E.27.c.1.8 enfilade trenches in (A).	50	12			
4th F.A.BRIGADE (10th London Bty)	10.45.am. 10.45.am.	Works and Trenches in (A). Works and Trenches in (B).			30 30		
6" HOWITZERS	10.45.am.	Works and Trenches in (A).				30	
60-pr. 5" Gun.	10.45.am.	Works and Trenches in (B).					30

30th Nov.1915.

J. de V. BOWLES, Major,
Bde. Major, 48th Div. R.A.

Appendix B

48th DIV. ARTY.

The following is a fairly accurate estimate of enemy's shelling of our Villages yesterday, and of our reply :-

HOSTILE ARTILLERY

Hour	Locality Shelled	No. of Shell
12.45.pm.	HEBUTERNE	12
	SAILLY	2
2.5.pm.	FONQUEVILLERS	10
3.5.pm.	SAILLY	2
4.20.pm.	HEBUTERNE	35
to	SAILLY	40
5.15.pm.	COLINCAMP	20
8.am.	HEBUTERNE	40
to	SAILLY	40
9.am.	COLINCAMP	?
Total :-	HEBUTERNE	87
	SAILLY	84
	FONQUEVILLERS	10
	COLINCAMP	30
	COURCELLES	14
		225

Nearly all 77mm 4.2"
a few 5.9" no 8.2".

OUR REPLY

Hour		Locality Shelled		No. of Shell
4.pm. to	1.F.A.B.	PUISIEUX	18-pr.S.	38
			18-pr.HE.	18
			60-pr.HE.	20
	Heavies	-	-
		SERRE	18-pr.S.	2
1.12.pm. &	2.F.A.B	GOMMECOURT	18-pr.S.	9
4.10.pm.	4.F.A.B.		18-pr.HE.	3
			5"How.HE.	4
8.am.		PUISIEUX	60-pr.HE.	20
"		BUCQUOY	60-pr.HE.	20
Total :-		PUISIEUX		94
		GOMMECOURT		16
		BUCQUOY		20
		SERRE		2
				132

J. de V. BOWLES, Major,
Bde. Major, 48th Div. R.A.

9th Dec. 1915.

Appendix C cont

48th DIV. ARTY.

REPORT ON WIRE CUTTING BY 1st S.M.F.A. BRIGADE

10th Dec. 1915.

A Section of 1st Gloucester Battery, R.F.A. situated at K.15.d.3.4 carried out wire cutting operations at the Point K.17.d.2.5, firing 100 Shrapnel from 11.20.am to 11.55.am.

NATURE OF WIRE

About 4 yards in depth and 3 to 4 feet high, stretched on stakes. Not new wire.

METHOD OF OBSERVATION

Battery Commander at K.16.c.1.7, Forward Observing Officer at K.17.c.1.7½ with an Infantry Officer, who confirmed his report in every particular.

AMMUNITION

100 Shrapnel specially selected from lots in possession of Battery about 3 weeks. Uncapped fuzes.

LIGHT

Good at first but somewhat misty at the end.

METHOD OF FIRE.

After establishing the range and fuze, bursts of 10 rounds were fired, and report from F.O.O. at end of each burst.

GUN RANGE .... 1925 yards.

FUZES

Burst extremely accurately. Proportion of grazes about 40%, the remainder all very low air bursts except 3 too high.

EFFECT

A lane 8 to 10 yards in width was cut through the wire; a clean cut was made with the exception of a few posts left standing in front with possibly a few strands of loose wire attached to them, but no wire of any considerable length was seen and no stretched wire.
(N.B. Only 100 rds. fired as against 150 last time).

RETALIATION

Enemy retaliated with about 15 to 20 rounds on our front line trenches all along, from a Battery believed to be behind LA LOUVIERE FME K.18.d.5.7½, though no flashes were seen.

J. de V. BOWLES, Major,
10th Dec.1915.   Bde. Major, 48th Div. R.A.

SECRET

Appendix D

BOMBARDMENT F. for THURSDAY, 16th December, 1915.

UNIT	Time Shapnl.	Time H.E.	TASK	AMMUNITION ALLOWED 18-pr.S.	18-pr.HE.	5"How.HE.	6"How.AP.
2nd F.A.BRIGADE	12.55.pm.	1.pm.	Enfilade Trenches E.28.b. E.29.a.	50	50		
Roving Gun	12.55pm.	1.pm.	E.28.c.6.5 – E.28.d.2.10	50	30		
Roving Gun	12.55pm.	1.pm.	Enfilade trenches E.28.c.South of Road	40	20		
Roving Gun	12.55pm.	1.pm.	Enfilade K.3.d.6.8 – K.4.a.2.3	40	20		
Wire Cutting	12.55pm.		E.28.c.5.3	100			
3rd F.A.BRIGADE A Rover	12.55pm.	1.pm.	Enfilade K.3.d.7.8 – K.3.d.10.4	20	20		
149th BRIGADE	12.55pm.	1.pm.	Bombard CEMETERY & Trench K.4.d.5.6	Remainder of Allowance	30		
4th HOW. BRIGADE		1.pm.	Enfilade German Trenches in E.28.b.			50	
37th DIVISION	12.55.pm.		A burst of fire at 12.55.pm. and again at 1.15.pm. to enfilade Communication Trenches leading up to Fire Trenches in E.28.b. & E.29.a.				
6" HOWITZERS		1.pm.	Bombard Works at K.3.d.8.8 and E.28.d.2.10				20

14th Dec. 1915.

J. de V. BOWLES, Major,
Bde. Major, 48th Div. R.A.

SECRET

B.M. No. 121.

Copy No. 12

Appendix E

BOMBARDMENT G. for TUESDAY, 21st December, 1915.

			AMMUNITION ALLOWED			
UNIT	TIME	TASK	18-pr.S.	18-pr.HE.	5"How.	6"How.
3rd F.A.BRIGADE	2.15.pm.	Trenches in the rectangle K.4.d.0.4, K.4.d.9.8, K.5.c.6.1, K.11.a.2.7. One Section to enfilade from A Rover Gun Position.	50	100		
		One Section to cut wire at K.4.d.3.4	100			
4th F.A.BRIGADE	2.20.pm.	Works at CEMETERY K.4.d.9.8 Trench K.4.d.3.7 - K.4.d.10.3			50	
16th SIEGE	2.20.pm.	Works at K.4.c.9.4 K.4.d.2.5 K.4.d.5.3				30

Copy No.   1.   3rd F.A.Bde.
 "   "   2.   4th F.A.Bde.
 "   "   3.   16th Siege
 "   "   4.   48th Division.
 "   "   5.   4th Div. Arty.
 "   "   6.   37th Div. Arty.
 "   "   7.   17th Bde. R.G.A.
 "   "   8.   8th Squad.R.F.C.
 "   "   9.   144th Inf. Bde.
 "   "   10.   145th   do
 "   "   11.   143rd   do

J. de V. BOWLES, Major,
Bde. Major, 48th Div. R.A.

20/12/15.

Appendix 6

SECRET

B.M. 126.

Copy No.

BOMBARDMENT J. for FRIDAY, Dec.31st 1915.
==*=*=*=*=*=*=*=*

To exercise Divisional Artillery in lifting fire

PHASE 1. A.

UNIT	TASK	Time	18-pr.S.	18-pr.HE.	5"	Heavy	Remarks
1st F.A.BRIGADE (1 sect) (less 1 Battery)	Wire cutting K.17.d.3.5 Bombard 1st Line Trenches in K.17.b.	Noon Noon	100 48	16			Bombardment of front line trenches to commence with 2 rds.gun fire with Shrapnel from each Battery, followed by Section Fire 30 secs. Shrapnel & H.E.
3rd F.A.BRIGADE	Bombard 1st Line Trenches in K.11.c. K.11.d.	Noon	48	16			
4th F.A.BRIGADE (less 1 Battery)	Bombard 1st Line Trenches in K.17.b. K.11.c. K.11.d.	12.2pm			50		Battery fire 20 secs.

PHASE 1. B.

1st F.A.BRIGADE (less 1 Battery)	Bombard 2nd Line Trenches in K.17.b.	12.25pm	30	30			Bombardment of 2nd Line trenches to commence with 1 rd.gun fire Shrapnel from each Bty. followed by Section fire 20 secs. S.& HE
3rd F.A.BRIGADE	Bombard 2nd Line Trenches in K.11.c. & K.11.d.		24	30			
4th F.A.BRIGADE (less 1 Bty)	Bombard 2nd Line Trenches in K.17.b. K.11.c. K.11.d.	12.26pm			50		Bty. fire 20 secs.

PHASE 1. C.

1st F.A.BRIGADE (less 1 Bty)	PHASE 1. A. repeated	12.45.pm.	24				Gun Fire
3rd F.A.BRIGADE	do		24				do
4th F.A.BRIGADE	do	12.45.pm.			12		Bty. fire 20 secs.

PHASE 1. D.

UNIT	TASK	Time	18-pr.S.	Time	18-pr.HE.	5"	Remarks
1st F.A.BRIGADE (less 1 Bty.)	Bombard 3rd Line Trenches K.17.b. and K.18.a.	12.50pm	30		16		Bombard 3rd Line Trenches to commence with 1 rd. Gun Fire from each Battery, followed by Section fire 30 secs.
3rd F.A.BRIGADE	Bombard 3rd Line Trenches from HEBUTERNE-BUCQUOY Road inclusive to CHEMIN CREUX exclusive.		24		16		
4th F.A.BRIGADE	Bombard 3rd Line Trenches from HEBUTERNE-BUCQUOY Road to HEBUTERNE-PUISIEUX Road inclusive	12.51pm				40	Bty. fire 20 secs.

PHASE 2.

UNIT	TASK	Time	18-pr.S.	Time	18-pr.HE.	5"	Remarks
1st F.A.BRIGADE 3 Btys.less 1 Sectn)	Form Barrage along Communication Trench K.17.d.3.1 - K.18.d.3.9	1.10pm	40				Commencing with a round of Gun Fire followed by Section Fire 10 secs.
3rd F.A.BRIGADE 2 Btys.	Form Barrage along Communication Trench K.11.a.2.6 - K.5.d.6.9		40				
4th F.A.BRIGADE	Bombard enemys trenchs BOIS ROSSIGNOL LINE K.6.c. K.12.b.	1.30pm				20	Bty. fire 20 secs.
2nd F.A.BRIGADE (less 1 gun) 1 Bty. 4th BDE.	Roving gun cut wire at K.3.b.8.0 To be ready to turn on any objective during Bombardment by order G.O.C.R.A.	12 noon	50			28	
			30				

| HEAVY ARTILLERY | Trenches in K.4.d. | 12.40pm | | 8" Hows. | ..... | 20 rds. | |
| | Trenches in BOIS ROSSIGNOL K.12.b.1.8 - K.12.b.3.5 | | | 9.2"Hows. | ..... | 10 rds. | |

Copy No. 1. 1st Brigade   5. 37th Div. Arty.   10. 8th Squad.R.F.C.
        2. 2nd   "   6. 31st Hy.Brigade   11. 143rd Inf.Bde.
        3. 3rd   "   7. 3rd Army Hy.Group   12. 144th "
        4. 4th   "   8. 48th Division   13. 145th "
                            9. 4th Division.

Bde. J. de V. BOWLES, Major,
Bde. Major, 49th Div. R.A.

30/12/15.

Confidential War Diary

of

48th Divisional Artillery

VOL ~~XVIII~~ II

January 1st to January 31st 1916.

W. Barne. Maj. BM.
for. CRA 48th Divl Arty

4/2/16

WAR DIARY or **INTELLIGENCE SUMMARY.**

Army Form C. 2118.

January 1 — 31

Vol XVIII

(Erase heading not required.) Headquarters 48 S.H. Devonyn RA

Instructions regarding War Diaries and Intelligence Summaries are contained in F.S. Regs., Part II. and the Staff Manual respectively. Title pages will be prepared in manuscript.

Place	Date	Hour	Summary of Events and Information	Remarks and references to Appendices
BUS (EN ARTOIS)	1/Jan/1916.		1. German messenger active from Commecourt wood replied to by our Battery and 5" How Batty. Germans spotted sniper to which we replied by shelling Bucquoy and Poisieux.	Sent eight
	2.		Except for a fast messenger place German Battery was not active. Our 5" Howitzer claim to have got a direct hit on the messenger.	Fair sight
	3.		The German Battery opened a lively fire on our trenches E of Hebuterne which was greatly answered by our 18 pdrs and Heavy Artillery. See Appendix A attached	force
	4.		Retiring machine gun had 7am all day.	
	5.		Messenger active from Commecourt engaged by 2 FAB, 5 How. Several shelling of German machine positions	
	6.		Light very bad. Thick mist and rain all day. 4 SMFAB. Examined with 4.5 "Howitzer". 2 guns taken out of action at 9.01 am & brought straight into action the other two remain in action temporarily — & 3 guns withdrawn & replaced by others.	

WAR DIARY or INTELLIGENCE SUMMARY

Army Form C. 2118.

Jan 1 – 31 Vol XVIII

Place	Date	Hour	Summary of Events and Information	Remarks and references to Appendices
B.S. (EN ARTOIS)	7/1/16		Activity of German minenwerfer from COMMECOURT, opposite L: 1st F.A.B. and 2 F.A.B. Corps Bombardment performed by many to light. Gun laid by 1 F.A.B. opposite LA LOUVIERE. F.M.E.	Indifferent afternoon Mistley
	8/1/16		14.3 h.p. B.G.F. field Trench mortars to slow German minenwerfer in COMMECOURT. 1st M.O.B. which replied vigorously at 9.20 a.m. and 2 F.A.B. from 50 shells into German trench just N. of FONQUEVILLERS–COMMECOURT R'd. 3rd M.F.A.B. fired 20 5" shells into German trench just north of the point. The 8" Howitzer attacked 20 rounds, the place the minenwerfer was seen firing from. Much damage was done by minenwerfer to the German trenches immediately between the fire of the Battery & the minenwerfer. SAILLY & HEBUTERNE. 1 F.A.B. replied in POISIEUX at 12.13 from 2 ph gun fire from each gun at 1 p.m. our heavy Artillery shelled POISIEUX and BOEQUOY. It 2 p.m. German again fired on SAILLY at 2.6 p.m. a reconnaissance Bombardment of the German line opposite 1B attacked. Great damage being inflicted on their trenches their reply was feeble & mild shire was cut in fire from 3.5 to 3.40. Germans again shelled SAILLY 1 F.A.B. immediately replying on each occasion, at 4 p.m. Corps Arty bombarded BOEQUOY & POISIEUX	Light good

1577 Wt. W10791/1773 500,000 1/15 D.D.& L. A.D.S.S./Forms/C.2118

Army Form C. 2118.

WAR DIARY
or
INTELLIGENCE SUMMARY. Vol XVIII
(Erase heading not required.)

HEADQUARTERS. 49 DIV. ARTY.

Jan 1 - 31 Jan

Instructions regarding War Diaries and Intelligence Summaries are contained in F.S. Regs., Part II. and the Staff Manual respectively. Title pages will be prepared in manuscript.

Place	Date	Hour	Summary of Events and Information	Remarks and references to Appendices
9/1/16. BUS EN ARTOIS		9ᵃ	Artillery inactive —	Rain
		10"	Registration by NEW H.S. Hows. Usual working parties & roads shelled.	Frosty
		11.	Runaway 4 gun 5" Hows come into action. 5" Howitzers +	Frosty
		12.	Usual working parties engaged enemy's batty inactive.	
		13.	VII Corps Bombardment Trenches on the Western edge of GOMMECOURT Wood and in the neighbourhood of BERNE COURT Cemetery - 9.2 Hows with whom our 18prs cooperated did much damage to German Trenches in response inflicted about 70 77 mm Shells on W Section and 1/2 Battery had some rounds the Batty. See Appendix C attacked.	Genl Stepmn
		14.	Lecture on Demonstration in Battle of LOOS by Tem. Lt. Col. Hon m a Wingfield at VII Corps H.Q. attended by 8 Officers 49 & 50 Div Artys. General Ross Johnson wires Major went to COBRIS to view experimental shooting.	Front firing
		15.	No Artillery activity	
		16.	Germans shelled Habuterne and Fonquivers replied on GOMMECOURT. A great day.	Fine

1577 Wt.W10791/1773 50',000 1/15 D.D.&L. A.D.S.S./Forms/C. 2118.

WAR DIARY
or
INTELLIGENCE SUMMARY.
(Erase heading not required.)

Army Form C. 2118.

Jan. 1 — 31
Vol XVIII
Headquarters 46 Div Arty

Place	Date	Hour	Summary of Events and Information	Remarks and references to Appendices
1915.	17.			
	18.		8" howitzers shelled W point of GOMMECOURT wood at supposed machinegun position. 3rd Bde co-operated. Slight retaliation by enemy on HEBUTERNE.	fine
	19.		Enemy trench howitzers active between 1 am & 3 am. Silenced by 2nd & 4th Bdes.	fair
	20.		Enemy trench howitzers again active in early morning & dealt with by 2nd & 4th Bdes. CRA 55th Divn came to see OPs in Cape Hetunney positions.	fair
	21.		French howitzers on GOMMECOURT wood active at midday. 2nd Bde & 4 H.B. replied on front-line trenches.	fine
	22.		Bombardment of enemy trenches in cooperation with III Corps HA Group — See attached programme of bombardment (Appendix D). Enemy shelled our trenches East of HEBUTERNE and the village very no damage.	fair
	23.		3 F.A.B. in cooperation with 144 Inf Bde shelled successfully an enemys patrol at Z hedge S of GOMMECOURT wood. Hostile retaliation unsuccessful. Opened our trenches S.E. of HEBUTERNE.	fine good

1577 Wt.W10791/1773 50,000 1/15 D.D. & L. A.D.S.S./Form/C. 2118.

Army Form C. 2118.

WAR DIARY
or
INTELLIGENCE SUMMARY.   Vol. XVIII

(Erase heading not required.)

Jan. 1 - 31

Headquarters 48 Div Arty

Place	Date	Hour	Summary of Events and Information	Remarks and references to Appendices
BUS (en ARTOIS)	24/1/16		Usual registration. Hostile artillery inactive.	Most Rain
	25/1/16		At 2.5 am Hostile artillery heavy shelled our front trenches E of FONQUEVILLERS just N of FONQUEVILLERS COMMECOURT Rd A small party of Germans rushed our front trench but a change finisher than expending a Lewis Gun. Two 2FA13 No change further than captivity a Lewis Gun. At 2.7 at 2.10 there a barrage on their night lines. Hostile fire 4.FA13. Shelled enemys front trenches. Hostile fire 4.FA13. Shelled enemys front trenches. At 2.46 am 2 FA13 and 4 FA13 ceased at 2.30 am. At 2.46 am 2 FA13 and 4 FA13 Bombarded German front line trenches. Enemy used trench mortars. German front line trenches. Enemy used trench mortars. German arty. 77mm 105mm 150mm and trench mortars then trench mortars successfully engaged on wire. The fire of German guns fell on each side of front trenches unusually was comparatively feeble.	Heavy most at times
	26/1/16		No special activity on either side - a misty dull day - At 3.20 pm. the enemy fired 5 salvos of 3 guns each, apparently that 5th How Batty left section.	

Wt. W10791/1773 500,000 1/15 D.D.&L. A.D.S.S./Forms/C. 2118.

Place	Date	Hour	Summary of Events and Information	Remarks and references to Appendices
BVS	27/1/16	At 7.20 pm.	G.A.S Signal received — Brigades were informed and 1st Bat (Glos) & 2nd Bat (Worc) opened fire — 3rd Brigade (War) did not open as infantry reported no gas on their front — The enemy's reply was insignificant —	
		8.25 pm.	"Alarm" from division was received and the correct procedure carried out.	
		8.55 pm.	"Stand down" was received from the division the alarm having been a false one. The wind was blowing in the wrong direction at the time — ie from NE to E.	
	28/1/16	7.30 a.m.	G.A.S Signal again received which again turned out to be a false alarm — Wind was from N to E as yesterday — The 3rd Battery, 2nd	
		8.30	Brigade sent out that gas alarm was a false one — Brigade opened fire —	
	29/1/16	6.40 a.m.	G.A.S Signal again received. This time it turned out to have come from South of ALBERT had no connection with 48 D.S. front —	
		7.30 a.m.	Units were told this — but it came through again at 8 a.m. & 10 a.m. No gas was smelt on our front. A quiet day — rather misty —	

Army Form C. 2118.

WAR DIARY
or
INTELLIGENCE SUMMARY.

Jan 1-31   Vol VIII

(Erase heading not required.)

Instructions regarding War Diaries and Intelligence Summaries are contained in F.S. Regs., Part II. and the Staff Manual respectively. Title pages will be prepared in manuscript.

Place	Date	Hour	Summary of Events and Information	Remarks and references to Appendices
BVS	30/1/16	4 a.m.	The 1st Brigade opened fire in connection with a feint attack S of CHEMIN CREUX which was designed to help infantry enterprises into the German trenches further north at K4 C04 + K4 C 3,5. — The 2nd + 3rd Bdes Cooperated in the enterprise — see Appendix E. The enterprises were not a success owing to mist & darkness — The whole day very misty.	
	31/1/16		nothing to report.	

48th DIV. ARTY.

B.M. CIRCULAR NO. 129.

Headquarters,
    R.A., 7th Corps.

The following is an account of activity on 48th Division front today.

At 1.30.pm. German Artillery bombarded our front line trenches from K.17.c. to K.10.d. with two 3-gun Batteries, a 5.9" from direction of BUCQUOY and a 4.2" from N. of PUISIEUX putting in all about 250 shells.

The following retaliation took place :-

Time	No. of Shell	Nature of Gun	Target
1.35pm	91	18-pr.	1st & 2nd Line Trenches in K.17.b. & d.
2.10pm	81	5"How.	do. do. do.
2.35pm	8	6"How.	K.17.d.2.8
2.45pm	10	60-pr.	LA LOUVIERE FME.
2.40pm.	24	do	do do
3.40pm.	10	8"How.	K.17.b.
	224		

****

The following active Batteries were also engaged by Corps Artillery :-

114th Hy.Battery.	2.pm.	L.8.d.2.5
	3.30.pm.	L.8.a.1.9
48th Hy. Battery	2.30.pm.	L.19.c.5.8
"		L.19.b.2.6
	3.30.pm.	L.13.d.1.5
	3.20.pm.	L.14.a.5.0
"		L.8.d.2.5

3rd Jany.1916.

J. de V. BOWLES, Major,
Bde. Major, 48th Div. R.A.

Appendix A

Appendix B

48th DIV. ARTY.

B.M. CIRCULAR NO. 134

1.   A combined Bombardment of the enemy's Trenches and Gun Positions will be carried out by the 4th and 48th Divisional Artillery, the 7th Corps Artillery (less 19th Brigade) and the 3rd Army Heavy Artillery Group, on Friday 7th January, commencing at 1.35.pm.

Time table for 48th Divisional Artillery attached.

2.   Signal time will be taken at 1.pm.

3.   Hostile activity to be immediately reported to this office.

4.   Signal lines to be cleared for tactical reports only, between 1.30.pm. and 3.pm.

5th Jany.1916.
J. de V. BOWLES, Major,
Bde. Major, 48th Div. R.A.

postponed to 8th Jany

Ref: Trench Map 1/10,000
2nd Edition 57 N.E.
1 & 2 (parts of)

Copy No. ......

CORPS BOMBARDMENT Friday 7th January, 1916.

49th DIVISIONAL ARTILLERY

UNIT	TIME	TASK	AMMUNITION ALLOWED			Remarks
			18-pr.S.	18-pr.HE.	5"How.	
1st F.A.BRIGADE						
1 Section	1.35.pm.	Wire Cutting K.17.d.2.5	150			
2 Batteries (less 1 Sectn.)	2.5.pm. to 2.15.pm.	Shell 1st and 2nd Line Trenches in K.17.d.	40	60		
1 Battery	- do -	All Communication Trenches within area K.17.b.1.2, K.17.d.4.1, K.18.d.3.9 inclusive.	40	40		
3rd F.A.BRIGADE Roving Gun "A" position	2.5pm to 2.15.pm.	Enfilade enemy's second line trench K.17.b.4.5 to K.17.d.5.5½	30	20		
4th F.A.BRIGADE 1 Bty. 5"Hows.	2.5-2.15pm.	1st & 2nd Line Trenches K.17.d.			60	
1st F.A.BRIGADE (less 1 Section)	2.15.pm. to 2.20.pm.	Lift to 3rd Line Trenches in K.18.a. & c.	40	50		
4th F.A.BRIGADE	2.15.pm.	Bombard 3rd Line Trenches from K.17.b.9.9½ to K.18.c.5.5 inclusive.			60	

5/1/16 Copy No. 2. 7th Corps Arty
"   "   3. 48
"   "   4   "

J. de V. BOWLES, Major,
Bde. Major, 49th Div. R.A.

48th DIV. ARTY.

B.M. CIRCULAR NO. 140.

1. A combined Bombardment of the enemy's trenches will be carried out by the 48th & 37th Divisional Artillery, the 7th Corps Artillery (less 19th Brigade) and the 3rd Army Heavy Artillery Group on Thursday 13th January, commencing at 10.40.am.

    Time Table for 48th Divisional Artillery attached.

2. Signal time will be taken at 10.am.

3. Hostile activity to be immediately reported to this Office.

4. Signal wires to be cleared for Tactical Reports only, between 10.30.am. and 12.30.pm.

12th Jan.1916.

J. de V. BOWLES, Major,
Bde. Major, 48th Div. R.A.

Secret

Ref: Trench Map 57D.NE.
Sheets 1 & 2.

B.M.140.

Copy No.

CORPS BOMBARDMENT Thursday 13th Jan.1916.
=*=*=*=*=*=*=*=*=*=*=*=*=*=

48th Divisional Artillery

UNIT	TIME	TASK	AMMUNITION ALLOWED				REMARKS
			18-pr.S.	18-pr.HE.	4.5"S.	4.5"HE.	
2nd F.A.BRIGADE 1 Section	10.40am	Wire Cutting E.28.c.7.7	150				Shrapnel in rapid bursts at irregular intervals. H.E. into trenches.
2nd F.A.Brigade	11.10 to 11.30am.	Bombard Trenches in E.28.b.c.& d.	50		100		
4th F.A.BRIGADE 1 Bty. 4.5".	11.10 to 11.30.am.	Bombard Trench E.28.c.7.6 to E.28.c.9.8				30	Rapid burst of Shrapnel co-operating with 9.2's doing same task.
		E.28.b.2.1 to E.28.b.8.6				50	
		Enfilade trenches in triangle K.4.d.1.7, K.4.d.9.7, K.4.d.8.4	30	40			
3rd F.A.BRIGADE	10.48am.		30				
	10.48am	RETTEMOY FARM	30				

Copy No.2 7th Corps R.A.   7. 17th Bde.R.G.A.   12. 4th Division. Als
      3.   1st F.A.Brigade   8. 37th Div.Arty.   13. 8th Squad.R.F.C.
      4.   2nd   "   9. 31st Heavy Bde.   14. 143rd Inf. Bde.
      5.   3rd   "   10. 3rd Army Hy.Group   15. 144th "   "
      6.   4th   "   11. 48th Division   16. 145th "   "

J. de V. ROWLES, Major,
Bde. Major, 48th Div.R.A.

12/1/16.

Appendix C

Ref. Trench Map 57D.NE.
Sheets 1 & 2.

SECRET

BOMBARDMENT K. SATURDAY January 22nd 1916. 48th DIV. ARTY B.M.145.

Copy No. ....

UNIT	Time	TASK	18-pr.S	18-pr.HE	4.5"HE	Remarks
			Ammunition Allowed			
2nd F.A.BRIGADE	2.30pm	Enfilade Trenches in K.3.d.	25	50		In co-operation with 6"Hows. doing same work.
	2.50pm	Wire cutting K.3.d.7.7	100			
3rd F.A.BRIGADE	2.30pm	Bombard front line trenches from K.4.c.02.40 to K.4.c.3.8		50		
	2.30pm	Bombard trenches between K.11.a.5.2 and K.11.c.8.5		50		In conjunction with 8" Hows. doing same task. Pay special attention to point K.11.c.9.8 7.6
	2.50.pm.	Wire Cutting in K.11.c.	100			
	3.pm.	Bombard work at K.4.d.2.5	25			In conjunction with 9.2"Hows. who are bombarding this point at same time.
4th HOW.BRIGADE	2.30pm	One battery to bombard front line trenches in K.4.c.			60	
	2.30pm	One battery to bombard trenches between K.11.a.5.2 & K.11.c.8.5			50	In co-operation with 8" Hows. who are doing same task.
16th SIEGE BTY.	2.30pm	Enfilade trenches K.3.d.7.8 to K.4.a.1.2 paying special attention to pt. K.3.d.7.8				

The above allotment of ammunition is additional to the weekly allowance.

NOTE The 8" Hows. at 2.30pm will bombard trenches between K.11.a.5.2 & K.11.c.8.5
The 9.2" Hows. at 3.pm.will bombard the work at K.4.d.2.5

Copy No. 1. 1st F.A.Bde.   6. 37th Div.Arty.   11. 143rd Inf.Bde.
"   2. 2nd "   7. 4th Div.Arty.   12. 144th "
"   3. 3rd "   8. 3rd Army H.Group 13. 145th "
"   4. 4th "   9. 48th Division   14. R.A. 7"Cor
"   5. 17th Hy.Bde.   10. 8th Squad.R.F.C. 15. 19th Army Bde.
                                                16. 31 "

                                  S.C. for
                                  Major,
                                  Bde. Major, 48th Div. R.A.

20th Jan.1916.

Appendix D

SECRET

48th DIV. ARTY.

B.M. CIRCULAR NO.145.

1. A combined bombardment of the enemy's trenches will be carried out by the 48th Divisional Artillery, and the 3rd Army Heavy Artillery Group on Saturday 22nd January, commencing at 2.30.pm.

    Time Table for 48th Divisional Artillery attached.

2. Signal time will be taken at 1.pm.

3. Hostile activity to be reported immediately to this office.

4. Signal wires to be cleared for Tactical Reports only, between 2.20.pm. and 4.pm.

20th Jan.1916.

S.C. for Major,
Bde. Major, 48th Div. R.A.

3rd S.M.F.A.BRIGADE

REPORT OF ARTILLERY ACTION - NIGHT 29th/30th-1.16.

1.   2.40.am. F.O.O. and Telephonist with Infantry reached "Z" Hedge (about point K.3.d.9.2).
Telephonic communication established between F.O.O. and 3rd F.A.Brigade Cmdr.

    2.45.am. Communication established between 2nd & 3rd F.A.Brigade H.Qrs.

    3.am. G.O.C. 143rd Inf. Brigade decided 5th R.Warwick not to attack and I instructed O.C. 2nd F.A.Brigade to be ready to barrage first line enemy trench between points K.4.a.0.2 and K.4.a.2.4 and to use Howitzers as arranged under my orders.

    3.1.am. Parties 6th Gloucesters ordered to advance. Artillery warned.

    4.am. First barrage asked for and opened by a Section 2nd Worcester Battery, Section 1st Warwick Bty. & 2nd Warwick Bty. at rate of Section fire 5 secs.

    4.0'30 secs. Barrage fire slowed down to Section Fire 10 secs.

    4.1.am. F.O.O. asked for quicker rate of fire - increased to Section Fire 5 secs.

    4.2.am. 3rd Warwick Battery opened on enemy 2nd Line Trench K.11.a.32.85 to K.11.a.60.45 Section Fire 15 secs. in support of 4th Gloucester Regt. bombing party.

    4.3.am. 3rd Warwick Battery slowed down to Section Fire 30 secs.

    4.4.am. 4.5"Hows. opened on selected points.

    4.6.am. 3rd Warwick Battery slowed down to Section Fire 40 secs.

    4.10.am. Enemy 77mm guns opened desultory fire on trenches K.9.b.N.W. from direction of PUISIEUX.

    4.12.am. 2nd and 3rd Brigade barrage rate of fire altered to Section Fire 20 secs.

    4.15.am. Enemy 77mm Battery altered its fire to about points K.3.d.N.W. and road K.1.d.S.E.

    4.16.am. Enemy machine gun opened fire high over K.9.b.7.5.

    4.20.am. Stop received from F.O.O. and acted on.
Commence 2nd barrage from F.O.O. and opened at rate of Section Fire 15 secs.
O.C. 2nd Brigade ordered to continue barrage with 2nd Worcester Battery.

    4.21.am. Enemy opened shell fire on K.10.d.1.1.

    4.23.am. 3rd Warwick Battery opened 2nd barrage on front trench K.11.a.2.7 to K.11.a.4.4.

    4.25.am. 4.5" Hows. and 77mm guns opened fire on Sector J. - about 50 rounds.

2.

    4.26.am.   F.O.O. reported parties returning from "Z" hedge.
                2nd Barrage stopped.

    4.27.am.   Enemy opened fire with 77mm H.E. shell on "Z" hedge about K.3.d.S.E. from direction of RETTEMOY FME.

    5.45am.   2 rds. gun fire from batteries 3rd Brigade on roads leading E. out of GOMMECOURT in conjunction with Corps Artillery firing on points :-
                Road N. of BRAYELLE FME. E.24.c.1.3.
                Road about E.30.a.central.
                RETTEMOY FME. and approaches E.30.d.N.E.
                Road about F.25.d.S.W.

2.   Number of 18-pr.Q.F. and 4.5" How. rounds fired throughout above operations :-

        18-pr.   ...   3rd F.A.Brigade   357 Shrapnel
        Q.F.   ...   2nd   do   50   "
                                                  7   H.E.
        4.5"How. ... 4th   do   116 H.E.
                                       Total 530 rds.

3.   Telephonic communication between F.O.O. and Artillery Bde. Commander remained intact throughout.

4.   F.O.O. reports barrage fire accurate and fuzes good - all bursting low.

5.   Flashes of enemy guns only visible as flares in sky through thick mist.   Impossible to take accurate bearings.

6.   Enemy's Artillery reply was desultory and unsystematic, no real barrage being opened to impede retirement of our assaulting parties.

                                                 sd/ A.R.B.COSSART, Lt.-Col.,
                                                              R.A.
30/1/16.   Cmdg. 3rd S.M.F.A.Bde.

Original

Confidential War Diary

of

Head Qrs 48th Divisional Artillery

Vol: ~~XXXXIX~~   12.

1st February to 29th February 1916

1.3.16

H Barne. Major
for CRA 48th Divn

WAR DIARY or INTELLIGENCE SUMMARY

Army Form C. 2118

HqRs 48 Bde — 1 – 29 Febry 1916 — Vol XIX

Instructions regarding War Diaries and Intelligence Summaries are contained in F.S. Regs., Part II. and the Staff Manual respectively. Title Pages will be prepared in manuscript.

Place	Date	Hour	Summary of Events and Information	Remarks and references to Appendices
BUS	1/2/16	7 am	Very misty & nothing much to be seen – The mist cleared off in the afternoon but came down again about 5 pm – The 1st Hanoverian Battery supported a bombing entertainment by the Y's East of the railway between 9-10 pm. (See Appendix A) –	
	2/2/16		1-10. A misty day; nothing to report – all quiet.	
	3/2/16		Fairly clear day – all quiet.	
	4/2/16	2 pm	The Q.O.O.H. Batt. carried out a bombardment of enemy trenches in square M.11. The 3rd Army HyArty took part in the bombardment. Apparent satisfactory. (Appendix B) The enemy made little reply.	
	5/2/16		Nothing to report – all quiet –	
	6/2/16		Nothing to report –	
	7/2/16		Nothing to report.	
	8/2/16		The German artillery were very active today – firing from about known positions mostly, and apparently registering – The activity of the German artillery continued all day – more German observation balloons were up during the day, evidently assisting & ascending. Apparently registration was being carried out.	

WAR DIARY or INTELLIGENCE SUMMARY

Army Form C. 2118

Headqrs 48th Bde. R.F.A.

1 – 29 February 1914

Vol XIX

Place	Date	Hour	Summary of Events and Information	Remarks and references to Appendices
BVS.	10 Feb.		German artillery still active – nothing special to report.	
	11 Feb.		German artillery still more active than usual.	
	12 Feb.		German artillery still more active than usual.	
	13 Feb.		A quiet day – rather hostile artillery activity.	
	14 Feb.		In the morning hostile artillery activity was fairly large – be bombarded Enemy 1st system of trenches on N.W. edge of GOMMECOURT WOOD at 12 midnight of 13/14 Feb., in preparation for an infantry enterprise proposed for a few days time	
	15 Feb.		A quiet day	
	16 Feb.		Very wet weather – very little firing	
	17 Feb.		Not very much firing – nothing to remark	
	18 Feb.	1.30 a.m.	A very violent bombardment by the Germans – during which a party of German Infantry entered our trenches at K.22.d. + carried away 12 men + 1 machine gun. See Report for action of the Artillery. Afterwards quiet for the rest of the day.	See Appendix C
	19 Feb.		A quiet day till 6.15 p.m. when an attack was made by a party of the enemy under cover of a heavy bombardment on our trenches S. of TOUVENT FARM.	See Appendix D

WAR DIARY or INTELLIGENCE SUMMARY

Army Form C. 2118

Head Qrs 48 Div R.A.

1 – 29 Feb'y 1916

VIII & IX

Place	Date	Hour	Summary of Events and Information	Remarks and references to Appendices
BUS LES ARTOIS	Feb 20		Bombardment in conjunction with Corps & Army Artillery	
		10.30 p.m.	A deal of enemy activity in BONNECOURT village being noticed, the Division ordered the village to be bombarded which was done by 150 rounds fifth How Bde at 10.30 p.m. 2nd Bde co-operated on enemy front & 2nd line in their sector 10.0 S & 50 H.E. Enemy retaliated with 77 mm & trench mortar bombs on FONQUEVILLERS.	Fine
	Feb 21		Quiet day	
	Feb 22		Quiet day. Snow showers	
	Feb 23		Quiet day. Snow	
	Feb 24		Quiet day. Snow	
	Feb 25		Quiet day. Snow	
	Feb 26		Quiet day. Frost.	

Army Form C. 2118

Instructions regarding War Diaries and Intelligence Summaries are contained in F. S. Regs., Part II. and the Staff Manual respectively. Title Pages will be prepared in manuscript.

WAR DIARY
or
INTELLIGENCE SUMMARY
(Erase heading not required.)

Vol XII   H.Q. 48 Sge Arty   1 – 29 Feb'y 16

Place	Date	Hour	Summary of Events and Information	Remarks and references to Appendices
BUS-LES-ARTOIS 1916.	Feb 29		Quiet day. Snow.	fair misty
	28		Enemy shelled FONQUEVILLERS about 4 pm. 4th (Army) Bde retaliated on GOMMECOURT. Minenwerfer active – Front line near GOMMECOURT WOOD shelled by 6 inch howitzer 5.30 pm.	
	29	11 am	Western point of GOMMECOURT WOOD, m.g. emplacement, bombarded by 6 inch howitzers.	

Appendix A

Ref. 48th. Div. No.G.X.1017.

1st. Warwick Bty. 3rd. S.M.F.A. BRIGADE

Night 1st./2nd. February, 1916.

9.15.pm. to 9.30.pm. 30 rounds Shrapnel to endeavour to cut wire at Northern arm of Y. Sap (K.3.d.60.50).

9.30.pm. to 9.40.pm. pause.

9.40.pm. Barrage 2nd. line enemy trench K.3.d.2.8 to K.4.c.2.7. A percentage of these shell will burst against trees over German first line trench. 2 guns only employed. Rate of fire 0. to 15 seconds Gun fire.15" onwards Section Fire 5" unless Infantry require a quicker rate.

When assaulting party returns to our lines barrage front line German trenches K.3.d.7.8 - K.3.d.90.45 - K.4.c.35.80 - K.4.c.5.7 with 3 guns. 3 rounds Section Fire 15 seconds. If there is repeated rifle fire this barrage to continue for a few more rounds.

1/2/16.   (Sd) A.R.B. Cossart, Lt. Col. R.A.

SECRET

Appendix B

48th DIV. ARTY.

B.M. CIRCULAR No.150

1. A combined bombardment of the enemy's trenches will be carried out by the 48th Divisional Artillery, and the 3rd Army Heavy Artillery Group on Friday, 4th February 1916, commencing at 2.pm.

   Time Table attached.

2. Signal time will be taken at 1.30.pm.

3. Hostile activity to be reported immediately to this office.

4. Signal wires to be cleared for Tactical Reports only, between 1.45.pm. and 3.pm.

3rd Feb.1916.

Major,
Bde. Major, 48th Div.R.A.

SECRET

Ref. Trench Map 57D.NE.
Sheets 1 & 2.

SECRET

Copy No.

48th DIV. ARTY. B.M.150

BOMBARDMENT L. Friday 4th February, 1916.

UNIT	Time	TASK	AMMUNITION ALLOWED			REMARKS
			18-pr.S.	18-pr.HE.	4.5"HE.	
1st F.A.BRIGADE	2.-2.30pm	Wire Cutting in K.11.d.	80	-		One section
	2.-2.10pm	Enfilade communication trenches between road HEBUTERNE-K.12.c.0.3 and the Southern limit of Square K.17.b.	20	-		In co-operation with 3rd Army Heavy Group & 4th Bde.- Rapid bursts at irregular intervals.
	2.20-2.30pm	Bombard 2nd Line Trenches between road HEBUTERNE-K.12.c.0.3 and HEBUTERNE-PUISIEUX Road.	20	30		
	2.30-2.40pm	Lift to 3rd Line & Barrage communication trench K.17.b.3.2½-K.18.c.5.9.	20	30		
3rd F.A.BRIGADE	2.-2.10pm	Enfilade trenches and communication trenches between HEBUTERNE-BUCQUOY road & road HEBUTERNE-K.12.c.0.3	20	-		In co-operation with 3rd Army Hy.Group & 4th Bde.- rapid bursts at irregular intervals.
	2.20-2.30pm	Bombard 2nd line trenches between HEBUTERNE-BUCQUOY road & road HEBUTERNE - K.12.c.0.3.	20	30		
	2.30-2.40pm	Lift to 3rd Line Trenches on same front.	20	20		

UNIT	Time	TASK	Ammunition Allowed			Remarks
			18-pr.S	18-pr.HE	4.5"HB.	
4th F.A.BRIGADE	2.-2.30pm	Bombard 2nd Line Trenches between HEBUTERNE-PUISIEUX & ANCHONNE-BUCQUOY Road.		70		
	2.30-2.40pm	Lift to CHEMIN CREUX behind 3rd Line Trench.. & to Comm. Trench K.11.b.1.6 - K.5.c.5.5.		30		
	2.-2.30pm	Bombard K.11.c.7.8 - K.11.d.0.4 front and rear line of small closed work.	As allotted by H.A.G.			This is a work which Infy. have specially asked to be bombarded.
3rd ARMY H.A.G.	2.-2.30pm	Bombard front line trenches in vicinity of CHEMIN CREUX.				

This allotment of ammunition is additional to the weekly allowance.

```
Copy No. 1. 1st F.A.Bde.    6. 37th Div.Arty.      11. 143rd Inf.Bde.
         2. 2nd   "          7. 4th Div. Arty.      12. 144th   "
         3. 3rd   "          8. 3rd Army H.Group.   13. 145th   "
         4. 4th   "          9. 48th Division.      14. R.A. 7th Corps.
         5. 17th Hy.Bde.    10. 8th Squad.R.F.C.    15. 19th Hy.Bde.
                                                    16. 31st
```

J. K. Dick
Bde.Major, 48th Div.R.A.

5/2/16.

Appendix C

48th. DIV. ARTY.
185

Headquarters,

 R.A., 7th. Corps.

   Herewith report called for on action of guns on the night of 17th/18th. February, 1916.

1. It is essential that the original request for fire should be as definite as possible in the circumstances. To ensure this in future the F.O.O. sleeping at Battalion Headquarters has been ordered to take down the Battalion Commander's instructions in writing. He must also keep his Battery continually informed of the situation.

2. A Lamp Station is useless if it cannot be reached during a bombardment, and if necessary a communication trench must be made.

3. 2nd. SM.Brigade — The extent to which the 2nd. Battery was being shelled should have been ascertained before leaving it out when the Barrage was asked for.

4. 125th. Brigade — The rate of fire was perhaps hardly commenserate with the requirement of the situation after the G.O.C. 144th. Brigade had stated that his trenches were being heavily shelled. However, the general tendency is to fire rather more than the situation demands and this, I think, is very much to be deprecated as likely to leave the Battery short of ammunition at the critical moment.
 The Brigade Commander should, I think, have concentrated the fire of another Battery on the front being shelled, after D/125 reported that this front was quiet.

         (sd) H D O Ward
             Brig.-Genl.,
19th. Feb.1916.   C.R.A., 48th. Division.

REPORT OF ARTILLERY ACTION NIGHT 17/18th. FEB.1916.

Front of the 143rd. Infantry Brigade

    Attached Artillery   2nd. S.M.Brigade R.F.A.
                                 4th. S.M.How.Brigade.

1.30.am.   The Germans opened a fairly heavy fire on FONQUEVILLERS and to the North of it. This was reported by the F.O.O. 3rd. Battery, 2nd. Brigade, and was passed on to the Headquarters of the 2nd. Brigade. The F.O.O. 3rd.Battery, 2nd. Brigade, had all his wires cut and was unable to get communication in any direction. The shelling near his Station which was close to the Barrier on the FONQUEVILLERS - GOMMECOURT ROAD was so intense that he was unable to get his lamp to the strong place made for visual signalling.

1.33.am.   The 1st. Battery, 2nd. Brigade, received a message from one of the Company Headquarters of the 7th. Warwicks asking "for retaliation on the 37th. and 48th. Divisional front"; this message was sent through the Infantry telephone operators, and the senders name is unknown. The Company Headquarters are linked up by telephone and any one of them can be plugged through to the R.A.Operator. 6 rounds were fired on this call.

1.38am.   The 4th. How. Brigade was asked to retaliate by the 7th. Warwicks.

1.47am.   They did so at 2 selected points.

1.40.am.   In the meantime, on his own initiative, Major Taylor commanding the 2nd. Battery of the 2nd. Brigade had opened in retaliation for the firing on FONQUEVILLERS, which had been reported to him by his flash observation officer. He fired 3 rounds gun fire, and then ceased fire. The Battery was shelled almost at once and reported the fact to the Headquarters 2nd. Brigade. The shelling was not a serious one.

1.40.am.   General James called up the 2nd. Brigade and asked for a Barrage.

1.45.am to
1.50.am.   Barrage was opened.
        The 2nd. Battery was not employed, but the 3rd. Battery was used to cover its zone. This was owing to the report that the 2nd. Battery was being shelled.

1.50am. to
2.8am.   "D" Battery, 4th. Howitzer Brigade, were asked for retaliation by the 7th. Warwicks. This had been carried out by 2.8.am.

2.10am.   Owing to a message received from the G.O.C. 143rd. Infantry Brigade, the Brigade Major R.A. called up the 2nd. Brigade and ordered the 2nd. Battery to open fire, this was done at once. The barrage fire was subsequently slowed down, and at 2.30am. all fire had ceased.

3.38am.   The 2nd. Brigade carried out a bombardment as asked for by the G.O.C. 143rd. Infantry Brigade.

Ammunition Expended	2nd.Brigade R.F.A.	
	1st. Battery	243 S.
4th. How.Brigade	2nd. "	135
5th. Bty. 33HE.	3rd. "	203

Front of the 144th. Infantry Brigade

Attached Artillery - 125th. Brigade R.F.A.
37th. Division.
"D" 4th. Howitzer Brigade
late 37th. Division.

1.50.am.   "D" 125th. Brigade received a message from its O.C., who sleeps in FONQUEVILLERS, that FONQUEVILLERS and the trenches to the North of it were being shelled, and that it had started about 1.35.am; this was repeated to the Headquarters of the 125th. Brigade at the time given 1.50am.

1.52.am.   The O.C., 8th. Worcesters, reported to "B" 125th. Brigade that their trenches were being heavily shelled. "B" 125th. Brigade opened at once "Battery fire 10 seconds", slowing down to Battery fire 30 seconds, and subsequently to Battery fire 1 minute, finally ceasing at about 2.45.am.

2.am.   "D" Battery, 125th. Brigade, was ordered to retaliate by the O.C. 125th. Brigade.

2.5.am.   The G.O.C. 144th. Infantry Brigade reported to the O.C. 125th. Brigade that trenches 56 to 60 were being heavily shelled.

2.7.am.   "D" Battery 125th. Brigade opened fire with 1 gun, the other guns being kept on their S.O.S. lines

2.15.am.   "D" 125th. Brigade received a message from their telephonist at the Signal Office of a Company of the 7th.
2.45.am.   Worcesters that all was quiet and ceased fire on command of the O.C. who was at FONQUEVILLERS.

2.50.am.   All was quiet.

Ammunition Expended

	S.	HE.
125th. Brigade		
"B" Battery	120	
"D" "	18	4
4th. Brigade		
"D" Battery		32
Total	138	36

(sd) H.D.O. Ward

19th. Feb.1916.
Brig.-Genl.,
C.R.A., 48th. Division.

Headquarters

48th. Div.Artillery

Report on operations on night of 19th. February :-

At about 5.45.pm. F.O.O. 127th. Battery, R.F.A., received information from O.C. Lancashire Fusiliers that about 100 Germans were working on their wire opposite our trench 83 (K.29.c.6.1). He at once opened fire on them.

About 5 minutes after this, a heavy bombardment of our 1st. line trenches, communication trenches and of the 125th. and 126th. Batteries positions was opened by the enemy, with Shrapnel, H.E. and Trench Mortars.

The front bombarded by the enemy, extended from K.23.d. in the North, to the Quadrilateral (K.35.a.) or the whole of the front covered by the 29th. Brigade, R.F.A. I am informed it extended further South to the REDAN.

As soon as the enemy bombardment began the 125th. and 126th. Batteries opened fire on their barrage lines on the front line German trenches.

I then ordered the Section of the 86th. How. Battery R.F.A., to fire on the enemy's 2nd. and 3rd. line trenches. This was done at 6.5.pm.

All Batteries opened fire at a rate of Battery Fire 5 secs.

Gas was reported but this was not likely in view of the direction of the wind. Gas shells were fired along the line roughly from K.34.a.9.2 - K.28.d.4.0 to K.28.b.8.0.

The left Battalion's centre and left company were being heavily shelled and trench-mortared during this bombardment. That is in the neighbourhood of JONES TRENCH and NAIRNE AVENUE.

The O.P. of the 127th. Battery was also shelled with Gas and H.E. shells. This Battery's Telephone wires were cut about 20 to 30 minutes after the bombardment commenced but communication was maintained through 126th. F.O.O.

About 6.40.pm. the enemy bombardment grew less intense, and our fire was slowed down to Battery Fire 20 secs. At 7.pm. to Battery Fire 1 minute. At 7.15.pm. firing ceased.

There were no casualties in the Brigade.

The batteries were shelled with 4.2" How. and 77mm guns, but no gas shells were used against them.

About 600 rounds were expended by this Brigade, and 42 by the Section of the 86th. How. Battery during the bombardment.

20th. Feb. 1916.
sd/ W.M.Stirling,Lt.Col. RFA
Commanding 29th. Brigade, R.F.A.

Report on hostile raid carried out by the enemy on the
evening of 19th. February 1916 against part of the line
held by the 2nd. Bn. Lancashire Fusiliers.

After almost two days incessant bombardment on the part of the enemy, of our trenches S. of TOUVENT FARM, a large party of the enemy were seen at 5.30.pm. on 19th. Feb. 1916 working on their wire along their front line trench just N. of the SERRE-MAILLY Road (K.29.d.). The O.C. Lancashire Fusiliers at once ordered the machine guns, Lewis Guns and Artillery, to open fire on this party, which was promptly carried out, with apparently good success.

This was followed almost immediately by a heavy bombardment by the enemy of our front and support line trenches S. of TOUVENT FARM. Later a barrage was formed with gas and other shells, in the vicinity of the reserve company, who were forced to put on their smoke helmets. Fire was also lifted to the neighbourhood of LA SIGNE Fme and further still to the SUCERIE - MAILLY Road where another barrage was formed for some minutes.

The hostile artillery continued their bombardment until 7.pm. when it practically ceased.

During this bombardment a party of the enemy estimated at about 100 strong entered a small part of our trench (trench 82) which had been previously rendered easy of access by a heavy bombardment early in the morning, by heavy trench mortars directed on this one spot. Large craters had been formed and the wire was badly damaged. This place having been thus damaged was only held by a listening post of two men supported close in rear by a post of 7 men

The enemy on entering, after disposing of this listening post, as well as the group in rear, turned with the evident intention of bombing northwards along the front line trench. But all, from the Brigade Commander downwards, had received warning of the possiblity of such an enterprise occurring on the part of the enemy and were consequently prepared.

Capt. Gamon, Lancashire Fusiliers, the Officer in Command of the Company taking the situation well in hand, at once ordered Lt. MacMullan to move up the platoon to the counter-attack. This was promptly carried out and after a hard hand to hand fight drove the enemy out of the trench at the point of the bayonet.

The whole operation was well carried out, and as the Company supports moved forward to the counter-attack, the men of the Reserve Company, still wearing their smoke helmets moved slowly forward to replace them.

Our casualties were 7 killed, 1 officer and 17 men wounded, 1 Officer and 4 men missing.

The enemy's casualties are unknown, but are believed to be heavy as throughout this period the Artillery kept up a very effective barrage in front of and along their trenches. So far 7 dead Germans have been counted lying out in front of our trenches, whilst more dead may yet be found in the numerous shell holes and in the trenches themselves, which are in a bad state.

Nothing was taken away by the enemy.

The two Lewis guns which fired from this trench had been removed early to a safer position in rear.

The blocking of our trenches and the wire in front greatly impeded the progress of our counter-attack.

G.x.1062
20/2/16.

sd/ D.Burt-Marshall, Capt.,
General Staff, 48th. Divn.

Original Vol XIII

Confidential War Diary

of

Head Qrs 48th Divisional Artillery

Vol. ~~XX~~

1st — 31st March 1916

_____ CAPTAIN,
STAFF CAPTAIN, 48th DIVL. ARTILLERY.

for

1st April 1916.

Br Genl
CRA 48th Division

WAR DIARY
or
INTELLIGENCE SUMMARY

Army Form C. 2118

Vol: XX Hqrs. 1.8th Divisional Arty
1 – 31 March 1916

(Erase heading not required.)

Instructions regarding War Diaries and Intelligence Summaries are contained in F. S. Regs., Part II. and the Staff Manual respectively. Title Pages will be prepared in manuscript.

Place	Date	Hour	Summary of Events and Information	Remarks and references to Appendices
BVS	1/3/16		Fine weather. No hostile artillery machine. Nothing to report	
	2/3/16		Hostile artillery more active than usual - in evening 2 sect: moved to 29th Bde p.o.w.	
	3/3/16		Showery weather. but view moderately clear - In evening 2 sections moved to 29th Bde p.o.w.	
	4/3/16		Snow. View completely obscured till 4.45 pm. At 5.20 pm. a gun drawn by a tractor	
	5/3/16		& pair was seen moving towards PUISIEUX on the BUCQUOY-PUISIEUX road. The 4.5"H.M. took on the front of the left section 29th Bde (4.50 S.F.) at 12 midday.	
	6/3/16		A clear day. Batteries busy registering new zones.	
	7/3/16		Snowing till 11 a.m. - Then clear. Batteries still registering new zones.	
		6.31 – 8.45	Enemy bombarded trenches of the battalion immediately on Right of 4.6 D.S.	
	8/3/16		A misty day. Visst. difficult.	
	9/3/16		Slight haze. nothing to report	
	10/3/16		nothing to report	

Army Form C. 2118

WAR DIARY
or
INTELLIGENCE SUMMARY

(Erase heading not required.)

Army of ....

Vol IX   1 - 31 March 1916

Instructions regarding War Diaries and Intelligence Summaries are contained in F. S. Regs., Part II. and the Staff Manual respectively. Title Pages will be prepared in manuscript.

Place	Date	Hour	Summary of Events and Information	Remarks and references to Appendices
BVS	11/3/16		Misty, light haze all day - nothing to report	
"	12/3/16		Clear from 10 a.m. onwards. Enemy shelled 3rd Warwick Battery (K 20 d 4 3) & killed 3 & wounded 1 man who subsequently died. German Aeroplane very active -	
"	13/3/16		Misty in morning - afterwards clear -	
"		12.30 p.m.	The Germans brought down our 9in Aeroplane in L.25.C.2.5 - was engaged by 1st B'de during night, but it had been removed by next day.	
"	14/3/16		Clear day - nothing to report.	
"	15/3/16		A bombardment spread out over the day was carried out by the 2nd, 3rd, 4th B'des and the 10th Corps H.A.G.	Appendix "A"
"	16/3/16		1st B'de carried out a ft bombardment on the same lines as yesterday - spread out over day.	
"	17/3/16		Hostile Artillery were more active than usual -	
"	18/3/16		Nothing particular to report. Enemys guns were active -	
"	19/3/16		2 a.m. a hostile enterprise was undertaken against our trenches in K 23 b - A barrage was made in different places along the front, as far north as E 2 8 - and the enemy entered trenches K 23.	

Army Form C. 2118

WAR DIARY
or
INTELLIGENCE SUMMARY
(Erase heading not required.)

Army Troops 40th Division

Volume XX   1 – 31 March 1916

Instructions regarding War Diaries and Intelligence Summaries are contained in F. S. Regs., Part II. and the Staff Manual respectively. Title Pages will be prepared in manuscript.

Place	Date	Hour	Summary of Events and Information	Remarks and references to Appendices
DHQ	19/3	2 am	Batteries of all the Brigades fired – The 1st Brigade commencing at 2.3 a.m. – Previous warning of the probability of this Enterprise had been sent to 1st Bde about 11 p.m. –	See Appendix B
"	20/3/16		Nothing to report.	
"	21/3/16		Misty in afternoon – nothing to report	
"	22/3/16		Nothing to report	
"	23/3/16 1 am		The Div. Artillery cooperated with the 143rd & 145th Inf. Bdes in a small infantry enterprise – Three parties were to get into the German Trenches N. & Not. South of the Bennis in the GOMMECOURT – FONQUEVILLERS road T. Sortie of the SUNKEN road in K.17. – Only one party succeeded in getting through the German wire – the one N. of the Bennis. The Artillery supported was upheld to be satisfactory – The enemy retaliated on the 8th W.R. Battery in K.7.c.11. killing 2 men, wounding 1 officer & 4 others, one of the latter very severely –	Appendix C
	24/3/16		Snow fell night 23/24th – nothing to report.	

Army Form C. 2118

46 Divl Arty H.Q.

WAR DIARY
or
INTELLIGENCE SUMMARY

1 – 31 March 16   Appendix XX

(Erase heading not required.)

Instructions regarding War Diaries and Intelligence Summaries are contained in F. S. Regs., Part II. and the Staff Manual respectively. Title Pages will be prepared in manuscript.

Place	Date March	Hour	Summary of Events and Information	Remarks and references to Appendices
B.H.S.	26		Rd 46 Dvn 1-45 Divl Arty move from B.H.S. LES-ARTEUS to COUIN	Snow
	27		Quiet day.	Snow
COUIN	28		Quiet day	Fair
	29		Quiet day	Fair
"	30		Quiet day. Body of hostile cavalry observed near HEBUOT	Misty
"	31		Several hostile Richallons up. Quiet day.	Fine

SECRET

48th. DIV. ARTY.

B.M. 267/1.

BOMBARDMENT - 15th. March, 1916.

1. A Bombardment will be carried out by the 48th. Divisional Artillery and the 10th. Corps Heavy Artillery Group. The firing will be spread out through the day at suitable times.

2. (a). 10th. CORPS HEAVY ARTILLERY GROUP.

   1. Bombard GOMMECOURT.
   2. Bombard triangle K.4.d.18.74 - CEMETERY - K.4.d.7.5.
   3. Bombard Second Line Trenches North of SUNKEN ROAD.

   Ammunition as allotted by H.A.G.

   (b). 2nd. S.M.F.A.BRIGADE
        3rd. S.M.F.A.BRIGADE

   Bombard selected strong points between SUNKEN ROAD and the North limit of the Division.

   Ammunition 100 Shrapnel and 100 H.E. per Brigade.

   (c). 4th. S.M.HOW.BRIGADE

   Bombard selected points on same front as in (b).
   Ammunition 50 H.E.

3. Units will report when bombardment has been completed.

14th. March, 1916.

Barne
Major,
Bde. Major, 48th. Div. R.A.

Copies to :-

1st. S.M.Bde.	Northern Counter Bty.Group.	143rd. Inf.Bde.
2nd. "	10th. Corps H.A.G.	144th. "
3rd. "	48th. Division.	145th. "
4th. "	R.A. 10th. Corps.	

REPORT ON ACTION OF ARTILLERY - Night 18th/19th. March, 1916.

1st. F.A. Brigade - Right Sector.

2.am.	A Heavy Bombardment started, apparently on front trenches
2.3.am.	Left Battalion. All Batteries opened barrage on German Trenches - rate Section Fire 15 seconds. When the situation
2.10.am.	came clearer the barrage lines of two right batteries were each shifted one place northwards, so as to concentrate one more battery on the threatened front. At the same time fire
2.15.am.	was quickened to Section Fire 10 seconds. Lachymatory shells were reported by F.O.O. at the Left Battalion Headquarters - almost immediately afterwards the wires were cut. In response
2.36.am.	to request by Infantry Brigadier fire was slowed down to
2.40.am.	Section Fire 20 seconds. The right gun 2nd. Battery went out of action from an oversize shell. This caused a temporary slackening of fire while barrage lines were being re-adjusted.
2.55.am.	1st. Battalion front reported heavy rifle fire - 40 rounds rapid fire were turned on. After this they quietened down and at 3.am. "ceased firing" was given.
3.15.am) 3.20.am)	Later, with the object of catching enemy parties, sudden bursts were opened on approaches SERRE-HEBUTERNE Road and behind STAR WOOD. During all this time the 1st. Battery, 1st. S.M. Brigade, was shelled; but the counter batteries engaged the hostile batteries at once, and apparently slackened their fire.

3rd. F.A. Brigade - Centre Sector.

2.am.	The enemy opened a heavy bombardment on our trenches G. Sector and Southwards - on this, at the request of the R. Battalion of the Centre Sector, the 3rd. Warwick Battery opened on
2.3.am.	night lines at a rate of Section Fire 5 seconds (at 2.15.am. it slackened the rate and by 2.30.am. was firing Section Fire 1 minute).
2.4.am.	The 3rd. F.A.Brigade called up Infantry Brigade and was informed as to where the bombardment was taking place. At this time one battery only was firing but almost at once another, the
2.4½.am.	8th. W.R.Battery, was asked to fire "as for an S.O.S. call" from the Centre Battalion Headquarters. The origin of this message has not yet been traced. In response to it the Battery
2.5½.am.	opened Section Fire 5 seconds, which it maintained till 2.15.am.
2.6.am.	when it was slowed down. Shortly after the 8th. W.R.Battery had opened the G.O.C. Centre Brigade asked for the barrage to be thickened opposite the Right Battalion, and the O.C. 3rd.
2.10.am.	S.M.Brigade turned a section of the 2nd. Warwick Battery on to
2.10½.am.	this front. After a very few rounds a "S.O.S." message from the Left Company of the Centre Battalion was received by the R.A.Operator at Battalion Headquarters, who transmitted it to the Battery; consequently the Battery opened at Section Fire 5 seconds and kept it up for a few minutes.
2.15-2.30am.	As things were getting quieter fire was gradually slackened off, and in the case of the 8th. West Riding Battery and the 2nd. Warwick Battery it ceased at 3.am. In the case of the
2.35.am.	3rd. Warwick Battery the rate of fire was quickened to Section Fire 10 seconds at the request of the Infantry, and 10 minutes
2.45.am.	later on receiving "G.A.S." signals from the Centre Battalion
2.46.am.	was further quickened to Section Fire 5 seconds. However,
2.50.am.	a short time after, the O.C. slowed the rate down again, and
3.15.am.	eventually he ceased fire at 3.15.am.

2nd. F.A. BRIGADE - Left Sector.

2.am.	A Heavy Bombardment began apparently towards the South, but the F.O.O. of the 3rd. Worcester Battery reported that it was also on his zone, so the O.C. 3rd. Worcester Battery opened Section Fire 10 seconds. After firing for five minutes the O.C. 3rd. Worcester Battery had heard nothing definite from his Infantry but continued firing.
2.5.am.	
2.10.am.	
2.10.am.	The O.C. 2nd. Worcester Battery on his own initiative opened fire at Section Fire 5 seconds, but slowed down to Section Fire 10 seconds after speaking to the Infantry.
2.15.am.	The O.C. 1st. Worcester Battery opened fire 5 minutes later at the request of the Infantry.
2.15.am.	In the meantime both the first and 2nd. Worcester Batteries had received a "S.O.S." message from the F.O.O.s at the same Battalion Headquarters who had both misunderstood a remark of the Adjutant. The mistake was found out by the Battery Commanders before any special action was taken. It was, however, reported to the Brigade and to the C.R.A.
2.40.am.	By this time things were quieter and "cease fire" was given.

4th. S.M.HOW. BRIGADE - covering the whole front.

2.am.	The bombardment appeared to be toward the South, and the 4th. Howitzer Battery (the Southern one) opened fire on its night lines.
2.6.am.	
2.4.am.	The 7th. Battalion Warwicks in the meantime had asked for assistance and D/Battery (the Northern Section) opened on its Night Lines, and later on on GOMMECOURT as well.
2.14.am.	The 5th. Battery was ordered to open on the SUNKEN ROAD.
2.33.am.	The 144th. Infantry Brigade was now able to let the O.C. 4th. Brigade know the threatened point and the 4th. Battery was ordered to concentrate on it.
2.35.am.	Things were quietening down, and a few shell were put into the approaches at LA LOUVIERE and STAR FARM.
2.45.am.	By now all was quiet.

War Diary   *Appendix C*

SECRET

48th. DIV. ARTY.

B.M.267/2.

The attached Scheme will be carried out during night of March 22nd/23rd.

Zero time will be communicated later.

Please acknowledge.

20th. March, 1916.

W. Barne.
Bde.Major,
for C.R.A., 48th. Division.

SECRET

Ref.Trench Map 57D.NE.
2nd.Edition 1/10,000.

49th.DIV. ARTY.
B.M.267/2.

1st. PHASE
Infantry leaving trenches and crossing open

UNIT	TIME	TASK	AMMUNITION ALLOWED					REMARKS
			18-pr S.	18-pr H.E.	4.5" H.E.	Heavy	
2nd.Brigade							
3rd.Bty.	0 – 6 min.	Barrage from K.4.a.1.2 to E.28.c.55.40	144				Section fire 5 seconds.
1st.Bty.	0 – 6 min.	Barrage from E.28.c.55.40 to E.28.b.7.5.	144				Section fire 5 seconds.
3rd.Brigade							
1st.Bty.							
1 Section	0 – 6 min.	Barrage from K.4.a.25.16 to K.4.a.95.85.	36				Section fire 10 seconds.
1 Section	0 – 6 min.	Barrage from K.4.a.1.2 to E.28.c.55.40	72				Section fire 5 seconds.
2nd.Brigade							
2nd.Bty.							
1 Section	0 – 6 min.	Barrage from K.4.a.95.85 to E.29.a.0.4	36				Section fire 10 seconds.
1 Section	0 – 6 min.	Barrage from E.28.c.55.40 to E.28.b.7.5	72				Section fire 5 seconds.
4th.Brigade							
1 How.	0 – 6 min.	Barrage from K.3.b.7.0 to K.3.b.9.0.			8		1 round every 45 secs.
1 Section	0 – 6 min.	Barrage from E.28.c.6.4 to E.28.c.9.0 (along the road)			12		Section fire 30 secs.
1 How.	0 – 6 min.	Barrage at point E.28.b.86.64			8		1 round every 45 secs.

2nd. PHASE

Cutting Enemy's Wire and entering Trenches

UNIT	TIME	TASK	AMMUNITION ALLOWED			REMARKS
			18-pr. S.	18-pr. H.E.	4.5" H.E.	Heavy	
2nd.BRIGADE 3rd.Bty.	6 min - 36 min	Keep one gun on K.4.a.1.2					1 rd. every 20 secs.
1st.Bty.	6 " - 36 "	Nil					
3rd.BRIGADE 1st.Bty.	6 " - 36 "	Barrage from K.4.a.25.16 to K.4.a.95.85	320	90			Section fire 5 secs. for 2 mins. then 10 secs.
D/125 1 Gun	6 " - 36 "	Curtain at E.28.b.9.5	30	70			
2nd.BRIGADE 2nd.Bty.	6 " - 36 "	Barrage from K.4.a.95.85 to E.29.a.0.4	320	70			Section fir 5 secs. for 2 min. then 10 sec
4th.BRIGADE 1 How.	6 " - 36 "	Barrage from K.3.b.7.0 to K.3.b.9.0			48		1 rd. every 45 secs.
1 Section	6 " - 36 "	Barrage from E.28.c.6.4 to E.28.c.9.0 (along the road)			72		Section fire 30 secs
1 How.	6 " - 36 "	Barrage at point E.28.b.86.64			48		1 rd. every 45 secs.

3rd. PHASE

Crossing open after leaving Enemy's Trenches

UNIT	TIME	TASK	18-pr. S.	18-pr. H.E.	4.5" H.E.	Heavy	REMARKS
2nd. BRIGADE 3rd.Bty.	36 min.– 46 min.	Barrage from K.4.a.1.2 to E.28.c.55.40.	144				2 min. sec. fire –5 secs. 8 " " 10 " & afterwards according to situation.
1st.Bty.	(for as long as required).	Barrage from E.28.c.55.40 to E.28.b.7.5.	144				2 min. sec. fire –5 secs. 8 " " 10 " & afterwards according to situation.
3rd.BRIGADE 1st.Bty.	"	Barrage from K.4.a.25.16 to K.4.a.95.85.	32	8			Section fire 30 secs. for as long as required
2nd.BRIGADE 2nd.Bty.	"	Barrage from K.4.a.95.85 to E.29.a.0.4	32	8			Section fire 30 secs. for as long as required
4th.BRIGADE 1.How.	36 min.– 46 min.	Barrage from K.3.b.7.0 to K.3.b.9.0			14		1 rd. every 45 secs.
1 Section	(for as long as required).	Barrage from E.28.c.6.4 to E.28.c.9.0 (along the road)			20		Section fire 30 secs.
1 How.		Barrage at point E.28.b.86.64			14		1 rd. every 45 secs.
		Total Ammunition required	352	16	48	196	

1st. 2nd. & 3rd. P H A S E S - CORPS ARTILLERY

UNIT	TIME	TASK	AMMUNITION ALLOWED	REMARKS
COUNTER BATTERY Group 16th.Brigade. (Ge Phillip)	O-onwards	Bombard hostile battery positions F.14.a.0.2 - F.19.b.2.2 - F.19.c.5.1 Afterwards to stand by to engage hostile batteries firing.	12 Up to 30.	A salvo at each position.
17th.Brigade.	O-onwards	Bombard hostile battery positions L.1.a.1.03 - L.7.a.5.0 - K.6.b.7.6 Afterwards to stand by to engage hostile batteries firing.	12 Up to 30	A salvo at each position.

Half an hour after completion - 1 round of gun fire from 1st. & 3rd. Batteries
2nd. Brigade on Front Trenches and repeat at irregular intervals till daylight.

Copy No. 1. Office Copy   No. 7. 1st.F.A.Bde.   No.13. 145th.Inf.Bde.
       2. War Diary   8. 2nd.   "   14. 36th.Div.Arty.
       3.   "   9. 3rd.   "   15. 37th.   "
       4. 48th. Division   10. 4th.   "   16. R.A. 7th.Corps.
       5. R.A. 10th. Corps   11. 143rd. Inf.Bde.   17. 16th. Siege Bty.
       6. H.A.Group 10th.Corps. 12. 144th.   "   18. R.F.C.
                                                             19. Northern Counter Btn Group

(signed) W Bann
Bde.Major,
for G.O.C.R.A., 48th.Division.

Numbers COMMECOURT
from R4 7.0 - R4 4 0.6

In addition
(16 Aug Mallon) 0 - onwards
6" How

15 rounds
Heavy H.E.

HQ RA 48 Div

Vol XIV

Army Form C. 2118

WAR DIARY or **INTELLIGENCE SUMMARY**

(Erase heading not required.)

Head Quarters 48th Div: Arty 1 – 30 April 1916 Volume XXI

Instructions regarding War Diaries and Intelligence Summaries are contained in F.S. Regs., Part II and the Staff Manual respectively. Title Pages will be prepared in manuscript.

Place	Date	Hour	Summary of Events and Information	Remarks and references to Appendices
BOUZINCOURT	1		Light day. Enemy active with trench mortars & minenwerfers in neighbourhood of the QUADRILATERAL.	
	2		Misty morning. Light afternoon great. Somewhat enemy activity on BEAUMONT – HAMEL – GRAND bois. Hostile Artillery active.	
	3		Heavy rain 11.30 am then clear. Hostile Artillery active. Minenwerfers active in early morning.	
	4		Thick during morning. Then clear. Hostile Artillery fire normal.	
	5		Minenwerfers active in the evening & engaged by 4.5" howitzers. Hostile artillery fire normal.	
	6		Misty – observation difficult – Heavy bombardment head to South just after 9.0 pm – Evident effort from infantry in 31st Div sector. Rifle & MG fire on our trenches & section of trenches opened on communication trench leading from SERRE – Lighted convoys & transport passing to South. Some of our & French troops near HEBUTERNE during bombardment.	
	7			

Army Form C. 2118

WAR DIARY
or
INTELLIGENCE SUMMARY
(Erase heading not required.)

Instructions regarding War Diaries and Intelligence Summaries are contained in F. S. Regs., Part II and the Staff Manual respectively. Title Pages will be prepared in manuscript.

Place	Date	Hour	Summary of Events and Information	Remarks and references to Appendices
COUIN	7		Quiet day. Fine.	
	8		Fine night - good. Quiet.	
	9		Fine night good. Quiet day.	
	10		Quiet. Observation difficult	
	11		Quiet day. Fine. Observation difficult	
	12		Fair. Observation difficult. Enemy has strengthened wires of 2nd line trench N of COMMECOURT. Hostile artillery very quiet.	
	13		Quiet day - Observation good in afternoon.	
	14		Quiet day - fine - Enemy shelled our new trench K.16.L.	
	15		Enemy shelled our new trench K.16.L. with 100 77mm & 10.5 cm shell.	

Army Form C. 2118

WAR DIARY
or
INTELLIGENCE SUMMARY
(Erase heading not required.)

Instructions regarding War Diaries and Intelligence Summaries are contained in F. S. Regs., Part II. and the Staff Manual respectively. Title Pages will be prepared in manuscript.

Place	Date	Hour	Summary of Events and Information	Remarks and references to Appendices
	16		MAJ. E.D.G. LYON took over duties of Bde. Maj. R.A. Enemy active with trench mortars in E.28.a.	
	17	10 PM	Bombardment by our 18 PDR & 4.5" Hows. on K.4.d., K.11.d., K.11.c., K.24.b., K.11.a. Very wet, high wind.	
	18		Very wet, high wind. Quiet day	
	19		Storms, high wind. Quiet day	
	20			
	21	7.40 am	2/3 Battery shelled. 60 5.9. no damage altho' two direct hits were obtained. A good deal of hostile shelling on K.10. E of HEBUTERNE.	
		5.30 PM	3rd Bde & 4"/75th bombarded SUNKEN ROAD & front & second line trenches from K.11.a. 2.7 to K.11.c. 8.5. Reported effective.	
	22		Hostile aeroplane dropped 5 bombs about HEBUTERNE & FONQUEVILLERS - increased shelling by enemy on 48th Divl. front.	
	23.	12.55 AM 4.25 PM	3rd S.M. Bde bombardire trenches in K.11.d., K.11.b., K.12.d. " " CEMETERY & GOMMECOURT WOOD (S.W.)	

Army Form C. 2118

WAR DIARY
or
INTELLIGENCE SUMMARY
(Erase heading not required.)

Instructions regarding War Diaries and Intelligence Summaries are contained in F.S. Regs., Part II and the Staff Manual respectively. Title Pages will be prepared in manuscript.

Place	Date	Hour	Summary of Events and Information	Remarks and references to Appendices
	23	3.15 pm	1/2 B⁴ had 2 direct hits by 10.5 cm. shell. Considerable damage to equipment & pits. 5 men suffering from shock & cuts. Enemy Arty. active all day.	
	24		Considerable enemy Arty. fire in neighbourhood of HEBUTERNE 1 sect. 37ᵗʰ B⁴ (attached from 29ᵗʰ D.A.) came into action K20 d 2.0.	
	25	12.10 am	6" Siege silenced Prinnenwerfen K17 b 1 6.	
		6 am	60 blr near SAILLY shelled with 110 5.9's. One gun slightly damaged.	
		3 pm	Bombardment by 48ᵗʰ D.A. & 6" "Stores up front line trench. E 28 b in conjunction with IV D.A.	
		9 pm	2ⁿᵈ & 3ʳᵈ Bdes bombarded GOMMECOURT & tracks E — SUNKEN ROAD & tracks from ROSSIGNOL FARM & LA LOUVIERE FARM	
	26			
	27	5.50 am	Enemy Arty. active on HEBUTERNE section	
		7 am	3/1 B⁴ shelled with 4.2 & 5.9. One pit damaged slightly	
	28	10.30 am	3/3 shelled from BIEZ WOOD Zero 5° 9 + 4.2. Four direct hits wh. did not penetrate Emplacements. 2ᵈ LANES 2/2 wounded	

Army Form C. 2118

WAR DIARY
or
INTELLIGENCE SUMMARY
(Erase heading not required.)

Instructions regarding War Diaries and Intelligence Summaries are contained in F. S. Regs., Part II and the Staff Manual respectively. Title Pages will be prepared in manuscript.

Place	Date	Hour	Summary of Events and Information	Remarks and references to Appendices
	29.		Hostile Arty less active except Minenwerfer	
	30.		Hostile Arty much quieter – trench mortars much quieter.	

Confidential War Diary

of

HeadQuarters, 48th Divisional Artillery

Volume ~~XXII~~

1st to 31st May 1916

1st June 1916

[signature]
MAJOR,
BRIGADE MAJOR, 48th DIVL. ARTILLERY.

WAR DIARY or **INTELLIGENCE SUMMARY**

Army Form C. 2118

Headquarters 48th Div Arty

Volume XXII   1 – 31 May 1916

Place	Date	Hour	Summary of Events and Information	Remarks and references to Appendices
	1 May	9 a.m.	Enemy's Artillery active in HEBUTERNE. 1st Warwicks B4 shelled – no damage.	
	2		Enemy Artillery quiet	
	3		Some hostile trench mortaring on HEBUTERNE + FONQUEVILLERS.	
	4		Hostile Arty quiet – D/165 relieved D/169 in K.20.d – D/169 relieved by 31st D.A.	
	5		Hostile Arty normal.	
	6		Hostile Arty quiet except some trench mortar bombs on right front of 4th Div.	
	7		Hostile Arty quiet – Relief of 1 sect each of 1/3, 2/3, 2/1, 5/4, D/4 by 56th D.A. Sect 2/1 moved into empty position (D/3) at K.20.d	
	8		One sect each of 1/2, 2/2, 3/2 relieved by 46th D.A. – Sect D/4 Hows FONQUEVILLERS relieved by 56th D.A. Sect 5/4 came into action at K.14.d	

WAR DIARY

Headquarters 48th Div Arty

or

INTELLIGENCE SUMMARY

Volume XXII   1 – 31 May 1916

Army Form C. 2118

Place	Date	Hour	Summary of Events and Information	Remarks and references to Appendices
	9	night	Hostile Arty quiet all day. Remaining sects of 1/3, 2/3, 2/1 relieved by 58th DA. 9th sect of 2/1 moved to postion K 20 d (D/3s)	
		10 am	Arty Command handed over from 48th DA to 58th DA.	
		5/4 Hrs: B/5 in action (4 Hows) K 14 d		
	10	night	Hostile Arty quiet	
		10 am	Arty Command handed over to 46th DA. by 46th DA.	
		night	Remaining sects 1/2 2/2 3/2 relieved by 48 DA	
		4/4 Hrs B/5 pulled out to rest at ST LIEGER.		
	11		Enemy Arty quiet	
	12		Enemy Arty active on NEUBUTERNG between 7am & 8 am	
	13		Hostile Arty active in morning against 'G' sects	
	14		Quiet day	

WAR DIARY or INTELLIGENCE SUMMARY

(Erase heading not required.)

Army Form C. 2118

Headquarters 48th Div Arty

Volume XXII 1 – 31 May 1916

Place	Date	Hour	Summary of Events and Information	Remarks and references to Appendices
	15		Hostile Arty fairly active round HEBUTERNE	
	16	am 12.30 till 2.30 am	Very heavy bombardment of whole Div'l front by 4.2, 5.9 + minenwerfer till 2.30 am. Enemy raided our trenches opposite K.23.b.6600 – about 60 casualties + own trenches much damaged.	Appendix "A"
		7.30 am	Enemy fired 430 4.2s at position K.20.d.2.0 (on loan to 56th Div) two direct hits by Blind shells – very little damage to pits + none to materiel or personnel. 58th evacuated pos. at night. Enemy balloon observed the fire.	
	17		Hostile Arty inactive – new supposed trench in K.16.b. dug during the night	
	18		Quiet day – our 9.2 How fired 35 rds at the POINT K.23.b. – enemy didn't reply. Enemy took no notice	
	19		Quiet day	
	20		Quiet day	
	21		Slight Arty activity by Enemy.	

WAR DIARY
or
INTELLIGENCE SUMMARY

(Erase heading not required.)

Army Form C. 2118

Headquarters. 48th Brigade

Volume XXII   1 – 31 May /16

Place	Date	Hour	Summary of Events and Information	Remarks and references to Appendices
	22		Slight activity by Hostile Arty on PAPIN & QUARRIES.	
	23		QUARRIES shelled. Survey post destroyed	
	24		Quiet day	
	25		Enemy Arty active on HEBUTERNE	
	26	4.30 p.m.	SAILLY heavily shelled for 10 minutes	
	27		Enemy Arty active all day – 11.25 p.m. Enemy bombed our new trench near SUNKEN ROAD & bin burrow off by machine gun fire	
	28		Hostile Arty active on our trenches – 10.25 p.m. Short but heavy bombardment of 56th Div trenches on our left.	
	29		Enemy T.M.s active on K 23.	
	30		Quiet day except for T.M.s. One 9.2 Stones bombarded the HOOK K 23 b	
	31.		Hostile Arty quiet – 9.2 Stones again bombarded the POINT K 23 b & 1.8.	

Appendix A

SECRET.

48th. DIV. ARTY.
B.M. 382.

Headquarters,
R.A., 8th. Corps.

With reference to the raid last night :-

1. Enemy shelling commenced at 12-25 a.m. and ceased at 2-30 a.m.

The barrage extended along the whole front, from about K.10.d. to K.29.a., thus including flanks of 56th. and 31st. Divisions, and consisted chiefly of 77mm. and Minenwerfers for some time. After about 30 minutes, the barrage was raised 400 yards, and was mainly composed of 10.5cm. and 77mm. The 18-pr. positions in K.20 were shelled the whole time with a slow rate of fire, by 10.5 cm. and 77mm, the latter appeared to be fired at a very long range.

No estimate can be formed of the number of shell fired.

2. 1st., 2nd. and 3rd. Gloster Batteries all commenced firing immediately - by request of Battalion Headquarters - Section fire 10 secs.

D/165 Bty. did not open fire until 12-54 a.m., as the infantry did not want them to.

2nd. Gloster Bty. was soon stopped by the infantry.

12-45 a.m. 1st. Gloster Bty., at request of infantry slowed down to Section fire 40 secs.

5th. Warwick (Howitzer) Battery at first fired on night lines, and subsequently on THE POINT and SUNKEN ROAD.

6" Siege fired on SUNKEN ROAD, and later were put on to THE POINT at request of infantry.

3/ Total

3. **Total rounds fired** –

      4.5" How. .... 91.
      18-pr. .... 624.
      6" How. .... 16.

4. **Communications.**

1st. Gloster Battery were in communication with Battalion Headquarters, and also with Right Company, G Sector, all the time.

2nd. Gloster Battery were in communication with Battalion Headquarters throughout, and with the Company. HQ.

3rd. Gloster Battery were in communication with Left Company, "G" Sector all the time, but out of communication with Battalion Headquarters from 12-50 to 1-20 a.m.

The wire from D/165 Bty. to Group Headquarters was cut by shell fire, and communication lost for 20 minutes.

The line to the detached post in centre of G Sector (where the enemy entered our trenches) was not working after 12-30 a.m.

5. **Result of raid.**

145th. Infantry Brigade report that the front line trenches opposite THE POINT, K.23.b., were blown in, and a good deal of damage done to communication trenches.

    Casualties :-   Killed 14
                        Wounded .... 40.
                        Missing .... 9. (of whom 6 are supposed to be prisoners).

16th. May 1916.

Brig-General,
C.R.A., 48th. Division.

48 original Vol 16

Confidential War Diary

of

Headquarters, 48th Divisional Artillery

Volume XXIII

1st. to 30th June 1916

30th June 1916.

[signature]
Major
Bde Major 48 Div Arty

Army Form C. 2118

WAR DIARY
or
INTELLIGENCE SUMMARY

(Erase heading not required.)

Head Quarters
48th Divisional Artillery
Volume XXIII   1 – 30 June 1916

Instructions regarding War Diaries and Intelligence Summaries are contained in F. S. Regs., Part II. and the Staff Manual respectively. Title Pages will be prepared in manuscript.

Place	Date	Hour	Summary of Events and Information	Remarks and references to Appendices
Couin	1 June		Slight shelling of HEBUTERNE	
	2		Hostile Arty fairly active on whole front.	
	3	midnight	Hostile T.M. active. Bombardment by 143rd B. F-east road by 31st D.A. result 2 Germans killed, none captured.	
	4		Enemy Arty quiet except T.Ms. 243rd, 13th relieved 240th in action	
	5		T.M. activity on K.23 – otherwise quiet day	
	6		Quiet day	
	7		242, 13th went St Riquier for Field day on 9th	
	8		Quiet day	
	9	6-7 am	A/243 shelled by 5.9s – 120 rds – no damage – otherwise quiet day.	
	9		Enemy Arty registering our trenches round HEBUTERNE	
	10		Quiet day	

Army Form C. 2118

WAR DIARY
or
INTELLIGENCE SUMMARY

Headquarters 1/8 Worc Regt

(Erase heading not required.) Volume XIII 1-30 June 1916

Instructions regarding War Diaries and Intelligence Summaries are contained in F.S. Regs., Part II. and the Staff Manual respectively. Title Pages will be prepared in manuscript.

Place	Date	Hour	Summary of Events and Information	Remarks and references to Appendices
	11		Very noticeable registration of our trenches by Enemy Arty. Slight TM activity	
	12		Quiet day	
	13		Quiet day. 2/8th 2/4 2 B's relieved 2/8th 2/4 3 B's in action	
	14		Quiet day — {3/1 SDA ⎱ A/171 relieved by A/242 48 SDA & returns to 31st Div Arty Control	
	15	1 am	Quiet day — 7th Worcester attempted a raid just N. of POINT K176 but failed — went the enemy with torpedoes & returned — complete failure — C/242 had emplacement hit by 4·2 shells during the night — 7 killed.	
	16		Quiet day	
	17		Quiet day	
	18		Slight Arty activity on HEBUTERNE	
	19		Enemy Arty fairly active on whole Div front	
	20		Quiet day	
	21st		Enemy Arty showed some activity on HEBUTERNE — many shell were duds.	

Army Form C. 2118

Headquarters
48 Div.H.Q.
Volume XIII 1-30 June 1916

WAR DIARY
or
INTELLIGENCE SUMMARY
(Erase heading not required.)

Instructions regarding War Diaries and Intelligence Summaries are contained in F.S. Regs., Part II. and the Staff Manual respectively. Title Pages will be prepared in manuscript.

Place	Date	Hour	Summary of Events and Information	Remarks and references to Appendices
	22.	10 p.m	Some registering by Enemy's Arty. French 75 Bty arrived & went into action K.20.a.1.9. on attachment to 48th Divn.	
	23		Quiet day.	
	24		1st day of bombardment — in morning enemy replied by shelling on front trenches. Generally speaking there was very little retaliation. Stokes had 2 bursts of fire on it in the day.	
	25		2nd day of bombardment. Some enemy retaliation off on own Batteries in K.20.d & K.14.d. 3 enemy observation balloons blown up.	
	26	10 p.m	3rd day of bombardment — 48th Div discharges gas 10/15 mins — Enemy put a very strong barrage on our front line — Crime trenches — otherwise not much from the Arty fire. Div. J.H.'s attempted raids at K.17.d.1.1 + also below the POINT — they stated the wire was not cut & they could not get through. Party was 60 men. Casualties 1 wounded.	

1375 Wt. W593/826 1,000,000 4/15 J.B.C. & A. A.D.S.S./Forms/C. 2118.

Army Form C. 2118

WAR DIARY Headquarters
or
INTELLIGENCE SUMMARY 48 Divisional Artillery
(Erase heading not required.) Volume XIII 1-30 June 1916

Instructions regarding War Diaries and Intelligence Summaries are contained in F. S. Regs., Part II. and the Staff Manual respectively. Title Pages will be prepared in manuscript.

Place	Date	Hour	Summary of Events and Information	Remarks and references to Appendices
	27		4th day of bombardment.	
	28		5th day of bombardment. Assault postponed 48 hours } weather bad.	
	29		6th day of bombardment	
	30		7th day of bombardment	

WAR DIARY

C. R. A.

48th DIVISION.

J U L Y

1 9 1 6

Vol 17 Original

586/SD

Confidential War Diary

of

Head Quarters, 48th Divisional Artillery

Volume XXIV

1st to 31st July 1916

1st Augt 1916.

[signature]
Major
Bde Major 48 Div Arty

Army Form C. 2118

Headquarters
48th Divisional Arty

WAR DIARY
or
INTELLIGENCE SUMMARY

Volume XXV

(Erase heading not required.)

1 – 31 July 1916

Instructions regarding War Diaries and Intelligence Summaries are contained in F. S. Regs., Part II. and the Staff Manual respectively. Title Pages will be prepared in manuscript.

Place	Date	Hour	Summary of Events and Information	Remarks and references to Appendices
COUIN	July 1		Attack by 29th 4th & 31st Divs all failed. 56th on left attacked at COMMECOURT – also failed. 48th Div. sent 2 Batteries to 4th Div.	
	2		48th Div. moved to MAILLY MAILLET for attack wh was cancelled 11 p.m. Div. Arty remained in their positions. 48th Div. returned to COUIN	
	3			
	4		Div Arty ordered to shell enemy communications all night	
	5		31st Bgde Arty went out to 40th Div took over their front. Enemy Arty fairly active on HEBUTERNE – SAILLY	
	6		Two raids attempted by our Tps – both failed owing to action on enemy communications & keeping wire open	
	7		Bombardment by 48th Div in N Sector – v. slight retaliation	
	8		Quiet day	

Army Form C. 2118

Head Quarters
48 Divisional Arty
WAR DIARY or **INTELLIGENCE SUMMARY**
(Erase heading not required.)

Volume XXIV

1 – 31 July 1916

Place	Date	Hour	Summary of Events and Information	Remarks and references to Appendices
	9		241 & 243 H.Q. moved to COURCELLES	
	10	5pm	Intense bombardment by 48th D.A. of German front line – 145 Tpts. Bks day was turned on left sector in front of old line.	
	11	10pm	Intense bombardment by 48th D.A. – feeble reply.	
	12		Quiet day	
			Quiet day	
	13		143rd Bty Bde moved to 25th Div at BOUZINCOURT – 115 & 236 to relieve 144 on	1 off
		6pm	Intense bombardment of enemy front line by 48th D.A.	
		11pm	2 Raids by our Infy. Northern one failed – S. one got in but brought back no prisoners	
		3am	Gas let off by 4th Div in the night – very little retaliation on our front. Enemy communication shelled all day in burst.	
	14		Quiet day	
	15		38th Welsh Div took over from 48th Div. 46th D.A. remained	

Head Quarters
48th Div Arty

WAR DIARY or INTELLIGENCE SUMMARY

HQ RA 48 Div HSD

Army Form C. 2118

Volume XXIV

1 – 31 July

(Erase heading not required.)

587

Place	Date	Hour	Summary of Events and Information	Remarks and references to Appendices
	16		48th Div HA left for BOUZINCOURT. Quiet day, hostile Arty inactive.	
	17		Orders recd for 38th DA to relieve 48th DA on 20th. 48th DA to relieve 12th DA in action on 21st.	
	18		Quiet day – very misty & observation bad.	
	19		Quiet day – 38th DA arrived at 48th DA wagon lines.	
	20		38th DA took over 48th DA guns – on relief 48th DA withdrew to wagon lines. Orders issued for 24th Bde to be attached to 49th Div. OC sent to HEDAUVILLE to report to CRA 49th Div.	
	21		48th DA took over from 12th DA – 48th Div attacked Pt 79 with 145 Bde.	
	22		48th Div attack now Pts 11, 79, 60, 23, 90, in conjunction with Australian attack on POZIERES – partially successful.	
	23		Attack continues. Attack on Pts 62, 90, 94 arranged for 2.30 pm afterwards cancelled.	

Head Quarters
4th Div Arty

WAR DIARY
or
INTELLIGENCE SUMMARY

Volume XXIV

1 – 31 July 16 *(Erase heading not required.)*

Army Form C. 2118.

588

Hour, Date, Place	Summary of Events and Information	Remarks and references to Appendices
23 July 2.35 pm	Rt. Group (Lt Col Lossart) repulses counter attack in R.34 central. Enemy retires in disorder.	
12 mn.	Enemy attack on X.2.c.8.6 – 23rd Div & Left Group drive them back.	
24 July 8.30 am	2. Pioneers reconnoitred POZIERES & found studs 1m. Aus. Div. crossing the village making up to CEMETERY	
8.40 am	4 guns reported in dust holes M.40 on 50 m X 3m	
	German held POZIERES heavily.	
10 am	Rt. Z Corps State going P. Edey is to prevent counter attacks in R.36 & 18 & helping all movements	
	South	
6 M	Rt & Left guns now shell into MARTINPUICH	

Army Form C. 2118.

Head Quarters
48th Divisional Artillery

WAR DIARY
or
INTELLIGENCE SUMMARY.

Volume XXIV

1 – 31 July 16 (Erase heading not required.)

Instructions regarding War Diaries and Intelligence Summaries are contained in F.S. Regs., Part II. and the Staff Manual respectively. Title pages will be prepared in manuscript.

Hour, Date, Place	Summary of Events and Information	Remarks and references to Appendices
24 July 10.10 pm	Reserve Army orders that German front line is to be bombarded for 5 minutes — answered for 10.30 pm	
25 July 1.45 am	145 Bde attacked Stuff Rdt – practically successful	
26 July 4.10 am	Our front 25 front 143 Bde between Enfans Pt 54	
6.30 am	4p Bombardt 143 B to two batteries X 3 c 8.7 & R 34 c and X 36. f 9 , & X 3 b 5.4	
9 pm	Right Group to cooperate the LEIPZIG SALIENT Orders rec'd. that 12 Div will relieve 48 Div btw a 2pm by Reserve Army	
27 July	Fighting continues for various trenches	18
28 July	12 D.A. took over from 48 gun R.A. – latter went to Corps reserve night 28/29 July	

Head Quarters
4th Divisional Arty

WAR DIARY
or
INTELLIGENCE SUMMARY.

Army Form C. 2118.

Volume XXIV

1 – 31 July 16 *(Erase heading not required.)*

Hour, Date, Place	Summary of Events and Information	Remarks and references to Appendices
29 July	4thDA moved to AMPLIER & bivouaced there	
30 July	4thDA moved onto ST OUEN to rest there.	
31" "	Rested at ST OUEN	

[signature]
Brig Genl
4th Div Arty
31-7-16

SECRET

Copy No. 6

48th. DIVISIONAL ARTILLERY OPERATION ORDER - No. 1.

1. 144th. and 145th. Infantry Brigades will attack the enemy on the line X.3.b.3.1 - X.3.b.9.0. on the night of 22/23rd. July. The attack will be preceded by a bombardment and the Infantry will be withdrawn temporarily from certain points to enable the Heavy Artillery to fire.

2. The dividing lines between Brigades for the attack will be trench 70 - 02 in X.3.c. to 145th. Brigade inclusive.

3. The following zones will be allotted to Groups :-
   Right Group 48th. Div.Arty. co-operating with 145th. Bde. from X.3.c.0.0, X.3.b.3.1, X.3.d.3.0, X.3.b.1.1, X.3.c.7.9, X.N.a.4.0.
   To Right Group is allotted Communication Trench - X.3.b.1.1 - 3.4. - 8.9. - R.34.c.3.1.

   Left Group 48th. Div.Arty. co-operating with 144th. Bde. :- from X.3.a.4.0 - 5.2. (strong point) X.2.b.9.4 - 9.0. - 6.2. - 2.0. - X.2.a.8.9. - X.8.c.3.0.
   To Left Group is allotted the "Ration Trench" running from X.3.a.0.5 - R.33.d.2.0 - 7.0.

4. The 111th. Brigade R.F.A., 25th. Divn., is connected to Right Group 48th. Div. Arty. and can be called on to assist the Right Brigade with 2 Batteries on the area X.3.b.1.1 - 3.9. X.3.b.1.1 - 3.1. and the trenches in X.4.a. & c.

5. Right Group 4.5" Hows. will block the following communication trenches during tomorrow :-
   Ration Trench X.3.a.1.4.
   X.3.b.3.4.
   X.3.b.1.7.
   X.2.b.7.2, 9.0 and 6.2. by D/242

   Left Group 4.5" Hows. will block communication trenches :-
   X.2.a.7.6 and 9.6.
   X.2.b.5.9.

   Total ammunition allotted for above tasks is 200 rds.

6. Reference paras. 1 & 2., Groups will carefully register the following points and keep them under occasional fire by day and night :-

   Right Group Pts. -
   X.3.b.3.1 - 1.1. and 6.4.
   X.3.c.7.9 (there is a stop 40 yards S. of Pt.79 which precludes shooting on this point unless the stop is withdrawn).
   X.3.a.4.0 - 5.0.
   X.3.a.5.2 (strong point).

   Left Group :-
   X.2.b.62.80.
   X.2.b.8.8, 7.4, 5.5.
   X.2.a.9.1, 8.1, 3.0, 9.5, 5.5.

   From information received machine guns have been located at following points :-
   X.4.a.4.0 - 5.2.; X.3.d.2.8, X.3.c.7.0., X.3.a.5.0., X.4.c.7.5., X.3.b.3.5 - 3.2., X.3.d.1.9.

21/7/16.

Major,
Bde. Major, 48th. Div.R.A.

Copies to :-

No. 1, Right Group, 49th
" 2, Left Group, "
" 3, 49th. Div.
" 4, R.A. X Corps.
" 5, R.A. 25th. Div.
" 6, R.A. 49th. Div.
" 7, File.

48th Divisional Artillery.

C.   R.   A.

48th DIVISION

AUGUST 1 9 1 6

Artillery Operation Orders attached.

Original

Vol IX

Confidential War Diary

of

Head Quarters, 48th Divisional Artillery

Volume ~~XXV~~

1st to 31st August 1916

31-8-16

Major
Bde Major 48 D¹ Arty

Head Quarters
48th Divisional Artillery

WAR DIARY
or
INTELLIGENCE SUMMARY
(Erase heading not required.)

Army Form C. 2118.

Volume XXV

1 – 31 Augt 16

Hour, Date, Place	Summary of Events and Information	Remarks and references to Appendices
1 Aug 1916	Rested at ST OUEN.	
2 "	" "	
3 Aug – 8 Aug	" "	
9 Aug	D.A. marched to AMPLIER	
10–11 Aug	D.A. remained at AMPLIER – B.Cs went up to 12th DA front line to reconnoitre and remain there	
12 Aug	D.A. & 1st & 2nd 'A' Echelon DAC & 1 subsection 'B' echelon DAC marched to 12th DA Wgn lines near BOUZINCOURT. Such personel of Brigade went up to Bouzincourt in buses. 48th DA took over from 12th DA	
13 Aug	DAC marched to VARENNES & SENLIS. TM personel – DAC surplus personel to AVELUY & SENLIS by lorry. RA/HQ moved from AMPLIER to BOUZINCOURT	

Headquarters 4th Divisional Artillery

Army Form C. 2118.

WAR DIARY
or
INTELLIGENCE SUMMARY.   Volume XXV

(Erase heading not required.)

1 – 31 Aug 1916

Instructions regarding War Diaries and Intelligence Summaries are contained in F.S. Regs., Part II. and the Staff Manual respectively. Title pages will be prepared in manuscript.

Hour, Date, Place	Summary of Events and Information	Remarks and references to Appendices
13 Aug 11 pm	Enemy counter-attacked 6th Avenue trench which had been captured by us on night of 12/13 Aug – situation was obscure for some time but about midnight it was reported that the enemy had got all 6 Avenue trench and that 14 & 15 Jap Bn were organising a counter-attack to retake place at dawn. Meanwhile Div Arty Barrage S. enemy's front line and also 6th Avenue to prevent him consolidating.	
14 Aug 5.15 am	14 & 15 Bn counter-attacks failed	
10 pm	Left Brigade attacked X 2 b 44·55 – 62 failed Right Brigade to front down 6 Avenue & – R33 c 47 Successful – he regained possession of 6th Avenue to Australian Bn attacks from W. of Mouquet Farm failed	

Headquarters 4th Divisional Artillery

WAR DIARY
or
INTELLIGENCE SUMMARY
(Erase heading not required.)

1 – 31 Aug / 16   Volume XXV

Army Form C. 2118.

Hour, Date, Place	Summary of Events and Information	Remarks and references to Appendices
15 Aug.	Some Enemy shelling of 6th AVENUE & rear gun returns to gun lay 12th Bty. Firing to 24.1 from L-24.3.13.40	
12.15 am	14.5 attacks X2.2.59-74 } failed 14.4 attacks X2.2.74-62-20 } failed	
16 Aug.	1 am Bursts of fire 5' each - 200 yds per burst ordered on X2a. Orders recd. to prepare for attack from S on Pts. 62 - 39 & from E on 78, 59, 48 44, 62 on 17th. Later cancelled till 18th C/240 & B/240 guns burst L 25.8w when recovered from 10 pm.	
17 Aug.	Quiet day - B/243 gun 1 sect to A/243 & 1 sect to C/243 C/243 (6 gun) moved S. L - BOISSELLES to get better range A/242 gun 1 sect to B/242 & 1 sect to C/242 in preparation for attack on 18th gun teams moved late at night C/242 (6 guns) moved S to BOISSELLES to get better range.	

Headquarters   ● Original   ● Written

Army Form C. 2118

WAR DIARY
or
INTELLIGENCE SUMMARY

Volume XXV

1 – 31 August 16

(Erase heading not required.)

Instructions regarding War Diaries and Intelligence Summaries are contained in F.S. Regs, Part II. and the Staff Manual respectively. Title Pages will be prepared in manuscript.

Place	Date	Hour	Summary of Events and Information	Remarks and references to Appendices
	18 Aug	5 pm	18 Pdr barrage 0 to +5 – Infty advanced just behind the barrage wh was very successful. Both objectives taken with very small loss – barrage lifted at +10 to +45 & +20. Prisoners taken – +25 & 7 machine guns. Bombing parties went out once – whole operation very successful. 25th D.A. assisted 1st JKA – the batteries have been very much occupied. Quiet night & no counter attack.	
	19 Aug		Enemy shelled our new front lines & 6th Avenue heavily at times, Inf. bombed up trenches & started consolidation.	
	20		Batteries registered S. side of LEIPZIG SALIENT preparatory to an attack on it – bomb fighting N of the trenches just taken, continues.	
	21st	6 pm	Attack by 4th Glos on S. trenches of LEIPZIG SALIENT – 18 Pdr barrage 5 mins by 48th 25th & 49th D.A.'s then lifts. Completely successful – both objectives taken with small loss. Fighting round Pt 19 29 79 all night.	
		8 pm	Germans who were moving up for counter attack from N.E. dispersed by 48th & 25th D.A.	

Army Form C. 2118

Headquarters 1st Bn Arnoud Fulliers

WAR DIARY
or
INTELLIGENCE SUMMARY

Volume XV

1 – 31 Aug 16   *(Erase heading not required.)*

Instructions regarding War Diaries and Intelligence Summaries are contained in F.S. Regs., Part II. and the Staff Manual respectively. Title Pages will be prepared in manuscript.

Place	Date	Hour	Summary of Events and Information	Remarks and references to Appendices
	22		Prisoners taken in fighting of 21st reported to amount to 123. Early in morning, Enemy recaptured Pts 19 & 29.	
		10pm	Enemy counter attacked from R 32 c 33 on to Pt 29 – Captured and were promptly ejected.	
	23	3pm	Attack by 145 Bde on Pt 79 & 31. Unsuccessful. Heavy shelling of CRUCIFIX CORNER – road side lanesup. Quiet night.	
	24	4.10pm	Attack by 25th Div (7th Inf Bde) on HINDENBURG TRENCH R 31 c 6.8 to R 31 d 74. 25th & 49th DIV co-operating. Objective carried at very small cost. 150 prisoners.	
	25	5.7pm	Counter attack by enemy on HINDENBURG TRENCH failed (whole 25th Div) heavy casualties to Welsh & Lincs. Reg ts. (25" How) from shell fire – all quiet by 7.30pm – 46th B.A. assisted 25th B.A. with barrage.	

Headquarters, 2⁰¹ Divisional Artillery

WAR DIARY
or
INTELLIGENCE SUMMARY
(Erase heading not required.)

Volume XXV

1 – 31 August 1916

Army Form C. 2118

Place	Date	Hour	Summary of Events and Information	Remarks and references to Appendices
	26		Projected attack by 25th Div on trench N of HINDENBURG cancelled, owing to heavy losses & damage to trenches & batteries on 25th. — attack by enemy on N. of LEIPSIG SALIENT driven off.	
	27		Attack by 145 & 143 Bde 48th Div on R32d, R32d 23–03, R32c 91– X2a 79 R32c 31–33 completely successful – all objectives gained. 25th Div & 49th DA cooperated in the barrage. Zero was 7 p.m. Quiet night.	
	28		Verbal orders from R.A. II Corps 2nd i/ that all 16th DA guns went to hand them over to 49th DA. A 130/260 Bde each sent one sect. & C/242 one sect. into action in afternoon – all the rest went into action during the night.	
	29		CRA 48th & 149 RA zeroed at BOUZINCOURT. All batteries command of 48th DA handed over to 49th DA. TMs handed over to 25th DA.	

Army Form C. 2118

Headquarters 4th Divisional Artillery

WAR DIARY
or
INTELLIGENCE SUMMARY

(Erase heading not required.)

Volume XXV

1 – 31 August 16

Instructions regarding War Diaries and Intelligence Summaries are contained in F. S. Regs., Part II. and the Staff Manual respectively. Title Pages will be prepared in manuscript.

Place	Date	Hour	Summary of Events and Information	Remarks and references to Appendices
	30		Very weak. – RA HQ at BOUZINCOURT	
	31.		RA HQ at BOUZINCOURT	

[signature]
B.M. R.A.
4th Division

31-8-16

SECRET
Copy No. 5
B.M.455/2.

48th. DIV. ARTY. OPERATION ORDER - No. 3.

1. 48th. Div. Arty. will relieve 12th. Div. Arty. in action on morning of August 13th. as per Table "A".

2. The Div. Arty. will march from AMPLIER to V.12.central Wagon Lines on August 12th. - March Tables will be issued later.

3. The personnel of Groups and Batteries will march from V.12.central to CRUCIFIX CORNER on morning of August 13th. to take over 12th. Div. Arty. guns in action. Guides from 12th. Div. Arty. will be at CRUCIFIX CORNER at 7.am.

4. Guns will be handed over in their emplacements by 12th. Div. Arty. - the latter taking over 48th. Div. Arty. guns at V.12. central on morning of 13th. August. Stores of which 48th. Div. Arty. are deficient will not be handed over by 12th. Div. Arty. All Trench Maps, Secret Maps, Registrations and Trench Stores will be handed over by 12th. Div. Arty.

5. 12th. Div. Arty. will leave 1 Officer per Battery and 1 N.C.O. per gun to assist 48th. Div. Arty. till 5.pm. on 13th. August and 1 Officer and 1 Linesman per Battery till 11.am. on 14th. August.

6. Ammunition Supply will be taken over by 48th. Div. Arty. at noon on 13th. August - all ammunition in gun positions will be handed over by 12th. Div. Arty.

7. One Section "A" Echelon and one Sub-section "B" Echelon, 48th. D.A.C., will march to V.17.b.9.9 and V.11.d.4.9 respectively on August 12th. - time of march will be notified later. Remainder of D.A.C. will march from AMPLIER on August 13th.

8. Medium Trench Mortar Batteries and personnel of V.48 will leave AMPLIER at 7.am. by lorry on morning of 13th. August and proceed to AVELUY. 12th. Div. Arty. will hand over all 2-inch Trench Mortars in action complete, and will take over from 48th. Div. Arty. an equal number at AVELUY. 12th. Div. Arty. T.M.personnel will be taken away by the same lorries. V.48 will take over the 240.mm. T.M.'s in action from 25th. Div. Arty. on morning of 13th. August. On relief the personnel of 25th. Div. Arty. 240.mm. T.M.Batteries will come under the orders of 25th. Div. Arty.

9. Group Command will be handed over on completion of relief on 13th. August.

10. C.R.A. 48th. Division will take over command from C.R.A. 12th. Div. on completion of relief on 13th. August.

11. H.Q.R.A. 48th. Division will remain at AMPLIER till 13th. August and will open at BOUZINCOURT about 8.am. on that date.

Major,
Bde. Major, 48th. Div.R.A.

10th. August, 1916.

Copies to :-

No. 1. R.A. II Corps   6. 48th. D.A.C.
     2. 48th. Div. "G"   7. 48th. Div. Train
     3. 48th. Div. "Q"   8-16 Right Group 48th. Div.Arty.
     4. 12th. Div.Arty.   17-24 Left Group 48th. Div.Arty.
     5. 49th. Div.Arty.   10.25 T.M.O.
                   26 Filed.

27- R A 25th Div

48th. DIV. ARTY. B.M.455/1.

TABLE "A" - RELIEF OF 12th. DIV. ARTY. by 48th. DIV. ARTY.

48th.DIV.ARTY.		12th. DIV. ARTY.	MAP REF.	REMARKS
A/242	Relieves	A/65	W.11.d.7.8	
B/242	"	B/63	X.15.a.2.1.	RIGHT GROUP
C/242	"	C/63	X.13.b.5.7½.	Lieut.-Colonel COSSART
D/242	"	D/63	X.8.c.5.2.	H.Qrs. USNA REDOUBT - W.18.d.1.1.
D/241	"	D/62	X.13.b.8.1.	
A/240 ½ B/240	"	C/65 ½ B/65	W.11.b.8.1.	
A/243	relieves	A/62	X.13.b.1.2	LEFT GROUP
B/243	"	C/62	X.14.a.5.6.	Wagon Lines V.12.central
C/243	"	A/63	X.13.b.6.6.	Lieut.-Colonel WEST
C/240 ½ B/240	"	B/62 ½ B/65	W.12.c.3.2.	H.Qrs. DONNETS POST - W.12.d.8.3.
D/240	"	D/65	W.18.c.9.9½.	

SECRET

48th. DIV. ARTY. OPERATION ORDER - No. 5.

15th. August, 1916.

1. 48th. Division will tonight continue the attack. Objective to capture the end of spur in X.2.b. approximately Pts. 59, 48, 44, 62 & 20.

2. First objective of 145 Brigade will be the line 59 - 74 inclusive Second objective Pt. 48.

   First objective of 144 Brigade will be the line 74, 62, 20. Second Objective 44 & 48.

3. The Artillery of 48th. and 25th. Divisions will assist as per bombardment table attached.

4. Group Commanders will be with Infantry Brigadiers and have Liaison Officers with Battalions.

5. Flares will be shown 1 hour after the mist lifts in the morning (or at 5.30.am. if no mist) again at 8.am. and 12 noon. The position will also be marked for the Artillery at the same time. Distinguishing badges will be worn by the Infantry.

6. Zero will be 12.15.am. and the assault will take place at 12.30.am.

7. Acknowledge.

15/8/16.

Major,
Bde. Major, 48th. Div.R.A.

Copies to :-
Right Group, 48th. D.A.
Left Group   "
25th. Div.Arty.
49th. Div.Arty.
48th. Div. "G".
R.A. II Corps.

SECRET

48th. DIV. ARTY. B.M.458/2.

BOMBARDMENT TABLE

UNIT	Time	Objective	Rate of fire	Ammunition	Remarks
B/242	Zero to +15	X.2.b.7.4 to 100ˣ S. of 78.	2 rds.per gun per min.		Stops fire at +15.
B/243	Zero to +15 +15 onwards	X.2.b.7.4 to 4.4. X.2.b.4.8 to X.2.a.9.6	"		From +20 rate of fire 1 rd. per gun.
C/112 } 25 D.A. ½ B/112}	Zero to +15. +15 onwards.	X.2.b.4.4. to 100ˣ S.W. of 78. X.2.a.5.9. to 4.8.	"		From +20 1 rd. per gun per min.
A/110 25 D.A.	Zero to +15 +15 onwards	X.2.b.4.4. to 6.2. 100ˣ N. of X.2.b.4.4. to X.2.b.4.8.	"		From +20 1 rd. per gun per min.
D/112 25 D.A.	Zero to +15 +15 onwards	X.2.b.4.4. to 4.8. "	"		From +20 1 rd. per gun per min.
C/243	Zero to +15	X.2.b.6.2. to 2.0.	"		Stops fire at +15.
D/240	Zero to +15 +15 onwards	X.2.b.20-0½- X.2.a.9.6 X.2.b.0.3-0.4.- X.2.a.9.6	"		From +20 1 rd. per gun per min.
A/243	Zero to +15 +15 onwards	X.2.b.5.9.- R.32.c.9.1.-X.2.a.7.9 "	1 rd. per gun per min.		
C/240	Zero to +15 +15 onwards	X.2.a.7.6- R.32.c.9.1- R.32.d.0.3-25. "	"		

RIGHT GROUP
LEFT GROUP

15/8/16.

SECRET

48th. DIV. ARTY. OPERATION ORDER - No. 6.

17th. Aug. 1916.

1.   143rd. Infantry Brigade will continue the attack tomorrow, 18th. August, at 5.pm.
   1st. Objective X.2.b.62 - 20 - 03 - X.2.a.9.1 - 81 - X.2.c.3.9.
   2nd. Objective Points X.2.b.55 - 44 - 06 - X.2.a.96 - 76 - 56 - 43 - 22.
   3rd. Objective (in which 145th. Infantry Brigade will co-operate by bombing from Point 99 (J)) points X.2.b.59 - 48 and exploiting any successes in remainder of front.

2.   Infantry will be in several waves - first wave capturing, consolidating and reforming on the line of 1st. objective, the second and succeeding waves push on to 2nd. objective which the second wave will capture, consolidate and there reform. The third wave will secure 3rd. objective and be ready to exploit any successes gained in other parts of the front.

3.   Heavy Artillery continue constant bombardment to
   (a) Obliterate Quadrilateral X.2.b.0.3 - X.2.a.96 - 65 - 81 paying special attention to Strong Point X.2.a.7.6 -65 -64
   (b) To prepare for first Infantry Assault by obliterating line of first objective.
   (c) At Zero hour Heavy Artillery will lift to line 59 - 48 - 06 - 56 - 25.

4.   48th. and 25th. Divisional Artillery time table will be as under, the dividing line between the two being the trench line X.2.b.20 - 03 - 04, X.2.a.96 - 76 - 79 inclusive to both:-

48th. & 25th. DIVISIONAL ARTILLERY

RED Line.   0' till +5.   Barrage of H.E. and Shrapnel will be formed on first objective, German Front Line from 62 to 39 (3 rds. per min.).

BLUE Line.   +5.   Lift to Line just S. of 44 - 04 - 64 and half way between 22 and 39, with exception of guns on portion from 03 to 91 which will not lift till +7.

YELLOW Line.   +10.   Lift to Second Objective, line 74 - 55 - 44 - 06 - 96 - 22.

GREEN Line.   +15.   Lift to Line 100 yards North of Second Objective and slow down to 1½ rds. per minute.

BROWN Line.   +20.   Lift to line 68 - 59 - 48 - 46 - 16 and reduce to 1 rd. per min. Barrage will then be lifted at rate of 100 yards per 2 minutes till the line 03 - 56 - 33 - 31 - 19 is reached. Slow rate of fire will be continued on this line.

The 4.5" How. Batteries will block communication trenches running N. from 62. 03. 81. 39.
From O till +5 at following points - 48. 96. 65. 22.
Lifting at +5. to Line 12. 91. 79. 46. 25.

The Barrage Lines will be called respectively the Red, Blue, Yellow, Green, Brown Lines.

The 49th. Div. Arty. and French Batteries will co-operate with fire from O' till +10 Yellow Line from 96 - 22. From 68 to 06 frontal fire will be employed. No guns to fire East of Pt. 68.

+10. Lift on trenches in valley from NAB to MOUQUET so as to completely isolate part attacked.
The high ground in LEIPSIG SALIENT from which fire can be brought to bear will also be kept under fire from 49th. Div. Arty.

At +5. one battery of 25th. Div. Arty. and one of 48th. will come entirely under the orders of G.O.C. 143 Infantry Brigade. The B.C's of these Batteries to be at Brigadiers Observing Station

6.   O.C. left group will be with G.O.C. 143 Infantry Brigade.

7.   R.A.H.Q. will be at DONNETS POST.

8.   Acknowledge.

                                                               Major,
                                         Bde. Major, 48th. Div.R.A.

Copies to :-
     R.A. 2nd. Corps.
     Right Group
     Left Group
     48th. Div. "G".
     25th. Div. Arty.
     Lahore Arty.
     49th. Div. Arty.
     143rd. Infy. Bde.

SECRET

48th. DIV. ARTY. OPERATION ORDER - No. 7.

21st. Aug. 1916.

1. 48th. Division will continue the attack today, 21st. August. Zero time will be notified later.
    144th. Infantry Brigade will capture the German front and support trenches R.32.c.1.5. - R.31.d.81. - X.1.b.2.8. - X.1.a.98. - R.31.c.90. - R.31.d.30. - 62 - 84.

    (a) Left attack - front from top of bank X.1.b.59. to X.1.a.98. and support trench in rear starting from NAB Trench.

    (b) Right attack against R.31.d.81. approximately, and support trench in rear.
    These attacks will be made in several waves, the first wave capturing front trench, consolidating it, and there reforming; the second wave passing through the front and capturing the support trench.

2. 48th. and 25th. Div. Arty. will support the attack, dividing line between them being a line N. & S. through X.1.b.39. R.31.d.30 - 35.
    Bombardment table for 48th. Div. Arty. attached.
    49th. Div. Arty. will also cooperate on 2nd. and 3rd. line trenches.
    Heavy Artillery will fire on strong points in rear.

3. Smoke will be ready for use, but will only be let off by orders from Divisional Headquarters and from N. of the NAB.

4. From +5 onwards 48th. and 25th. Div. Arty. will each place one Battery at the disposal of the G.O.C. 144th. Infantry Brigade to fire on any special target the latter wishes. The B.Cs of these Batteries will be with G.O.C. 144th. Infantry Brigade.

5. O.C. Right Group will be with G.O.C. 144th. Infantry Bde.

Acknowledge.

Major,
Bde. Major, 48th. Div. R.A.

21st. August, 1916.

Copies to :-

R.A. II Corps.   49th. Div.R.A.   Heavy Arty II Corps
Right Group 48th.D.A.   48th. Div. "G".
Left Group   "   143 Inf. Bde.
25th. Div. R.A.   144 Inf. Bde.
Lahore Arty.   D.T.M.O.

SECRET

48th. DIVISIONAL ARTILLERY - BOMBARDMENT TABLE

UNITS	TIME	OBJECTIVE	RATE OF FIRE	REMARKS
4 Batteries A/240	0 to +5	X.1.b.39 - X.1.b.98.	3 rds. per gun per min.	
½ B/240	0 to +5	R.32.c.33 - 15.	3 rds. "	Fires H.E. only.
4 Batteries A/240	+5 to +10	R.31.d.30 - R.31.c.90.	3 rds. "	
½ B/240	+5 to +10	R.32.c.33 - 15.	3 rds. "	Fires H.E. only.
4 Batteries A/240	+10 to +15	R.31.d.35 - 07.	2 rds. per gun per min.	
½ B/240	+10 to +15	R.32.c.33 - 15.	1½ rds. "	Fires H.E. only.
4 Batteries A/240	+15 onwards	R.31.d.35 - 07.	1½ rds. " & slackens at +20 to 1 rd. & ceases at +30 or slow barrage kept on as required.	
½ B/240	+15 onwards	R.32.c.33 - 15.	"	Fires H.E. only.
1 Battery	0 to +5	Pts. R.31.c.90.	1 rd. per gun per min.	
1 Battery	+5 to +10.	Trench half way between R.31.c.90 and R.31.d.2.6.	1 rd. "	
1 Battery	+10 to +15	Pts. R.31.d.26 & 48.	1 rd. "	
1 Battery	+15 onwards	Pt. R.31.d.2.6 & 48.	1 rd. per gun per 2 mins. at +30 slacken to slow rate ceasing when situation allows.	
1 Battery	0 to +30	R.32.c.48. 58. 68.	1 rd. per gun per min.	
1 Battery	0 to +30	R.32.d.14. 25. 23.	1 rd. "	

SECRET

25/8/1916.

R.A. II Corps.
174.

II Corps R.A.

1. The 48th Division are attacking the line R.32.c.9.1., X.2.a.79., - R.32.c.31 - 33 this evening.

2. The H.A. will bombard during the day as follows:-

(a) Trench R.32.c.91 - X.2.a.79 - R.32.c.31 - 33.
500 rounds. 9.2" or 8" How.
200 rounds. 6" How.

(b) Trench R.32.c.56 - 65.
Trench R.32.c.58 - 68.
150 rounds. 9.2" or 8" How.
150 rounds. 6" How.

(c) Points R.32.a.08., 09., 28.
35 rounds 9.2" or 8", or 50 rounds 6" per pt.

(d) Points R.32.d.14., 25., 23.
35 rounds 9.2" or 8", or 50 rounds 6" per pt.

(e) Points R.31.b.32., 31., 51.
35 rounds 9.2" or 8", or 50 rounds 6" per pt.

(f) Points R.32.b.74., 84., 75 - 85 will be bombarded by the Vth Corps R.A.

3. Divisional Artilleries are to be ready to take advantage of any target that presents itself.

(Sgd) ---------- Major, R.A.
S.C.R.A. II Corps.

Copy to 48th Division.
48th Divisional R.A.

SECRET   48th Divnl. ARTY.

B.M.453/8.

PROPOSED BARRAGE FOR ATTACK OF LINE FROM
R.32.c.91 to 31.

A.   18-pr. Barrage from R.32.d.20., through 91 – 79 – 51
to 33., including Trench from 91 to 03 (48th Div. Arty.
36 guns).

B.   From R.32.d.12., through 03 to R.32.c.58 (25th D.A. 12
                                                guns enfilade).

       1 Bty. on Trench from R.32.c.33 – 26.   ) 25th Div.
       1 Bty. on Trench from R.32.c.53 – 56.   ) Arty.
       1 Bty. on Trench from R.32.d.23 – R.32.b.62) enfilade.

       4.5" Hows From R.32.d.23 – 39   )
                  "   R.32.a.30 – 28   ) 3 Batteries.
                  Pts.R.31.b.23., 32., 31)

       Heavies remaining on Pts. R.32.a.75-85, R.32.a.08 – 09.

C.   Barrage 18-prs. on Trench from R.32.c.27 to R.31.b.51.
To be as intense as possible.

       A. Barrage lifts 150^x to line R.32.d.12., through
03., to R.32.c.35.

       18-pr. Barrage to open at 3 rounds per gun per minute.
       At + 10 slow to 2 rounds., and
       At + 15 to 1 round per gun per minute.

       4.5" Hows. Rate of fire – 2 rounds per gun per minute.
       At + 10 slows to 1 round per gun per minute, and
       At + 15 "   " $\frac{1}{2}$ "   "   "   "   "   "

Map shewing Barrage attached.

                                        (Sgd) H.D.O. Ward,
                                              Brigadier-General,
25/8/16.   C.R.A., 48th Division.

SECRET

48th. DIVISIONAL ARTILLERY OPERATION ORDER - No. 9.

26th. August, 1916.

1. 25th. Division will attack the line R.31.d.48, R.31.a.91 - 73 - 42, today.

2. The Infantry will **assault** at Zero hour, the time of which will be notified **later**.

3. 25th., 48th. and **49**th. Div. Artillery will cooperate also Heavy Artillery **and** French Batteries.

   48th. Div. **Arty.** Bombardment Table attached.

4. Acknowledge.

26/8/16.

Major,
Bde. Major, 48th. Div. R.A.

Copies to :-

```
R.A. II Corps         Lahore Arty.
Right Group (48th)    49th. Div.R.A.
Left Group     "      48th. Div. "G".
25th. Div.R.A.        D.T.M.O.
25th. Division        H.A.
```

48th DIVISIONAL ARTILLERY -- BOMBARDMENT TABLE

18-POUNDERS

UNIT	TIME	OBJECTIVE	RATE OF FIRE	REMARKS
A/240 (4 guns)	0 to +7	R.32.c.2.7 - 16 - R.31.d.7.4. (within safety limits)	3 rds. per gun per min.	
	+7 to +15	do.	2 "	
	+15 Onwards.	do.	1 "	
C/240 B/242 (2 guns)	0 to +7	R.32.c.6.8 - 58 - 56 - 33 - 100 yards) N. of 31.)	3 "	
	+7 to +15	do.	2 "	
	+15 Onwards	do.	1 "	
B/242 (4 guns)	0 to +7	R.31.d.9.8 - 56. (within safety limits)	3 "	
	+7 to +15	do.	2 "	
	+15 Onwards	do.	1 "	
A/240 C/243 A/243 C/242 (2 guns)	0 to +7	R.32.c.2.7 - R.31.d.9.8 - 79.	3 "	
	+7 to +15	do.	2 "	
	+15 Onwards	do.	1 "	

Sheet 2.

4.5" HOWITZERS

UNIT	TIME	OBJECTIVE	RATE OF FIRE	REMARKS
1 Battery.	0 to +10	R.32.c.3.3 – 15.	2 rds. per gun per min.	
	+10 Onwards	do.	1 " " " "	
2 Batteries	0 to +10	Points R.31.d.7.9, 98, R.31.b.23, 45.	2 " " " "	
	+10 to +30	do.	1 " " " "	
	+30 Onwards.	do.	½ " " " "	

SECRET

48th. DIVISIONAL ARTILLERY OPERATION ORDER - No. 10.

27th. August, 1916.

1.   48th. Division will continue the offensive.

    145th. Infantry Brigade will this evening attack the line R.32.c.91 - 33.

    143rd. Infantry Brigade will attack the line R.32.d.23 - 25 - 14 - 03 - R.32.c.91. exclusive.

    The barrage for 145th. Infantry Brigade will lift at +3 and the barrage for 143rd. Infantry Brigade will lift at +4

    The dividing line between Brigades will be the line X.2.b.48 - R.32.c.91.

2.   25th. and 49th. Div. Arty. will cooperate.

    One Battery from Right Grpup 48th. Div. Arty. will be placed under the orders of G.O.C. 143rd. Brigade from +4, and one Battery from Left Group 48th. Div. Arty. under the orders of G.O.C. 145th. Brigade from +3.

    B.Cs. of each of these Batteries will be at the O.P. of the G.O.C. 143rd. & 145th. Infantry Brigades.

3.   Heavy Artillery will fire on the objectives till 5.pm. and after that hour on points in rear.

4.   Zero time will be 7.pm.

5.   ACKNOWLEDGE.

27/8/16.

Major,
Bde. Major, 48th. Div. R.A.

Copies to :-

R.A. II Corps.	25th. Division.
48th. Div. "G".	25th. Div. R.A.
Right Group	Lahore Arty.
Left Group	49th. Div. R.A.
143rd. Inf. Bde.	H.A. II Corps.
145th. "	D.T.M.O.

S.C.

SECRET

Sheet 1.

48th. DIVISIONAL ARTILLERY - BOMBARDMENT TABLE

UNIT	TIME	OBJECTIVE	RATE OF FIRE	REMARKS
B/242	0 to +3	R.32.d.03 - R.32.c.91.	3 rds. per gun per min.	
C/242	0 to +3	R.52.c.91 - X.2.a.79.	"	
A/243	0 to +3	X.2.a.79 (& system just N.W.) to Trench Junction R.32.c.5½.¼.	"	
C/243	0 to +3	Trench Junction R.32.c.5½.¼ to R.32.c.3.1.	"	
A/240	0 to +3	R.32.c.31 - 33.	"	Pres Shrapnel only
C/240	0 to +3	R.52.c.53 - 15.	"	

Sheet 2.

48th. DIV. ARTY. - BOMBARDMENT TABLE
18-Pounders

UNIT	TIME	OBJECTIVE	RATE OF FIRE	REMARKS
B/242	Z-3 to Z-7 Z-7 to Z-15 Z-15 onwards	R.32.c.8½.4. to 56. " "	3 rds. per gun per min. 2 " " " " " 1 " " " " "	R.32.c.8½.4. to 56. will be divided among all Batteries except A/240.
C/242	Z-3 to Z-7 Z-7 to Z-15 Z-15 Onwards	" " " "	3 " " " " " 2 " " " " " 1 " " " " "	
A/243	Z-3 to Z-7 Z-7 to Z-15 Z-15 Onwards	" " " "	3 " " " " " 2 " " " " " 1 " " " " "	
C/243	Z-3 to Z-7 Z-7 to Z-15 Z-15 Onwards	R.32.c.45 (within safety limits) to 56. " "	3 " " " " " 2 " " " " " 1 " " " " "	
A/240	Z-3 to Z-7 Z-7 to Z-15 Z-15 Onwards	R.32.c.8½.4. to 56. " "	3 " " " " " 2 " " " " " 1 " " " " "	
C/240	Z-3 to Z-7 Z-7 to Z-15 Z-15 Onwards	R.32.c.8½.4. to 56. " "	3 " " " " " 2 " " " " " 1 " " " " "	

Sheet 3.

48th. DIV. ARTY. - BOMBARDMENT TABLE

4.5" Howitzers

UNIT	TIME	OBJECTIVE	RATE OF FIRE	REMARKS
D/240) D/241)	0 to +3	Points R.32.c.15 - 16 - 27 - 38 - 58 - 68 - 39. and R.32.a.3.0.	2 rds. per gun per min.	
	+3 to +10	Points R.32.c.27 - 38 - 58 - 68 - 39 .. and R.32.a.30.	2 " " " "	
	+10 to +30	"	1 " " " "	
	+30 Onwards	"	½ " " " "	
D/242	0 to +10	Points R.31.d.98 - 79. R.31.b.30 - 51.	2 " " " "	
	+10 to +30	"	1 " " " "	
	+30 Onwards	"	½ " " " "	

48th. DIVISIONAL ARTILLERY

C. R. A.

48th. DIVISIONAL ARTILLERY

SEPTEMBER 1 9 1 6.

Army Form C. 2118

Headquarters 48th Divisional Artillery

WAR DIARY
or
INTELLIGENCE SUMMARY

(Erase heading not required.)

1 – 30 Sept 1916   Volume XXVI

Instructions regarding War Diaries and Intelligence Summaries are contained in F. S. Regs., Part II. and the Staff Manual respectively. Title Pages will be prepared in manuscript.

Place	Date	Hour	Summary of Events and Information	Remarks and references to Appendices
RAHQ at BOUZINCOURT	1		guns still under tactical control of 49th & 25th DsA	
"	2		"	
"	3		Attack on THIEPVAL by 49th & 25th Divs unsuccessful – 48th DA was lent being grouped under 49th & 25th DsA	
RAHQ at BOUZINCOURT	4		"	
"	5		"	
"	6		" detachment of 240, 241, 242, 243 Bdes were withdrawn to wagon lines, leaving a guard only on the guns.	
RAHQ at BOUZINCOURT	7			
"	8			
"	9			

Army Form C. 2118

Headquarters 48th Divisional Arty

WAR DIARY
or
INTELLIGENCE SUMMARY

(Erase heading not required.) Volume XXVI

1 – 30 Sept 1916

Instructions regarding War Diaries and Intelligence Summaries are contained in F. S. Regs., Part II. and the Staff Manual respectively. Title Pages will be prepared in manuscript.

Place	Date	Hour	Summary of Events and Information	Remarks and references to Appendices
	10	11 pm	R.A. H.Q. at BOUZINCOURT – Orders recd from R.A. II Corps that 3 Bdes 48 DA are to go into action to enfilade tank enemy E & W counter attk 12 PM on 12th	
	11		Reconnoitred positions near MESNIL & MARTINSART selected Group H.Q. at MARTINSART	
	12		Guns were moved to these new positions during the night excepting D/240, D/241, D/242, C/240, B/242. which went into other positions	
	13		Guns registration new barrages	
	14		" " Orders recd for 240 & 243 Bdes to withdraw from action on night of 14/15 Sept & to be in readiness to move forward at 2 hours notice from 6.30 am 15 Sept. Orders issued accordingly	

1875 Wt. W593/826 1,000,000 4/15 J.B.C. & A. A.D.S.S./Forms/C. 2118.

Headquarters 48th Divisional Arty

WAR DIARY
or
INTELLIGENCE SUMMARY

Volume XXVI

1 - 30 Sept 1916

Army Form C. 2118

Place	Date	Hour	Summary of Events and Information	Remarks and references to Appendices
	14	6.30pm	Attack by 32nd Inf Bde. 11th Divn on WONDER WORK - successful. 48th, 49th, 25th & 11th DTAs cooperating.	
	15	3 am	240 & 243 with B/241 withdrawn to Wagon Lines & ordered to remain at 2 hours notice. Officers reconnaissance patrols were sent on to find positions in X 3 d to fire on ZOLLERN TRENCH running W of COURCELETTE also to fix OPs.	
		2pm	240 & 242 ordered to rendezvous at USNA VALLEY & to be under orders of 2nd Canadian Div? Arty. (Apx D/241)	
		6.30pm	B/s got into position in X 3 d & X 9 b & started a barrage N W of COURCELLETTE to assist Canadian attack - the latter completely successful & all objectives gained. Barrage continues till 9pm - wagon lines at W 29 b. Portion of DAC came up.	
	16	2pm	B/s digging in - orders received from 2 Can RA. to register ZOLLERN REDOUBT in preparation for Canadian attack in evening.	

Army Form C. 2118

Headquarters 48th Divisional Artillery

WAR DIARY
or
INTELLIGENCE SUMMARY

(Erase heading not required.)

1-30 Sept 1916   Volume XXVI

Instructions regarding War Diaries and Intelligence Summaries are contained in F.S. Regs., Part II. and the Staff Manual respectively. Title Pages will be prepared in manuscript.

Place	Date	Hour	Summary of Events and Information	Remarks and references to Appendices
	16	5 pm	Canadian attack started — partially successful on ZOLLERN TRENCH but was not carried out on ZOLLERN REDOUBT.	
		7.30 pm	Barrage was stopped by order of 2 Cdn Div.	
	17	12.15 am	Night barrage ordered by 2 Can Div. on R23 d vo & R22 d 70.	
	18	12 noon	48th D.A. (2 Bdes) moved to R.A. II Corps control.	
			R.A.H.Q. moved to BOUZINCOURT	
			B/242 moved from Q22 b X10a 4.4	
			B/243 " " X3c64 — X3c 3.2	
			D/241 moved back into action at X3b87	
	19		MAJOR BROWNE C/240, LT WYLEY Adjt 240 Bde killed — Capt LAWRENCE RMC 240 Bde, Capt VALLANCY A/243 wounded — 1 OR wounded.	
	20		Quiet day — very wet — Batteries digging in	

Headquarters 48th Divisional Artillery

Army Form C. 2118

WAR DIARY
or
INTELLIGENCE SUMMARY Volume XXVI

(Erase heading not required.)

1 – 30 Sept/16

Place	Date	Hour	Summary of Events and Information	Remarks and references to Appendices
	21		Quiet day. Obj registus - HQ Rt & Left Group moved to USNA	
	22		A & C/241 moved from MARTINSART to X10a SW of PZIGZAGS.	
	23		Quiet day registration continues. weather improved	
	24		" " " " Fine & warm	
	25		" " " "	
	26	12.35 pm	Attack on ZOLLERN & STUFF REDOUBTS by 11th Div supported by 11th & 48th DA's and attack on THIEPVAL VILLAGE & SCHWABEN REDOUBT by 18th Div supported by 18th – 49th DA's. Very successful. 18th Div did not get SCHWABEN REDOUBT but did get 2nd objective vij ZOLLERN TR. to N. of THIEPVAL RD – 11th Div got all their objectives including STUFF REDOUBT. Conducon on the right took all objectives. Many prisoners taken, numbers not yet known, mostly from types. 180 DA L. Brouage extended for 11th Div from MOUQUET FARM northwards to REGINA TR. very successful.	
			Quiet night.	

Army Form C. 2118

Headquarters 4⁰ᵗʰ Divisional Artillery

WAR DIARY
or
INTELLIGENCE SUMMARY

Volume XXVI

1 – 30 September

(Erase heading not required.)

Instructions regarding War Diaries and Intelligence Summaries are contained in F.S. Regs., Part II and the Staff Manual respectively. Title Pages will be prepared in manuscript.

Place	Date	Hour	Summary of Events and Information	Remarks and references to Appendices
	27	3 pm	Attack on STUFF REDOUBT by 11ᵗʰ Div. Successful. 48ᵗʰ D.T.A. did barrage. During night bombing attack down HESSIAN TR. Failed to connect up with Canadians at R.21.d.99. 48ᵗʰ D.T.A. barraged REGINA TR. during night.	
	28	1 pm	Attack by 18ᵗʰ Div on SCHWABEN REDOUBT – successful. London Div barrage L-S.E.	
		6 pm	Attack by 11ᵗʰ Div on HESSIAN TR. postponed	
		11 pm	Orders rec⁰ from RA II Corps that 1 sect. fm 134. 48ᵗʰ DA will be relieved by 1 sect fm 134. 25ᵗʰ DA. on night of 29/30 Sept.	
	29	12 noon	11ᵗʰ Div attacks & took HESSIAN TR. & N. End of STUFF REDOUBT. 48ᵗʰ barraged.	
		1 pm	Enemy counter attack STUFF REDOUBT & retook it.	
		night	1 sect fm 134 48ᵗʰ DA relieved by 1 sect fm 134 25ᵗʰ DA & went to wagon lines	
	30	6.30	Enemy counter attack SCHWABEN REDOUBT & took part of it. Remaining sect. of D⁴⁰ relieved by 25ᵗʰ DA & went to wagon lines	

SECRET

48th. DIVISIONAL ARTILLERY - OPERATION ORDER No. 11

13th. Sept. 1916.

1. 11th. Division will capture the line R.31.d.98 - WONDER WORK - b.23 - b.03 - a.91 - c.78. on the afternoon of 14th. September (the portion b.03 - a.91 - c.78. being organised as a defensive flank and a block formed on the right about R.32.c.08.

2. The Infantry will reach their objective at Zero + 6.

3. The Infantry will light flares at Zero + 10 and at regular intervals of 10 minutes after that hour to show their positions to aeroplanes.   Should parties be without flares, men should wave their trench helmets whenever an aeroplane passes over them in daylight.

4. 11th., 25th. and 48th. Divisional Artillery and French Batteries will co-operate.

5. Zero will be 6.30.pm.

6. ACKNOWLEDGE.

Major,
Bde. Major, 48th. Div. R.A.

Copies to :-

18-pr. Group	11th. Div. R.A.
How. Group.	25th. Div. R.A.
R.A. II Corps.	49th. Div. R.A.
11th. Divn.	H.A. II Corps.

48th. DIVISIONAL ARTILLERY - BOMBARDMENT TABLE 18-POUNDERS

UNIT	TIME	OBJECTIVE	RATE OF FIRE	REMARKS
C/243 1 Sect. C/240	0 to +3	R.31.b.45 - 05 - a.94 - 55	3 rds.per gun per min.	
	+3 to +6	"	"	
	+6 to +8	(R.31.a.94 - 55 (R.31.b.06 - a.75 - 66.	"	
	+8 to +15	"	2 "	
	+15 to +30	"	1 "	
	+30 onwards.	"	¼ "	
C/240 (4 guns)	0 to +8	R.32.b.45 - R.32.a.77.	3 "	
	+8 to +15	"	2 "	
	+15 to +30	"	1 "	
	+30 onwards	"	¼ "	
A/243 A/242	0 to +8	R.32.a.28 - R.31.b.59 - R.31.a.77 - 67.	3 "	
	+8 to +15	"	2 "	
	+15 to +30	"	1 "	
	+30 onwards	"	¼ "	

BOMBARDMENT TABLE - 18-POUNDERS CONTD.

UNIT	TIME	OBJECTIVE	RATE OF FIRE	REMARKS
A/240	0 to +6	R.31.b. - 51 - 23	3 rds. per gun per min	
	+6 to +8	R.31.b.91 - 53 (within safety limits).	3 " " " " "	
	+8 to +15	" "	2 " " " " "	
	+15 to +30	" "	1 " " " " "	
	+30 onwards	" "	$\frac{1}{4}$ " " " " "	
B/342	0 to +5	R.31.b.60 - 51 - 31 - 32 - 23	3 " " " " "	
	+5 to +8	R.31.b.53 - R.32.c.39.	3 " " " " "	
	+8 to +15	R.31.b.91 - 53	2 " " " " "	
	+15 to +30	"	1 " " " " "	
	+30 onwards	"	$\frac{1}{2}$ " " " " "	

3.

BOMBARDMENT TABLE - 4.5" HOWITZERS

UNIT	TIME	OBJECTIVE	RATE OF FIRE	REMARKS
1 Bty.	0 to +6	R.31.b.45 - 25 - 05.	2 rds. per gun per min.	
	+6 to +8	R.31.b.99 - 78 - 88 - 59.	2 " " " " "	
	+8 to +15	" "	1 " " " " "	
	+15 to +30	" "	½ " " " " "	
	+30 onwards	" "	1 rd. per gun per 8 mins.	
1 Bty.	0 to +8	R.31.b.29 - 19 - R.31.a.77.	2 " per min.	
	+8 to +15	" "	1 " " "	
	+15 to +30	" "	½ " " "	
	+30 onwards	" "	1 rd. per gun per 8 mins.	
1 Bty.	0 to +8	R.31.b.06 - R.31.a.75.	2 rds. per gun per min.	
	+8 to +15	" "	1 " " " " "	
	+15 to +30	" "	½ " " " " "	
	+30 onwards	" "	1 rd. per gun per 8 mins.	

SECRET

48th. DIVISIONAL ARTILLERY OPERATION ORDER - No. 12.

14th. Sept. 1916.

1. To take advantage of any opportunity which may offer the 18th. Division will be ready to move at 6 hours notice after zero on 15th. September.

   1/1st. Yorks Dragoons and Reserve Infantry Brigade of 11th. Division will be ready to move on 15th. September at half an hour's notice from 6.30.am.

   Reserve Infantry Brigade of 49th. Division, Corps Cyclists, and two R.F.A. Brigades will be ready to move at two hours notice from 6.30.am. on 15th. September.

2. 240 Brigade R.F.A. and 243 Brigade R.F.A. (with D/241) will withdraw from action before daybreak on 15th. September and will proceed to their Wagon Lines and will be ready to move forward at 2 hours notice from 6.30.am. on 15th. September.
   Vehicles will be packed but horses will not be harnessed up.
   250 sandbags will be carried for each gun and arrangements made to carry water in petrol tins on the footboards.
   One day's forage and rations and emergency rations will be carried.
   An Officers reconnoitring patrol, consisting of 1 Officer 3 N.C.Os. and 2 cyclists, will be told off by each Brigade.

3. A proportion of 48th. D.A.C. will be ready to move forward on 15th. September.

4. Major FOWLER, D/240, will command 240 Brigade during the temporary indisposition of the Lieut.-Colonel Commanding 240 Brigade.

5. From zero on 15th. September, 242 Brigade R.F.A. will be available to assist the Counter Battery Group in neutralizing fire, and will be connected to the Wireless Station belonging to 22 Siege Battery R.G.A. 242 Brigade, R.F.A., will be prepared to answer "Area" calls throughout the day

6. Zero will be notified later.

7. ACKNOWLEDGE.

Major,
Bde. Major, 48th. Div.R.A.

Copies to :-
    18-pr. Group)   R.A. II Corps
    How. Group   ) 48th. D.A. H.A. II Corps
    H.Q. 243 Bde.   11th. Div. R.A.
    O.C. D/240.   49th. Div. R.A.
        48th. D.A.C.

SECRET

48th. DIVISIONAL ARTILLERY OPERATION ORDER - No. 14.

19th. September, 1916.

1. 11th. Division will today, 19th., attack the line
    R.33.a.77 - 47 - 27 - R.32.b.98 - 76 - 4½ - 5.

2. 48th. Div. Arty. will co-operate as shown in table attached.

3. 1st. Canadian Corps have been asked to assist with
    8 18-prs. on R.27.b.51 - R.27.c.97 - R.27.d.½.3 (within
    safety limits) and with 4 18-prs. on R.27.c.97 - 38.

4. Area calls will be taken up as usual and O.C. 240 Bde.
    will arrange that from 0.15 onwards a battery will respond
    to all N.F. targets within range.

5. Zero will be notified later.

6. ACKNOWLEDGE.

Major,
Bde. Major, 48th. Div. R.A

Copies to :-

    R.A. II Corps.   11th. Div.R.A.
    240 Bde.   H.A. II Corps.
    242 Bde.   49th. Div. R.A.
    243 Bde.   25 Div. R.A.

48th. DIV. ARTY. - BOMBARDMENT TABLE - 18-POUNDERS.

Unit	Time	Objective	Rate of Fire	Remarks
A/242 C/242	0.0 to 0.8. 0.8 to 0.15 0.15 to 0.30	R.32.b.7½.9 - R.26.c.9.3. " "	3 rds. per gun per min. 2 " " " " " 1 " " " " "	
2 Bties. of 240 or 243 bdes.	0.0 to 0.8. 0.8 to 0.15 0.15 to 0.30	R.27.c.54 - 38 - 29 - R.26.b.8.6 " "	3 " " " " " 2 " " " " " 1 " " " " "	
B/242	0.0 to 0.8. 0.8 to 0.15 0.15 to 0.30	Rifle pits R.27.c.½.5 - R.32.b.6.9½ " "	3 " " " " " 2 " " " " " 1 " " " " "	
B/243	0.0 to 0.8. 0.8 to 0.15 0.15 to 0.30	Rifle pits R.27.c.38 - R.26.d.97 - 6½.2½ - 50. " "	3 " " " " " 2 " " " " " 1 " " " " "	
2 Bties. of 240 or 243 bdes.	0.3 to 0.5. 0.12 to 0.14	R.27.b.51 - 25 - 17 - 09. "	Bursts of intense fire. " "	

BOMBARDMENT TABLE - 4.5" HOWITZERS.

Unit	Time	Objective	Rate of Fire	Remarks
D/240	0.0 to 0.10	R.27.c.54 - 60.	2 rds. per gun per min.	
	0.10 to 0.20	"	1 " " " "	
	0.20 to 0.30	"	1/2 " " " "	
D/242	0.0 to 0.10	R.27.c.97 - 38.	2 " " " "	
	0.10 to 0.20	"	1 " " " "	
	0.20 to 0.30	"	1/2 " " " "	

SECRET

48th. DIV. ARTY. OPERATION ORDER - No. 15

25th. Sept. 1916.

1.   II Corps will tomorrow, 26th. Sept., in co-operation with Canadian Corps attack and capture the ZOLLERN REDOUBT - STUFF REDOUBT, SCHWABEN REDOUBT crest line and THIEPVAL VILLAGE.

11th. Division on the Right, 18th. Division with 146th. Brigade Group attached on the left - 25th. Division in Corps Reserve.

2.   BOUNDARIES

    (a) Between II and Canadian Corps, the road running N. from R.28.c.22 inclusive to Canadian Corps

    (b) Between 11th. and 18th. Divisions, the line of trees running N. through R.32.a. inclusive to 18th. Division, thence to junction of HESSIAN TRENCH & MIDWAY LINE inclusive to 11th. Division.

3.   OBJECTIVES

1st. Objective
    (a) for 11th. Division -
    R.28.a.36 exclusive through R.27.c.54 - R.32.b.79 to about R.26.c.93.
    (b) for 18th. Division
    thence along road to about R.25.central.

2nd. Objective
    (a) for 11th. Division
    R.22.c.19 exclusive through R.27.a.59 to about R.26.b.02.
    (b) for 18th. Division
    thence to about R.25.b.34.

Final Objective
    (a) for 11th. Division
    R.22.c.19 exclusive - STUFF REDOUBT - along HESSIAN TRENCH to junction of latter with MIDWAY LINE inclusive
    (b) for 18th. Division
    thence through R.19.d.99 & 39 to about R.19.c.92.

When the line has been established on the final objectives strong patrols with Lewis Guns will be pushed forward to the REGINA TRENCH - STUFF TRENCH - SPLUTTER ROAD line.

4.   Each Division will attack with two Brigades in front and one in reserve. Strong supports will follow closely the attack, and reserves will move up automatically as the attack progresses.

2.

5. Apart from other arrangements for marking progress, front line Infantry will xxxxx show flares at Zero plus 1 hr. 45 mins. and again at plus 2 hrs. 15 mins., or at any time on demand being made from contact aeroplanes sounding Klaxon Horns or dropping white lights.
 11th. Divisional Infantry will wear a piece of tin on their backs and 18th. Div. will have yellow flaps to their haversacks.

6. 48th. Div. Arty. will co-operate with 11th. Division as per table attached.
 O.C. Left Group will find one battery which will be at the disposal of G.O.C. 34th. Infantry Brigade from plus 25. and the O.C. Battery will be with the latter.
 O.C. Right Group will find a Battery from plus 15 which will respond to all NF targets within range.
 O.C. Right Group will find a Liaison Officer to be at Headquarters Right Battalion 34th. Infantry Brigade.
 Lieut. BROOKE TAYLOR will perform the duties of Liaison Officer with the Canadian left Infantry Brigade.

7. Os.C. Groups will arrange for visual signalling to supplement the telephone.

8. Provided the situation allows, from 1 hr. - 1 hr. 5. and from 1 hr. 20. - 1 hr. 25. there will be no Artillery fire of any description in order to allow smoke and dust to clear.

9. Zero will be notified later.

10. ACKNOWLEDGE.

 Major,
 Bde. Major, 48th. Div. R.A.

Copies to :-

 Right Group   11th. Division.
 Left Group   11th. Div. R.A.
 R.A. II Corps 18th. Div. R.A.
 H.A. II Corps Canadian Div. R.A.
         S.C.

A M E N D M E N T
==*=*=*=*=*=*=*

Ref. attached table :-

The initial barrage will now be formed from R.28.d.04 to junction of road and HIGH TRENCH at R.27.d.2½.2½ from 0. to 0.2. at 4 yds. per gun per min.

From 0.2. to 0.4. the barrage will be on R.28.d.06 to R.27.d.15 at 4 yds. per gun per minute.

The barrages will be formed by 8 guns of Right Group on the right and 6 guns of Left Group on the left.

At 0.4. the above guns come into the barrage from R.28.a.36 to R.27.d.08.

Care will be taken that there is no fire East of the dividing line between squares R.27.d. & 28.c.

25th. Sept., 1916.

Major,
Bde. Major, 48th. Div. R.A.

48th. DIV. ARTY. - BOMBARDMENT TABLE - 18-POUNDERS

PHASE 1.

Unit	Time	Objective	Rate of Fire	Remarks
2 Btys. Right Group	0. to 0.14. 0.14 to 0.25	Trench R.28.a.3.6. to R.27.b.82. R.28.a.29 to R.27.b.8.5½.		
2 Btys. Right Group	0. to 0.12. 0.12 to 0.25	Trench R.27.b.82 to R.27.b.51 R.27.b.8.5½ - 5.4½.	rds. per gun per min.	
1 Bty. Right Group	0. to 0.5. 0.5. to 0.12. 0.12 to 0.25	Trench R.27.d.89 to 82. Trench R.27.b.63 - 87. Trench R.26.b.87 - 49.	0.0. to 0.15 - 4 rds. 0.15 to 0.18 - 3 " 0.18 to 0.25 - 2 "	
2 Btys. Left Group	0. to 0.8. 0.8 to 0.12 0.12 to 0.25.	Trench R.27.b.51 - R.27.d.08 R.27.b.51 - 01. R.27.b.55 - 01		
1 Bty. Left Group	0. to 0.5. 0.5. to 0.12. 0.12 to 0.25	Trench R.27.d.59 to R.27.b.51 Trench R.27.b.51 - 17. Trench R.27.b.34 - 17.		

PHASE II

Unit	Time	Objective	Rate of Fire	Remarks
5 Btys. Right Group	0.25 to 0.27	R.22.c.21 to R.27.b.5½.7	rds. per gun per min.	
3 Btys. Left Group	" to 0.27 "	R.27.b.5½.7 to R.27.b.03.	0.25 to 0.31 - 3 rds.	
5 Btys. Rt. Group	0.27 to 0.29	R.22.c.13 to R.27.b.5½.9½	0.31 to 0.39 4 "	
3 Btys. Left Group	" "	R.27.b.5½.9½ R.27.b.06.	0.39 to 0.50 2 "	
5 Btys. Rt. Group	0.29 to 0.31	R.22.c.15 to R.21.d.5½.2.	0.50 to 1.0 1 "	
3 Btys. Left Group	" "	R.21.d.5½.2 to R.27.b.09.		
5 Btys. Rt. Group	0.31 to 0.38	R.22.c.1½.9 to R.21.d.5½.4.	1.0. to 1.38 1½ "	Care must be taken that
3 Btys. Left Group	" "	R.21.d.5½.4 to R.27.b.09.	1.38 to 1.44 3 " from) there is no fire E. of
			Rt. Group. Boundary Road as the
			4 rds.from)Canadians are due to
			Left Group)reach trench at 0.33.
5 Btys. Rt. Group	0.38 to 1.44	R.22.a.12 to R.21.d.59	1.44 to 1.54 3 rds.	Searches between this
3 Btys. Left Group	" to 1.38.	Trench R.21.d.58 to R.21.c.97 *	1.54 to 2.0. 2 "	trench & line from
			(2.0. onward till	R.21.d.59 to 13. At
			ordered to increase	1.38 remains on trench
			or stop.	R.21.d.58 - R.21.c.97.
			$\frac{1}{4}$ rd	
5 Btys. Rt. Group	1.44 onwards	R.22.a.13 to R.21.b.5½.3.		*Searches between this line
3 Btys. Lt. Group	1.44 "	R.21.b.5½.3 to R.21.a.80.		& REGINA TRENCH till ordered to stop.

4.5" HOWITZERS

Unit	Time	Objective	Rate of Fire	Remarks
One 4.5" Bty. Right Group.	0. to 0.9.	Trench R.28.a.36 - R.27.b.87	rds. per gun per min.	
	0.9. to 0.22.	Trench R.27.b.87 - 49.	0. to 0.15 - 2 rds.	
	0.22 to 0.34.	Road R.22.a.11 - 26.	0.15 to 0.25 1 rd. 0.25 to 0.38 2 rds. 0.38 to 0.50 1 "	At 0.34. stops firing & becomes available for zone calls.
One 4.5" Bty. Left Group	0. to 0.9.	Trench R.27.b.63 - 87.	0.50 to 1.38 1 " per 3 mins. 1.38 to 1.54 2 " 1.54 to 2.0 1 "	
	0.9. to 0.22.	Trench R.27.b.49 - 38 - 17	2.0 onwards till ordered to stop or increase ¼ rd.	
	0.22 to 1.38	Trench R.21.c.97 - R.21.a.80 towards 75)		
	1.38 towards	Road R.21.a.82 towards 67.		
One 4.5" Bty. Left Group.	0. to 0.6.	Trench R.27.b.51 - 25.		
	0.6 to 0.22	Trench R.27.b.25 - 17.		
	0.22 to 1.38.	Trench R.21.c.97 - R.21.a.80 - towards 75.		
	1.38 onwards.	Road R.21.a.67 towards R.15.c.62.		

SECRET

48th. DIVISIONAL ARTILLERY OPERATION ORDER - No. 16.

29th. September, 1916.

1. 48th. Div. Arty. (less 241 Bde.) will be relieved by 25th. Div. Arty. as shewn in table attached on ~~nights~~ of [afternoons] 29/30th. September, ~~30th. Sept./1st. Oct.~~, arrangements for relief being made between Group Commanders direct.
   241 Bde. will be relieved by 18th. Div. Arty. under arrangements made by 49th. Div. Arty.

2. Guns in action will be handed over to 25th. Div. Arty. stripped, all sights and small stores being taken away by 48th. Div. Arty.
   All Maps and Secret Documents to be handed over.
   Ammunition at the guns will be taken over by 25th. Div. Arty. at noon 30th. September.

3. The 9.45 Heavy Trench Mortar on charge of 48th. Div. Arty. and now in AVELUY will be handed over to 25th. Div. Arty.
   Orders for 2" T.M.Batteries will be issued separately.

4. The Wireless Masts and Operators at Right and Left Group Headquarters will accompany 48th. Div. Arty. and will not be handed over to 25th. Div. Arty. The stations will not be dismantled till relieved by 25th. Div. Arty. wireless.

5. On completion of relief each night, 48th. Div. Arty. will proceed to their Wagon Lines.

6. Command of Batteries and Group Command will be handed over on completion of relief.

                  Major,
               Bde. Major, 48th. Div.R.A.

Copies to :-

   Right Group
   Left Group
   241 Bde. RFA.
   25th. Div.R.A.
   R.A. II Corps.
   49th. Div. R.A.

RELIEF OF 48th. DIV. ARTY. by 25th. DIV. ARTY.

48th. Div.Arty.	relieved by	25th. Div.Arty.	Remarks
A/240	"	Bty.of 112th.Bde.	1 Section on afternoon 29th. Sept. 1 " " " 30th. Sept.
B/240	"	Bty.of 112th.Bde.	ditto.
C/240	"	Bty.of 112th.Bde.	ditto
D/240	"	D/112 Bde.	ditto
A/243	"	Bty.of 111th.Bde.	ditto
C/243	"	Bty.of 111th.Bde.	ditto
A/242 ½ C/242	"	110th. Bde.	1 Section on afternoon 29th. Sept. 2 Sections " " 30th. Sept.
B/242 ½ C/242	"	110th. Bde.	ditto
B/243	"	Bty.of 111th.Bde.	1 Section on afternoon 29th. Sept. 1 " " " 30th. Sept.
D/242	"	D/110 Bde.	ditto
D/241	"	D/111 Bde.	ditto

Original

Vol 20

Confidential War Diary

of

Head Quarters 48th Divisional Artillery

From 1st to 31st October 1916

Volume XXVII

31.10.16

C.J. McDonnell
Lieut ft
Major
Bde Major 48 D.A.

Head Quarters 48th Divn Arty

WAR DIARY
or
INTELLIGENCE SUMMARY Volume XXVII

Army Form C. 2118

(Erase heading not required.) 1 – 31 Octr 7/16.

Place	Date	Hour	Summary of Events and Information	Remarks and references to Appendices
	Oct 1.		B4s in wagon line near ALBERT – took over stripped guns from 18th Dvn. Order recd to proceed to neighbourhood of WARLINCOURT on 2. Oct.	
	2	10am	CRA 48th Dvn Arty handed over command to CRA 25th Dvn. Hqrs Dvn Arty HQ. moved to HENU. B4s & DAC. marches to WARLINCOURT.	
	3.		B4s in billets – orders recd. to occupy positions allotted by RA VII Corps on night of 5/6 Oct.	
	4	12 noon	48th TMs took over 12 positions N.E. of HEBUTERNE from 33rd Dvn. TMs and two 9.45" TMs in position. Rain + mist – B4s engaged in preparing positions	
	5.		Quiet day – B4s engaged in preparing positions – Rt group put 1 Bde Each into action in 3 positions to begin wire cutting on 6th Oct.	
	6		Some wire cutting done – Brd communications + weather interferes	

Army Form C. 2118

WAR DIARY
or
INTELLIGENCE SUMMARY
(Erase heading not required.)

Instructions regarding War Diaries and Intelligence Summaries are contained in F. S. Regs., Part II. and the Staff Manual respectively. Title Pages will be prepared in manuscript.

Place	Date	Hour	Summary of Events and Information	Remarks and references to Appendices
	7th		Wire cutting carried out by both Groups and TMs — very high winds & aeroplane made the situation difficult.	
	8th		Wire cutting by 18Pdrs resumed with fair success. TMs did much damage to wire. At midday orders recd from RA VII Corps that TMs were to cease firing. OPs1 placed 2 forward guns in action at K10c62	
	9th		No wire cutting today.	
	10th		SA fired 500 rds at wire — some damage done.	
	11th		" " Owing to bad day no wire cutting.	
	12th		" "	
	13		Wirecutting resumed by both Groups — construction of forward OPs begun owing to extension of time.	
	14		Wirecutting resumed by Right group.	
	15		" Continued " "	

WAR DIARY
or
INTELLIGENCE SUMMARY.

(Erase heading not required.)

Army Form C. 2118.

Place	Date	Hour	Summary of Events and Information	Remarks and references to Appendices
	16	1 pm	Wire cutting continued by Groups. Orders received from VII Corps that 49th & 17th Divn Arty will be withdrawn taking over last from BHQ on night of 16/17 Oct & other sections on night of 17/18 Oct. 33D Divn Arty to go out as a whole on night of 17/18 Oct. Lgt Div Arty to cover the front from E.11.a. 95 L - SUNKEN ROAD K.19.a. as from 6 pm on 17 Oct.	
		Night	A/241 moved a sect. into rear of B/248 & D/246 position (49th Divn) and A/190 a sect into C/248 position. D/242 moved a sect into D/247 position. Rt group orders to regpts 17th Divn front on morning of 17 Oct.	
	17		Remaining sections moved to above positions.	
	18		Lgt Div Arty took over Arty Defence of the line L-SUNKEN ROAD relieving 33.D.D.A. Lgt Div. received orders to go out into G.H.Q. Reserve — guns to stay in under Lgt Div who took over the line held by 4oth Divn D.A.	

Army Form C. 2118.

WAR DIARY
or
INTELLIGENCE SUMMARY.
(Erase heading not required.)

Instructions regarding War Diaries and Intelligence Summaries are contained in F. S. Regs., Part II. and the Staff Manual respectively. Title pages will be prepared in manuscript.

Place	Date	Hour	Summary of Events and Information	Remarks and references to Appendices
	19th		Right Group cut wire near SUNKEN ROAD. D/240 moved to K8a 24 vacated by 33rd DA.	
	20th		Rt. Group T.Ms cut wire near SUNKEN ROAD.	
	21st		48th Div left – 49th W. Yorks taken their line to SUNKEN ROAD K.19.a. K8a D.H. remained covering 49th Div.	
	22		Enemy attempts to raid opposite FONQUEVILLERS and "Z" Hedge in front of HEBUTERNE – neither was successful – opposite latter 1 Off + 10 O.R. were found dead.	
	23.		Very foggy – observation impossible	
	24		Very foggy + rain – Rt. Inf. Wire cut by 2" T.Ms continued. Laundry found into 3 groups to correspond with	
	25		Quiet day – wire cutting near Gommecourt – Foncquillers Road.	
	26		Continued shoot on COTTAGE COPSE by three 9.45" mortars – 2" TMs – R.Gs + Right + Centre Groups. 9.45"/T.M. shooting not good owing to faulty ammunition	

Army Form C. 2118.

WAR DIARY
or
INTELLIGENCE SUMMARY.
(Erase heading not required.)

Instructions regarding War Diaries and Intelligence Summaries are contained in F.S. Regs., Part II. and the Staff Manual respectively. Title pages will be prepared in manuscript.

Place	Date	Hour	Summary of Events and Information	Remarks and references to Appendices
	27		Quiet day. 5-31 Hows B4 arrived from England on footing to 46th Div Art. B4 were put into huts in GRINCOURT	
	28		Wirecutting by R't & Left groups & T.M's. Southern Operations postponed to 1. hour.	
	29		Wirecutting by R't group. Quiet day.	
	30.		Southern operations postponed to Nov 5th	
	31		Wirecutting by Rt Group. Quiet day.	

Original

Vol 2

Confidential War Diary

of

Head Quarters 48th Divisional Artillery

from 1st to 30th November 1916

Volume XXVIII

[signature]
Major
Bde Major 48 Div Arty

1/12/16

11th Bde, 48th Divn. Arty.

Army Form C. 2118.

WAR DIARY
or
INTELLIGENCE SUMMARY.

(Erase heading not required.)

Volume XXVIII 1 - 30 Nov 1916.

Instructions regarding War Diaries and Intelligence Summaries are contained in F. S. Regs., Part II. and the Staff Manual respectively. Title pages will be prepared in manuscript.

Place	Date 1916	Hour	Summary of Events and Information	Remarks and references to Appendices
	November 1st		Quiet day. Wirecutting continued by 18 pdrs and medium trench mortars	
	2nd		C.R.A. and D.T.M.O. visited School of Mortars Third Army. Wirecutting continued. Night 2/3rd No. Right Group cooperated with 31st Divn Arty in connection with attempted raid on German trenches	
	3rd		M.G.R.A. Third Army visited OP's of Centre and Left Groups. Enemy heavily shelled HEBUTERNE in the evening	
	4th		Quiet day. 48th Divn Arty School opened. Brig General A.D.O. Ward gave opening address.	
	5th		Wire cutting continued by Right Group in front of FETTER. Hebuterne shelled at intervals.	
	6th		Quiet day. Wirecutting continued. 31st Divn made a "creeper" raid. In conjunction with 31st Divn, made a sham barrage on 1st + 2nd line North of SUNKEN ROAD, in conjunction with 31st Divn. Result, 5 prisoners and 30 boche believed killed.	

WAR DIARY
or
INTELLIGENCE SUMMARY.

Army Form C. 2118.

Place	Date	Hour	Summary of Events and Information	Remarks and references to Appendices
	1916 NOVEMBER 6th (Cont)		D/242 badly shelled, one gun pit hit & knocked in, five men wounded. Gun pit put out of action. BIENVILLERS shelled.	
	7th		Quiet day. No wirecutting on account of bad health.	
	8th		A/210 badly shelled. One gun knocked completely out. No casualties as detachments withdrawn. No wirecutting. Quiet day.	
	9th		Wet & misty	
	10th		night Enemy raided A9" Gun front at WELCOME STR but got no prisoners	
	11th		Wire cutting by Rn & Centre groups & TMs continued	
	12th		Ditto - very misty	
	13th		Attack by XIIIth & Vth Corps - zero 5.45am - very misty. 48th D.A. demonstrated from SUNKEN RD to K.11.a and from ROAD E.28.c to LITTLE Z - Smoke clouds formed etc. 3rd Bde on night took objectives but had to return later owing to failure of 3rd Bde on their right	

WAR DIARY
or
INTELLIGENCE SUMMARY.
(Erase heading not required.)

Army Form C. 2118.

Place	Date	Hour	Summary of Events and Information	Remarks and references to Appendices
	13th Oct.		BEAUMONT HAMEL & ST PIERRE DIVION taken by 51st & 63rd Div's 3500 prisoners approx.	
	14th	6 am	31st Div withdrew to their own front line owing to their position being untenable. 4th Bde Cdt wire cut K4a 22.51 fm road by 147 Inf Bde cut 10 pm. 49th Div road at K4a 22.51 postponed, no patrol made to reconnoitre gap. Right Sector of 49th front (SUNKEN ROAD to K3d79) handed over to 31st Div. 241 Bde became attached to & under orders of 31st R.A. & remained covering their present zone.	
	15th			
	16.		Enemy bombarded own trench in E11a. S.W. of MONCHY down a gas shell — deal of damage	
	17	2 pm	Organised bombardment by 242 Bde on trenches just S. of MONCHY in retaliation to shelling of our trench opposite BIENVILLERS. E11a on 16th.	
	18		Quiet day	
	19		Group of 46 R.B.A. became attached to 48 S.A. 49th Div took over new sector.	

Army Form C. 2118.

WAR DIARY
or
INTELLIGENCE SUMMARY.
(Erase heading not required.)

Instructions regarding War Diaries and Intelligence Summaries are contained in F.S. Regs., Part II. and the Staff Manual respectively. Title pages will be prepared in manuscript.

Place	Date	Hour	Summary of Events and Information	Remarks and references to Appendices
	20		H.A. fires on CHEMIN DES DAMES - cancelled later owing to bad light.	
		8 pm	Raid by 147 Inf Bde on K.9.a.22.51 very successful - many casualties inflicted - barrage very good.	
	21		Very foggy. Quiet day	
	22		Very foggy - orders red that 49th DIV will concentrate on 28th & 29th on NW of MEZEROLLES (W of DOULLENS) having been relieved on 26", 27" Nov by 49th RDA	
	23	5.30 am	Raid by Germans in Y.2. no enemy entered our trenches, but some casualties were caused by their bombardment.	
	24		Quiet day	
	25		Quiet day very foggy & wet.	
	26		Quiet day - 1st (est) fus Bn 146th DA relieved by 49". DA & proceeded bivouac lines - 146 DA group attacks 48". Similarly relieved by 49". 24/13th bde relieved by 31st DA. - 48" TMs relieved by HQ 4" TMs	

Army Form C. 2118.

WAR DIARY
or
INTELLIGENCE SUMMARY.
(Erase heading not required.)

Place	Date	Hour	Summary of Events and Information	Remarks and references to Appendices
	27	a/m	Relief of 48th DA by 49th DA completed – 48th DA moved to PAS.	
	28		48th DA remained in billets at PAS, ST AMAND & HENU (DHQ)	
	29		48th DA marched to MEZEROLLES – FROHEN-LE'GRAND – occupies outposts.	
	30th		48th DA remained in billets as on 29th.	
	–			

1577 Wt. W10791/1773 50,000 1/15 D. D. & L.   A.D.S.S./Forms/C. 2118.

Original

Vol 2

Confidential War Diary

of

48th Divisional Artillery Head Quarters

From 1st to 31st December 1916

Volume XXIX

31/12/16

C.W.V.
Major
Bde Major 48 D.A

Army Form C. 2118.

Headquarters 48th Divl Arty

WAR DIARY
or
INTELLIGENCE SUMMARY.

Volume XXIX
1 to 31 December 1916

(Erase heading not required.)

Place	Date	Hour	Summary of Events and Information	Remarks and references to Appendices
	1 Dec		48th D.A. moved to TALMAS & VILLERS BOCAGE - Hq at latter place	
	2nd		D.A. moved to MOLLIENS AU BOIS, PIERREGOT, BEHEN COURT, FRECHEN COURT. Hq at MIRVAUX	
	3rd		D.A. remained as on 2nd Dec	
	4th		One bat. of B4 took over from 1 sect. of B4 of 23rd D.A. round MARTINPUICH	
	5th		Remainder of 48th D.A. relieved 23rd D.A. & 1 Bty of 15th D.A.	
	6th		CRA 48th took over from CRA 23rd. 12 noon	
	7th		Quiet day. v. misty	
	8th		Quiet day v. misty	
	9th		Misty - Enemy working parties shelled by own Arty	
	10th		" "	

Army Form C. 2118.

WAR DIARY
or
INTELLIGENCE SUMMARY.
(Erase heading not required.)

Instructions regarding War Diaries and Intelligence Summaries are contained in F.S. Regs., Part II. and the Staff Manual respectively. Title pages will be prepared in manuscript.

Place	Date	Hour	Summary of Events and Information	Remarks and references to Appendices
	11th		Quiet day except for shelling of MARTINPUICH —	
	12th		Nothing unusual. D/72 relieved D/70 & 532 How Bde relieved D/71	
	13th		Quiet day — wind light	
	14th		" "	
	15th		1 Sect for Bty of A,B,C,D/241 relieved by 1 sect for Bty A,B,C/242	
	16th		Remainder of 241 relieved by 242. 15 Div. took over from 48th Div	
	17th	10am	C.R.A 15th Div. took over from C.R.A 48th Div. HQ moved to ALBERT.	
	18th		240 Bde = 242 Bde in the line 241 Bde at BEHENCOURT in rest.	
	19th		1 Sec A/70 relieved 1 sec C/241. C/241 wagon lines moved to BEHENCOURT	
	20th		Remainder of C/241 relieved by A/70.	
	21st		R.A H.Q at ALBERT with Divl HQ.	
	22-29			
	30		R.A/Hq moved to LAVIEVILLE. Half 240 Bde relieved by R.H.A 241 Bde	
	31		Remainder of 240 Bde relieved by remainder of 241 Bde — 240 Bde at BEHENCOURT.	

original

Vol 2

Confidential War Diary

of

48th Divisional Artillery Head Quarters

from 1st to 31st January 1917

Volume ~~XXX~~

31-1-17

Ch—
Major
Bde Major 48 Divn Arty

Original

WAR DIARY
or
INTELLIGENCE SUMMARY.

Headquarters R.A. 48 Div Army Form C. 2118.
1 to 31 January 1917   Volume XXX

(Erase heading not required.)

Instructions regarding War Diaries and Intelligence Summaries are contained in F. S. Regs., Part II. and the Staff Manual respectively. Title pages will be prepared in manuscript.

Place	Date	Hour	Summary of Events and Information	Remarks and references to Appendices
LAVIÉVILLE	1 Jan		H.Q. R.A. at LAVIÉVILLE. D/Lt Lord WYNFORD acted as C.R.A. vice Brig. Gen. H D.O WARD at R.A. III Corps.	
	to 13th Jan			
	11, 9 1h 8, 9 "		48th Div. Div A.M. moved to new ABBEVILLE for training. A/R. remaining behind.	
	13 Jan		1/2 240 relieved 1/2 242 in the line	
	14 Jan		Remainder of 240 released remainder of 242 & 242 at BEHENCOURT A/166 & C/188 arrived at MIRVAUX on posting to Army Bdes in III Corps.	
	15 "		2 × C/188 posted to form D/242 at BEHENCOURT as soon as possible. to complete D/242 to 6 gun Bty.	
	16th–20th		Nothing to note	
	20th		Reorganisation of D.A.C. complete – nucleus of 242 (A.F.B&) BAC formed at FRECHENCOURT	

WAR DIARY
or
INTELLIGENCE SUMMARY.

Army Form C. 2118.

Headquarters RA 48th 1 to 31 Jany 1917 Volume ***

Hour, Date, Place	Summary of Events and Information	Remarks and references to Appendices
21 Jan	1 Sect Jn 78th 240 & 241 relieved by 15th DA.	Grosagnulies
22"	Remainder 240 & 241 relieved by 15th D.A. & withdrawn	
22 - 25th	Nothing to note	
26th	48th Div Art & DAC moved to FOUILLOY AUBIGNY and	HAMELET
	RAHQ closed at LAVIEVILLE & opened at FOUILLOY	
27th to 31st	No change.	

Original

Vol 24

Confidential War Diary

of

48th Divisional Artillery Head Quarters

From 1st to 28th February 1917

Volume XXXI

1/3/17

C. Lyon, Major RA
Brigade Major RA 48 Divn

Volume XXXI

Army Form C. 2118.

WAR DIARY
or
INTELLIGENCE SUMMARY.

Headqrs RA 48 Divn

1 – 28 February 1917

(Erase heading not required.)

Hour, Date, Place	Summary of Events and Information	Remarks and references to Appendices
1. Feb 1917	RAHQ & Divl Arty at FOUILLOY & neighbourhood	
2. "	RAHQ & ½ Divl Arty moved to CAPPY – 48° Inf bth over the 2nd from 152 French Div	
3. "	Remainder of Divl Arty & DAC moved to CAPPY	
10 pm	½ Left Arty relieves ½ Arty of 152 French Div	
4. "	Heavy shelling of our front line & B.4 positions all day by the enemy. Raid by enemy on 143 & 144 Bdes. Breaks off slight from hostile enemy's lts. SAA movement of importance.	
6 pm	Arranged with French Corps for that portion of French Arty still in the line to remain for a further 24 hours as our guns not properly registered	
8 pm	Artr Command to remain with the French till evening to visit & shelling. Enemy used gas shell morning of 6 Feb.	

5th Feb. morning of 6 Feb.

Forms/C. 2118/10

Army Form C. 2118.

WAR DIARY
or
INTELLIGENCE SUMMARY.
(Erase heading not required.)

Instructions regarding War Diaries and Intelligence Summaries are contained in F.S. Regs., Part II. and the Staff Manual respectively. Title pages will be prepared in manuscript.

Hour, Date, Place	Summary of Events and Information	Remarks and references to Appendices
5. Feb.	48th DA registers — Quiet day.	
6 Feb. 8 am	CRA 40th took over Artᵃ Command for Col. HECQ	
7th & 8th Feb.	C/241 Artᵃ of 152 French Div. Registering continues.	
9th Feb.	The Brigade boundary was altered — necessitating A/240 & C/241 being transferred to Dₜ Sub Group	
10th – 13th Feb.	Quiet days — registering continues	
14th – 15th Feb.	Registering continues.	
16th Feb. night	Detached section of B/241 & C/241 pulled up to be ready to start wire cutting	
17th 18th Feb.	Two A.F. Brigades from 50th & 1st DA's ordered to be attached to 48th DA when required — positions reconnoitred for them, also for TMs	

Army Form C. 2118.

WAR DIARY
or
INTELLIGENCE SUMMARY.
(Erase heading not required.)

Instructions regarding War Diaries and Intelligence Summaries are contained in F.S. Regs., Part II. and the Staff Manual respectively. Title pages will be prepared in manuscript.

Hour, Date, Place		Summary of Events and Information	Remarks and references to Appendices
19th Feb		Wire cutting & destructive shoots by 4.5" Hows. Left subgroup moved up 1 inch 18pdr for wire cutting. Very wet.	
20 Feb.	9am	RAMP moved from CAPPY CHATEAU to BOIS OLYMPE. Recently 145 Inf Bde. covered by Rt. sub group failed – wire not cut – 1 OR slightly wounded. Trenches in bad state	
21 Feb		Trenches worse – registration continued	
22 Feb		A/26 C/72 & 13/242 of Army F. Art. Bde. from zoners near VAIRE moved up to wagon lines CAPPY in 4th Div Area.	
23 Feb		Quiet day – very misty. SOS on 143 Inf Bde front 8pm. false alarm.	
24 Feb.		Destructive shoots by Hows. & 4.5" Hows. 1egun.	
25th Feb.		Divl Art formed into 3 subgroups before – A/26 & 13/242. Moved up 1 sect each into position.	

(9 29 6) W4141—463 100,000 9/14 HWV Forms/C. 2118/10

Army Form C. 2118.

WAR DIARY
or
INTELLIGENCE SUMMARY.
(Erase heading not required.)

Instructions regarding War Diaries and Intelligence Summaries are contained in F.S. Regs., Part II. and the Staff Manual respectively. Title pages will be prepared in manuscript.

Hour, Date, Place	Summary of Events and Information	Remarks and references to Appendices
26. Feb.	B/242 moved up another section. D/241 sent forward sect of Battery at N15b 5778 C/242 sent " " " N4a 7030	
27 Feb.	B/242 moved up remaining section. C/72 moved 2 sects into forward position H11c85 during darkness. 1 am 48th DA bombarded enemy trenches for 3 mins.	
28th Feb.	5.25 am 48th DA bombarded enemy trenches in conjunction with operation carried out by XIV Corps.	

SECRET

III Corps G. For information

Copy No. 8.

48th DIV. ARTY. ORDER - NO.43.

31st January, 1917.

1. 48th. Div. Artillery will relieve the Artillery of the 152 French Divisions on the nights 3/4th and 4/5th. February.

2. At 8 pm. on 3rd February the advanced portion of the Batteries as shewn in attached Table "A" will arrive at positions. Table "A" also shows the number of emplacements to be vacated by French Batteries.
   One Officer from each Brigade will also report at 5 pm. to each Group Headquarters which is being relieved and will remain there as Liaison Officer. All guns put in on night of 3/4th February will be under the Command of French Group Commanders and will fire if required on the zone of the French Group to which they belong till 8 pm. 4th February.

3. At 8 pm. on 4th February the remaining guns of the 152 French Div. Artillery in the line will be relieved by 48th Div. Artillery and Artillery command will pass to C.R.A. 48th Division.

4. O.C. 242 Brigade with his Adjutant will proceed to Headquarters of 152 French Div. Artillery, HERBECOURT, on the morning of 4th February and remain there.

5. Trench Mortar Batteries of 48th Division will relieve Trench Mortar Batteries of French Division on the night of 2/3rd February under arrangements to be made between Trench Mortar Officers concerned.
   D.T.M.O. will arrange to put in six 2" Trench Mortars on the Divisional front as follows:-

   Two Mortars on North from X Bty.
   Two   "   Centre "   Y Bty.
   Two   "   South   "   Z Bty.

   9.45" emplacements will be taken over but no guns put in at present.
   Remainder of 2" Trench Mortar personnel and V/48 will remain in reserve at CAPPY till further orders.
   All Trench Mortar personnel will be conveyed from HAMELET to CAPPY Area on 2nd February under arrangements to be notified later.

6. Completion of reliefs each night will be notified to R.A.H.Q.

7. Position of R.A.H.Q. will be notified later.

8. ACKNOWLEDGE.

Copies to:-   sd/C.Lyon, Major,
   No.1   240 Bde.   Bde. Major, 48th Div. Arty.
   " 2   241 Bde.
   " 3   242 Bde.
   " 4   D.A.C.
   " 5   D.T.M.O.
   " 6   H.Qr.Coy.Train
   " 7   48th Div.
   " 8   R.A. III Corps
   " 9   Col.Commdt. Arty. of 152 French Div.

TABLE "A"

RELIEF OF ARTILLERY OF 152 FRENCH DIVISION BY 48th DIV. ARTILLERY ON NIGHTS 3/4th 4/5th FEBRUARY.

Brigade.	Bty.Position English Co-ordinates	Bty.Position French Co-ordinates	48th D.A. Bty.	Relieves French Bty.	No.of guns to be put in Night 3/4th	Night 4/5th	No.of positions required from French.
240	H34b75	8573	B/240	11th/52nd Regt.	2	2	2
H.Qrs. Dugout H34b93	N11a69	8956	B/240	Unoccupied	2	-	-
	H34d47	8468 8366	C/240	Unoccupied	4	2	-
	N4b14	8263	A/240	4th/52nd Regt.	3	3	1
	N5a28	8765	D/240	Unoccupied	4 Hows.	2 Hows.	-
241 H.Qrs. H28b03	H23a44	8791	A/241	Unoccupied	4	2	-
	H28b03	8281	B/241	10/52nd Regt. 12th/52ndRegt.	3	3	3
	H34d84	8568	C/241 D/241 (1 Sec)	1st/52nd Regt. 2nd/52nd Regt.	3	3 2 Hows.	3
	H23a222	8691	D/241	Unoccupied	2 Hows.	2 Hows.	-
242 H.Qrs. H26c15 N4b03	N4a75	8164	B/242	6th/52nd Regt.	2	2	2
	N4b63	8563	(1 Sec)B/242 D/242 (1 Sect)	Unoccupied	2 1 How.	1 How.	-
	N9d05	7349	A/242	Unoccupied	4	2	-
	N9d60	7646	D/242	Unoccupied	3 Hows.	1 How.	-

Original

Vol 25

Confidential War Diary

of

48th Divisional Artillery Headquarters

from 1st to 31st March 1917

Volume XXII

1/4/17

Major
Bde Major R.A. 48 Div

Headquarters Royal Artillery, 48th Division

Army Form C. 2118.

WAR DIARY
or
INTELLIGENCE SUMMARY.

1st to 31st March 1917
Volume XXXII

(Erase heading not required.)

Instructions regarding War Diaries and Intelligence Summaries are contained in F.S. Regs., Part II. and the Staff Manual respectively. Title pages will be prepared in manuscript.

Hour, Date, Place		Summary of Events and Information	Remarks and references to Appendices
1 March		B/4½ & C/240 heavily shelled – B/4½ had 1 gun destroyed. No casualties. Fine day & enemy aeroplanes very active.	
2 March		Wirecutting undertaken owing to bad light.	
3 March	2.30 am	Raid by 143. unsuccessful. B/4½ & 50th & 1st DAs fired in red. Wire not cut. Wire cancelled & B/4½ were not out till road & rent back.	
4 March		Wirecutting carried on for future raids	
5 March		A/246 ordered to come out of action & go to wagon lines & march to FOUILLOY on 6 March.	
6 March		Registration by aeroplane commenced & was cutting by 7MS & Masters of group.	

WAR DIARY
or
INTELLIGENCE SUMMARY.

(Erase heading not required.)

Army Form C. 2118.

Instructions regarding War Diaries and Intelligence Summaries are contained in F.S. Regs., Part II. and the Staff Manual respectively. Title pages will be prepared in manuscript.

Hour, Date, Place	Summary of Events and Information	Remarks and references to Appendices
7 March	Unevently continued.	
8 March 12.45 AM	1/4 Beds raided just N. of MAISONETTE & captured 2 prisoners	
9 pm	143 raided N. of MAISONETTE & captured 2 prisoners & 2 M.Gs. Our casualties slight.	
9 March	Quiet day & very misty	
10 March	Quiet day – TMs fired 150 rds without retaliation at our posns MAISONETTE. B/242 Cut wire. 2 Camouflage bombardments at 10pm & 11.30pm	
11 March	TMs Cut wire. B/242 went out of action to engage rear.	
12 "	5 am 'Camouflage' barrage on front & support lines by MAISONETTE. B/242 moved to VARG by order of RA III Corps.	

Forms/C. 2118/10

WAR DIARY
or
INTELLIGENCE SUMMARY.
(Erase heading not required.)

Army Form C. 2118.

Instructions regarding War Diaries and Intelligence Summaries are contained in F.S. Regs., Part II. and the Staff Manual respectively. Title pages will be prepared in manuscript.

Hour, Date, Place	Summary of Events and Information	Remarks and references to Appendices
13. March	Quiet day	
14. March	Quiet day – orders received from RA III Corps to recommence wire cutting on 15th in preparation to attack on 18th on MAISONETTE in cooperation with attack by French further S.	
15. March	Information rec'd that Enemy is retreating leaving rearguards. Orders rec'd from RA III Corps that 242 B'de will go out night of 18/19 March.	
2.30 am 17th March	Attack on MAISONETTE by 145 Inf. B'de – Quite successful. only small enemy rearguards – 13 prisoners taken – line consolidated along railway thus line – patrols pushed out towards town.	
17. March	Rearguard action towards PERONNE continues. 144 B'de joined up with 1st Div on our right.	
18. March	Mt ST QUENTIN & PERONNE occupied – no sign of Enemy anywhere.	

(9 20 6) W 4111–453 100,000 9/14 HWV Forms/C. 2118/10

WAR DIARY
or
INTELLIGENCE SUMMARY.
(Erase heading not required.)

Army Form C. 2118.

Hour, Date, Place	Summary of Events and Information	Remarks and references to Appendices
19 March	Inft Patrols pushed out to DOINGT WOODS – COURCELLES – CATELET. No sign of enemy & no hostile shelling. 4/241 moved to new position N. of RADEGONDE B/240 " " " 07 b N. of BARLEUX COPSE D/241 " " " near CHAPELLETTE D/240 " " " 07 a 1000× NE of BARLEUX	
20 March	Orders recd for Mobile Column to be formed under Command of Genl WARD & to push on to get touch with Enemy on 21st. C/240 & D/240 detailed & 2 Bos 145 Inf Bde	
21 March	Lt Col COLVILLE assumed duties of C.R.A. A×B/241 moved to position near ETERPIGNY – 1" Div withdrew from action & 48th took over their area. Mobile Col. formed under DOINGT	

WAR DIARY
or
INTELLIGENCE SUMMARY.
(Erase heading not required.)

Army Form C. 2118.

Place	Date	Hour	Summary of Events and Information	Remarks and references to Appendices
March	22.		A & B/240 moved back to invaginate CAPPY in reserve. WARD'S COLUMN in CATALET	
	March 23		Quiet day for Art. - reconnoitring continues.	
	24		Cav? (5th Div) relieve Ward's Column on the outpost line POEUILLY - FLECHIN - MARQUAIX.	
	25.		9 am 48th Div moved to QUINQUANCE - RAHQ to PERONNE	
	26.		WARD'S COLUMN disbanded - CRA reassumed command of 48th Div Art. 241 B'y & A+B/240 first into action N. of TINCOURT & near TEMPLEUX LA FOSSE to cover operations against LONGAVESNES.	
	27th		C/240 & D/240 assists 5th Cav Div in the capture of the high ground between ROISEL & LONGAVESNES. Cav occupied GUYENCOURT - VILLERS FAUCON + SAULCOURT. 14 R.H.A. still PERONNE. 240 B? HQ TINCOURT - 241 BUSU. HQ 241 moved to TEMPLEUX LA FOSSE	
	28"			
	29".		Quiet day - guns moved forward for attack on S? EMILIE	
	30"		40th Div (144 Bde) attacks S? EMILIE - successful. Village captured. 2/LT YIRRELL B/240 killed	

Army Form C. 2118.

WAR DIARY
or
INTELLIGENCE SUMMARY.
(Erase heading not required.)

Instructions regarding War Diaries and Intelligence Summaries are contained in F.S. Regs., Part II. and the Staff Manual respectively. Title pages will be prepared in manuscript.

Hour, Date, Place	Summary of Events and Information	Remarks and references to Appendices
31 March	46th Bns. pushed out patrols towards ESPEHY. without much opposition - preparatory to attacking the latter place	

Vol 26 Original

Confidential War Diary

of

48th Divisional Artillery Headquarters

From 1st to 30th April 1917

Volume XXXIII

1-5-17

C. Heyer
Major
Bde Major RA 48 Div

Headquarters 48th Divisional Artillery

Army Form C. 2118.

WAR DIARY
or
INTELLIGENCE SUMMARY.
(Erase heading not required.)

1st to 30th April 1917   Volume XXIII

Instructions regarding War Diaries and Intelligence Summaries are contained in F.S. Regs., Part II. and the Staff Manual respectively. Title pages will be prepared in manuscript.

Hour, Date, Place	Summary of Events and Information	Remarks and references to Appendices
1 April 5 am	4th Divn attacks EPEHY & PEIZIERES – successful & fully occupied also MALASSISE FARM. One 77mm gun & 20 prisoners captured. R.A.H.Q. at TINCOURT	
2 Ap.	Quiet day – guns moved up between VILLERS FAUCON &	
3 Ap.	EPEHY. Suffer attack on RONSSOY	
4 Ap.	37"S13 & 22.H13 came under us Div control	
5 Ap. 6.45 am	Attack by 144 Bde on RONSSOY – LEMPIRE-RONSSOY & BASSE BOULOGNE taken also 30 prisoners and 6 MGs. Dead estimated at 200	
6 Ap.	Quiet day – our Infy consolidating	
7 Ap. 9–10 am	A/240 & 104th D/240 fired on SUNKEN RD & 59 Div Inf. went over & patrol at 10 am. Enemy ↑. Patrol did not succeed. Otherwise quiet day	

Army Form C. 2118.

WAR DIARY
or
INTELLIGENCE SUMMARY.
(Erase heading not required.)

Instructions regarding War Diaries and Intelligence Summaries are contained in F.S. Regs., Part II. and the Staff Manual respectively. Title pages will be prepared in manuscript.

Hour, Date, Place	Summary of Events and Information	Remarks and references to Appendices
7 Ap.	All Swps & Heavy Bty reverted to HA III Corps.	
8 Ap.	Enemy shelled St Emilie & When FAUCON all night & early morning. 6th 240 13th started wire cutting & went 5 P.I. by demonstration	
9 Ap.	2/11 Bn & 42 nd Bty attached to 1st DA & went into action night of 9/10 th Ap. A & B/211 under 240 13th. C & D/211 under 241 13th. Bty first started near APAHS. 6.00 pressing & some guns taken. Quiet day on our front. 59 th Div occupied LE VERGUIER without opposition. Consequently their proposed attack for 10 p.m. cancelled.	
10 Ap.	Quiet day. Snow storm & high wind.	
11 Ap. 4.30 am 5 am	146 13th occupied cross roads F 29 b 05 59th Div advanced to Pouncy & L 5 d & took 2 MGs. but were driven out by a counterattack later.	

WAR DIARY
or
INTELLIGENCE SUMMARY.

(Erase heading not required.)

Army Form C. 2118.

Hour, Date, Place	Summary of Events and Information	Remarks and references to Appendices
12 Ap.	Snow & high wind	
7.45 pm	VIII Div attacked enemy front line	
9 pm	125 Bde. 42" Bde (attacked) advanced to No 12 COPSE & RED HOUSES & occupied both with little opposition	
13 Ap. 4 am	144 Bde attacked enemy front line from cross roads F 29 b 99 L- opposite START FARM Successful – 7 prisoners & 1 MG captures. Our casualties about 60. Enemy counter attacks twice with no success. Rest of day some shelling of captured line by the enemy – but we retained	
14 Ap.	Quiet day, fine weather but strong wind	
15 Ap.	59 Bde attack on VILLARET - Successful all objectives taken. A/211 & B/211 Artil. to 59th BDA.	
16 Ap. 10 pm	Quiet day – preparing for Inf. attack at night. 143 Inf Bde attacked the line LITTLE PRIEL FARM – CATELET former place – 241 Bde cooperating 143 got the high ground of X 21 a & CATELET Copse & 6 500 x S of but Enemy hole up a good deal of resistance.	

Forms/C. 2118/10

WAR DIARY or INTELLIGENCE SUMMARY

Army Form C. 2118.

Hour, Date, Place	Summary of Events and Information	Remarks and references to Appendices
16 Ap. 11.30 pm	1/5 13th attacks thelua GILLEMONT FARM — TOMBOIS FARM with 143 Bde. 2 Coys Co-operated. Attack on GILLEMONT pushed on to GILLEMONT FM. taken. Enemy put up heavy barrage on our trenches on right & on Inf could not leave them. 1/5 took 3 prisoners & 3 M Gs in TOMBOIS	Attack on GILLEMONT to Connect with TOMBOIS FM — TOMBOIS FM right & on Inf in TOMBOIS
17 Ap.	Quiet day.	
18 Ap.	Attack postponed on GILLEMONT FARM postponed owing to bad light	
19 Ap. 7.30 pm	Attack on Gillemont Farm by Oxfords failed	
20 Ap.	50 Bde attacks GONNELIEU & occupied it — Taking 2 Off & 30 OR. prisoners	
21 Ap.	Quiet day	
22 Ap.	1 Sect Each of A 240 & 13/24 pushes forward kept wire in front of Enemy trenches by GILLEMONT FARM & 140 Lewis tms in A76 & F12a	
23 Ap.	RA HQ moved to QUARRY K11a 7.5. C/221 moved up to Valley between RONSSOY & EPEHY. Registering by all BAs for attack by 144 Inf Bde next day.	

Army Form C. 2118.

WAR DIARY
or
INTELLIGENCE SUMMARY.
(Erase heading not required.)

Instructions regarding War Diaries and Intelligence Summaries are contained in F.S. Regs., Part II. and the Staff Manual respectively. Title pages will be prepared in manuscript.

Hour, Date, Place	Summary of Events and Information	Remarks and references to Appendices
24 Ap 3.45 am	144 Inf Bde attacked GILLEMONT FARM & captured it. Later were driven out by counter attack preceded by very heavy M.G. fire	
	144 Inf Bde also attacked THE KNOLL N. of above – attack failed	
	125 Inf Bde captured the high ground in X 29 d & took 1 MG.	
11 p.m.	144 Inf Bde renewed the attack on the GILLEMONT FARM & THE KNOLL 126 Inf Bde cooperating with latter. Our Inf advanced behind a barrage put up by 46 Divn Arty. Attack successful	
25 Ap 9 a.m.	Situation on KNOLL obscure but we & the enemy could after which were on each side of it. At 7 a.m. enemy counter attacked GILLEMONT FARM about 60 m east of our damage & lost heavily. Our post E of the farm fell back to E 4 corner of the farm. Rest of day AM Shells behind GILLEMONT & The KNOLL, also at night.	
26 Ap	Our Inf by consolidating. Attack prepared to take Copse in A 19 a.	
27 Ap 3.55 am	145 Bde attacked Copse in A 19 a. Wd hill 59 yds attacked quarry & Ry Embankment E of HARGICOURT. 59th opposition gained	
	145 Bde Inf any strong opposition did not press the attack.	

Army Form C. 2118

WAR DIARY
or
INTELLIGENCE SUMMARY
(Erase heading not required.)

Instructions regarding War Diaries and Intelligence Summaries are contained in F. S. Regs., Part II. and the Staff Manual respectively. Title Pages will be prepared in manuscript.

Place	Date	Hour	Summary of Events and Information	Remarks and references to Appendices
	28 Ap		Quiet day	
	29 Ap	8.30 pm	Relief of 40th DA by 42nd DA began - 1 section for BM relieved from B/240 & C/240 who remain in action under 42 DA. C/240 & D/240 ordered to go into action in 59th DA area, sent 1 pair each.	
			Section taking over from B/240 & D/240 (42nd DA) who went to 42nd DA.	
		6 pm	During the day B/240 position was shelled – no damage. 42nd DA bombarded KNOLL & VENDHUILE in schedule for artillery of ROUSSOY.	
	30 Ap	8.30 pm	Relief continues. Quiet day	

1875 Wt. W593/826 1,000,000 4/15 J.B.C. & A. A.D.S.S./Forms/C.2118.

Original

Vol 27

Confidential War Diary

of

48th Divisional Artillery Head Quarters

from 1st to 31st May 1917

Volume XXXIV

1/6/17

Major
Bde Major R.A. 48 Divn

Army Form C. 2118

Headquarters 48th Divisional Artillery

WAR DIARY or INTELLIGENCE SUMMARY

1st to 31st May 1917

Volume XXXIV

(Erase heading not required.)

Place	Date	Hour	Summary of Events and Information	Remarks and references to Appendices
	1 May	12 noon	Relief complete of 48th DA by 42nd DA. Quiet day.	
	2 May	10 am	CRA 42nd Div took over command from CRA 48th Div. HQRA 48th Div moved to TINCOURT. B&C/240 left in action under 42 DA. C&D/241 in action under 59th DA. Remainder at TINCOURT & MARQUAIX in rest.	
	3 May		Disposition as for 2nd May.	
	4 May		" " " "	
	5 May		" " " "	
	6 May		" " " "	
	7 May		Quiet day. " " " T.M. Batt. Off. C/Vaux X to the School of Instruction.	
	8 May		A/240 B/240 went into action in 42 Div Area & were tactically under O.C. 295" Bde (59th Div)	
			A/241 B/241 " " " " 59" " " " O.C. 296 " "	
			Rained all day.	
	9 May		C.R.A. left 4.30 pm, 16 hrs GOCRA 8th Corps.	
	10		59th Div Shoot off. B&C/240 went out of action & moved to Thilly waggon lines C & D/241 " " " " " " " " "	

Proportion of DAC for Horse Batteries forwarded to B.D.I.A.E.

Army Form C. 2118

WAR DIARY
or
INTELLIGENCE SUMMARY
(Erase heading not required.)

Instructions regarding War Diaries and Intelligence Summaries are contained in F. S. Regs., Part II. and the Staff Manual respectively. Title Pages will be prepared in manuscript.

Place	Date	Hour	Summary of Events and Information	Remarks and references to Appendices
	MAY 11		Batteries (with the exception of 1 section of B/240) limber 4.2" D.A. with drawn to their wagon lines. A & B/241 with drawn to their wagon lines – Proportion of one gun team proceeds to RUE.	
	12		Section of B/240 came out of action & proceeds to their wagon lines.	
	13		Quiet day nothing to report.	
	14		"	
	15		O.C's Bdes went over to "M" area to reconnoitre.	
	16		The D.A. moved to "M" area. Both Bdes + HQRA at BEUKENCOURT. D.A.Q. N.24 Central	
			Trench mortars returned from 4th Army School.	
	17		Battery commanders reconnoitred their positions	
	18		All batteries moved up to VELU. Two sections from each battery went into the line & took over from 1st Anzacs. Bde. H.Q. remained at BEURENCOURT.	
	19		Bdes took over from 1st Anzacs in the line. Remaining sections went into action.	
			24 D.13th J.H.Q. moved to J.20.c.98.	

WAR DIARY or INTELLIGENCE SUMMARY

Place	Date	Hour	Summary of Events and Information	Remarks and references to Appendices
	20 May	6am	GOCRA assumed command of RA - taking over from GOCRA 1st Army Div.	
	21 May		Quiet day. Orders recd from Div that guns will be sent to MAURICOURT and QUEANT by Spec. Coy R.E. at 2am on 22nd. All transport to...	
	22 May		Quiet day	
	23 May			
	24 May	9pm	A741 was withdrawn from a line wide reserve - the ready to reinforce any group of them a sect. really one hour before dawn daily 1-4°. In position to engage tanks.	
	25 May		RAHQ moved to near HAPLINCOURT - guns of 13th Army F.A. Bde. knocked out by enemy - no casualties.	
	26 May		D/240 moved position to J35 a 52 - 7MS shelled end of BEAUMETZ 2 killed - 7MS shelled end of BEAUMETZ	
	27 May	7am	4/13 - 13th Bde heavily shelled - from 3 un knocked out & 1 officer killed (Lt MAITLAND) / Off. wounded (Lt CHASE)	
	28 May		4/Army Bde in action by 113th Army How Bde J7c	

Army Form C. 2118

Army Form C. 2118.

WAR DIARY
or
INTELLIGENCE SUMMARY.
(Erase heading not required.)

Instructions regarding War Diaries and Intelligence Summaries are contained in F. S. Regs., Part II. and the Staff Manual respectively. Title pages will be prepared in manuscript.

Place	Date	Hour	Summary of Events and Information	Remarks and references to Appendices
	29 May		B/241 heavily shelled no damage. C/241 also shelled 1 gun damaged.	
	30 May		51st & 18th Ams (A.13th & one sect 45 How AFA were withdrawn from action	
	31 May		B/241 moved 1 sect to just W of Downes. C/241 1 sect to 1000x SW of LONGCRUN FARM. Quiet day.	

Original

Vol 28

Confidential War Diary

of

48th Divisional Artillery Headquarters

from 1st to 30th June 1917

Volume XXXV

30/6/17

Lyon
Major
Bde Major RA 48 Div

Army Form C. 2118.

Headquarters 48th Division 145 WAR DIARY or INTELLIGENCE SUMMARY. 1st to 30th June 1917

Volume XXXV (Erase heading not required.)

Instructions regarding War Diaries and Intelligence Summaries are contained in F. S. Regs., Part II. and the Staff Manual respectively. Title pages will be prepared in manuscript.

Place	Date	Hour	Summary of Events and Information	Remarks and references to Appendices
	1 June		Quiet day	
	2 June	12 noon	Artillery formed into 2 groups under Lt Col Eastwood (Right) & Lt Col Colville (Left). HQ 13th Aus. Bde. withdrawn. B/241 heavily shelled in a.m. & moved 1 sec. to J.14.d at night. B/240 no heavy shells. Lt. H.B. BARNES wounded & to hosp.	
	3 June		Lt BARNES died of wounds in hosp. "Quiet day."	
	4 June		Quiet day	
	5 June		Quiet day	
	6 June		Quiet day	
	7 June	8 pm	49th Bde shelled near MORCHIES - no casualties. 145 Bde raided enemy post by CANAL. 8 prisoners taken, 10 killed & post established. Our casualties 1 killed, 240 damaged for this attack. 8 wounded.	
	8 June		Quiet day	
	9 June		Quiet day	
	10 June		49. Bde (AFA) shelled 1 gun, A/241 2 guns C/240 2 guns into forward positions for wire cutting etc. in preparation for Chinese attack on night of 11/12 June. Chinese attack postponed.	
	11 June			
	12 June		Wire cutting test of 49th Am Bde & between J C. B/241 shelled - no casualties.	

WAR DIARY
or
INTELLIGENCE SUMMARY.
(Erase heading not required.)

Army Form C. 2118.

Instructions regarding War Diaries and Intelligence Summaries are contained in F.S. Regs., Part II. and the Staff Manual respectively. Title pages will be prepared in manuscript.

Place	Date	Hour	Summary of Events and Information	Remarks and references to Appendices
	13 June		Quiet day	
	14 June		Lost 13/241 shells - no damage. 48 SBA bombarded enemy front line as demonstration during V Corps attack on left.	
	15 June		Quiet day.	
	16 June		All day bombardment of trench in HAVRINCOURT area by 9.45 TMs & 45/how MIF & 42nd STA/Howrs. Excellent results.	
	17 June			
	18 June		Quiet day	
	19 June	1 am	Raid by 143 Bde v. successful. 10 PR. 7 O.R. taken prisoners. Order rec'd for relief of 48 SBA by 1st Aus. STA. R to be completed by night 23/24 June. Quiet day.	
	20 June		Quiet day. Raid at midnight by enemy repulsed by left 13th 14S 13th. 1 prisoner taken.	
	21 June		B/pdrs + D/pdrs shells. No casualties. BC of 1st Aus Div Art came up.	
	22 June	1 am	Raid by 143 Inf Bde on post in COPSE D.15c - unsuccessful. 2 O.Rs taken prisoner. 6 O.R. killed. Relief of 2 sects of Bty of 48 SBA by ditto of 1st Aus STA.	
	23 June	11 pm		
		11 pm	Relief of 48 SBA by 1st Aus. STA complete	

Army Form C. 2118.

WAR DIARY
or
INTELLIGENCE SUMMARY.
(Erase heading not required.)

Instructions regarding War Diaries and Intelligence Summaries are contained in F. S. Regs., Part II. and the Staff Manual respectively. Title pages will be prepared in manuscript.

Place	Date	Hour	Summary of Events and Information	Remarks and references to Appendices
	24 June	10 am	At command passed to C.R.A. 1st Aus Div A.L.	
			156 Div Art marched to the MONTAUBAN area. RAHQ opens at LOZENGE WOOD X27b 52	
	25 June to 30 June		156th RA returns to MONTAUBAN area	
			RA HQ at LOZENGE WOOD X27b 52.	

Duplicate

Confidential War Diary
of
48th Divisional Arty HeadQuarters

From 1st to 31st July, 1917

Volume XXXVI

La C L Lyon.
Major
Brigade Major R.A. 48th Division

Headquarters 48th Divisional Artillery

WAR DIARY
or
INTELLIGENCE SUMMARY

Army Form C. 2118

Volume XXXVI 1st to 31st July 1917

Instructions regarding War Diaries and Intelligence Summaries are contained in F.S. Regs., Part II. and the Staff Manual respectively. Title Pages will be prepared in manuscript.

Place	Date	Hour	Summary of Events and Information	Remarks and references to Appendices
	1 July to 4 July		48th Div Art resting in MONTAUBAN area — Ratio at LOZENGE WOOD X 27 b 53	
	5 July		48th D.A. marched to ENGLEBELMER T.M.S by train to 39th D.A.	
	6 July		48th D.A. " SARTON & THIEVRES	
	7 July		marched to REBREUVE area	
	8 July		marched to ST POL area (ROUCOURT, RANNECOURT ← ST MICHEL)	
	9 July		Rested	
	10 July		marched AMES AMETTES & NIEDERCHELU	
	11 July		marched to AIRE area	
	12 July		marched to STAPLE & WALLON CAPPEL	
	13 July		marched to GODEWAERSVELDE	
	14 July		all Bties & B.A.C marched to wagon lines in POPERINGHE — WESTAAN area	
			2nd Bde went into action with 39th D.A. (Gen D/169)	

Army Form C. 2118

WAR DIARY
or
INTELLIGENCE SUMMARY
(Erase heading not required.)

Instructions regarding War Diaries and Intelligence Summaries are contained in F. S. Regs., Part II. and the Staff Manual respectively. Title Pages will be prepared in manuscript.

R.H. & R.G.A. Records Section
8 - MAR 1919
WOOLWICH

Place	Date	Hour	Summary of Events and Information	Remarks and references to Appendices
	15 July		240 Bde went into action under 39 BDA - Troops remained in wagon lines	
	16 July		Heavy A/A bombardment began 18/40 registers	
	17 July		D/241 and 3 Hows into action	
	18 July		Remainder of D/241 went into action.	
	19 July		D/241 lost 2 Hows & 1 killed 5 wounded	
	20 July / 21 July		Bombardment continued.	
	22 July			
	23 July		D/240 shelled out & withdrawn. 3 Hows destroyed 1 killed 4 wounded	
	24 July		C/241 killed Lt J. HAMILTON badly wounded 3 O.R. slightly	
	25 July		Bombardment continues. 2 day postponed	
	26 July		RA/149 HQ came up to G.6.L. near 39 BDA	
	27 July		Various bombardments carried out	
	28 July 5 am		Chinese attack on Coy front. D/241 heavily shelled during night & am "blown up"	
	29 July		D/240 went up into action again. Heavy thunderstorm	

1875. Wt. W593/826 1,000,000 4/15 J.B.C. & A. A.D.S.S./Forms/C. 2118.

WAR DIARY
or
INTELLIGENCE SUMMARY
(Erase heading not required.)

Army Form C. 2118

Instructions regarding War Diaries and Intelligence Summaries are contained in F.S. Regs., Part II and the Staff Manual respectively. Title Pages will be prepared in manuscript.

Place	Date	Hour	Summary of Events and Information	Remarks and references to Appendices
	30 July	Y Day	4-5 Hour bombards all known hostile Bty's within range all night.	
	31 July	Z Day	Zero 3.50 am. 5th Army + French attacked. On 39th Front the attack was successful. All objectives being taken up to time. During aftn. the green line was lost by counter attack + our Inf. remained on line of ST JULIEN - GRAVEL t. journey. 241 Bde moved to N. of ST JULIEN + Lt. 240 Bde moved to S. of HILL TOP. Casualties during day. 2/Lt CRANE D/240 killed. 2/Lt FORSYTH(D/241)+ 4/BATTENBERG wounded, about 20 O.R. wounded. Prisoners taken by 39 Div. about 1500. 4 77 mm guns 1 + 2 How.	

R.H. & R.F.A. Records Office
8 - MAR 1919
WOOLWICH

XVIII Corps

Duplicate.

Confidential War Diary
of
48th Divisional Arty Head Quarters

From 1st to 31st August, 1917

Volume XXXVII

G. C. Lyon. Major
Brigade Major R.A. 48th Div'n

WAR DIARY
or
INTELLIGENCE SUMMARY.
(Erase heading not required.)

Army Form C. 2118.

Hour, Date, Place	Summary of Events and Information	Remarks and references to Appendices
1 Aug	Heavy Rain - all ground soaked - muddy - Boche counter attacks on 2nd JUNCTION were to form-up positions for continuation were taken but by night our Inf were clear of ST JULIEN AREA	
2 Aug	Heavy rain all day - Country becomes impassable. 34 Bty showing signs of new found position in No man's land near HAMPSHIRE FARM - preparing the withdrawal	
3 Aug	A/155 moved up to position SW of MONSTRAAT. Hq 241 relieved by Hq 240 Coy 81 Bty wounded. C battery of 122 R.H. relieved personnel of 72° (34-231)	
4 Aug	Boche bombed CANOPUS TR all day - room in Lord Kitchener Col CURLEY slightly wounded	
5 Aug	Fitful bombardment to Inf actions health improving	
6 Aug 10 am	L/Bdr + M/Bdr took over from 39 Bn + Hq RA Inf relief completed during B right - all falls 13th returned in order. Weather fine + ground getting harder Col CLIFFORD (126 Bde) put in command of 34 + 13 Bn temporarily	

WAR DIARY
or
INTELLIGENCE SUMMARY.
(Erase heading not required.)

Army Form C. 2118.
8 - MAR 1919
WOOLWICH

Hour, Date, Place	Summary of Events and Information	Remarks and references to Appendices
7 Aug	HQ 241 relieved HQ 240 in HILL TOP - 34 Bde Hqrs registered from new positions	
8 Aug	HQ 186 Bde to LA BELLE ALLIANCE - one Bty moved up to no man's land - also C/155 HQ +personnel of 34 Bde relieved HQ +personnel of 174 Bde (7.9) later to W.L.	
9 Aug	Major C.W. Todd + Lieut Fullerton A/240 killed	
10 Aug. 4.35 am	Bombardment by 48 D.A. fronts in conjunction with Operations by II Corps further South.	
11 Aug 10 am	48 D.A. fronts reorganised into 3 Groups - Rt Group (174 Bde +155) Lt Col Allanbye Centre Group (240 +241 Bde) Lt Col Colville left Group (186 +34 Bde) Lt. Col Kilner.	

WAR DIARY
or
INTELLIGENCE SUMMARY.
(Erase heading not required.)

Army Form C. 2118.

Instructions regarding War Diaries and Intelligence Summaries are contained in F.S. Regs., Part II. and the Staff Manual respectively. Title pages will be prepared in manuscript.

Place	Date	Hour	Summary of Events and Information	Remarks and references to Appendices
	11 Aug	3 pm	C.R.A. held Group commanders conference at R.A. H.Q.	
	12 Aug	5 pm	C.R.A. attended conference at XVIII Corps R.A. Heavy rain fell in the evening. C/166 moved up to forward position just short of O.6.2 on night of 12/13.	
	13 Aug		D/166 moved up to forward position. just short of no mans land - on night of 13/14. During the day enemy counter btys very active.	
	14 Aug	7 pm	Practice barrage carried out at 7 pm. Having gun at old positions of 155 Bde moved up to join their btys in forward positions on night of 14/15.	

Army Form C. 2118.

WAR DIARY
or
INTELLIGENCE SUMMARY.
(Erase heading not required.)

Instructions regarding War Diaries and Intelligence Summaries are contained in F.S. Regs., Part II. and the Staff Manual respectively. Title Pages will be prepared in manuscript.

Place	Date	Hour	Summary of Events and Information	Remarks and references to Appendices
August	15"	3 pm	Practise barrage carried out.	
	16"	4.45am	Div HQ opened at Albemarle H.Q. (C25d1530)	
		Zero hour	Barrage started well - all guns together	
			145"B'de attacked on Buit front	
			Situation rumoured serene at 6 am.	
			145 B'de relieved by 143/144 B'de - the latter working out towards 6	
		2.30am	Wires available from DO HiBou when own S.I. shrapnel barrage	
			by us - but were knocked out.	
	17"		Harassing fire kept up on all enemy approaches & communication during the day/night.	
	18"	4 pm	All available 18 Phr fired practise smoke barrage	
	19"		In the early morning our hy arty cooperating with Tanks in an attack on MON DU HiBOU, HILLOCK WMS, these being fd - we entirely successful attacking in the own barrage. Smoke screen was placed on hostile O.Ps.	

WAR DIARY or INTELLIGENCE SUMMARY

Army Form C. 2118.

(Erase heading not required.)

Instructions regarding War Diaries and Intelligence Summaries are contained in F.S. Regs., Part II. and the Staff Manual respectively. Title Pages will be prepared in manuscript.

Place	Date	Hour	Summary of Events and Information	Remarks and references to Appendices
August	20.		One sect of 23rd D.A. relieved one sect 39th D.A. - other guns being handed over in situ.	
	21.		Remaining sects of 23rd D.A. relieved remaining sections of 39th D.A. in action. Bank command passed at 5pm Lt Col Bethom. Thornhill DSO taking command of Rt bank - Lt Col Grove DSO taking command of left bank. 39th D.A. on relief proceeded to their W.L.	
	22nd	4.45	An attack on the SPRINGH16GD - WIN11239 Road & retaining the Wilton was launched at that hour - tanks co-operating - owing to the failure of the Tanks to reach their objectives the attack was not successful - 14th Division in 150° about of them together	
	23rd		Night of 22/23rd D/402 moved 4 guns forward to northern SW of MOUSE TRAP FARM	

WAR DIARY or INTELLIGENCE SUMMARY

Army Form C. 2118.

(Erase heading not required.)

Instructions regarding War Diaries and Intelligence Summaries are contained in F. S. Regs., Part II. and the Staff Manual respectively. Title Pages will be prepared in manuscript.

Stamp: B.H. & R.F.A. Records — 8 MAR 1919 — WOOLWICH

Place	Date	Hour	Summary of Events and Information	Remarks and references to Appendices
Yupt	24"		B+C 102 moved 1 sect each forward to position W of MOUSE TRAP FARM during the night 9.23p.m.	
	25"		On night of 24/25 R.S.C. 172 Bde completed more movement. B+C 241 Bde moved 1 step forward also A+D 102 during night of 25/26. All forward were completed	
	26	4 pm 4.30 pm	from the true being - 102 Bde + 172 Bde all being a forward position with 11 D.A. + 61st D.A. Penetrated trenches + hostages with 11 D.A. + 61st D.A. Heavy rain fell during the evening	
	27	1.55 pm	Zero hour of attack. UNCOUVER + SPRINGFIELD captured - strewn not and fallen they not + guard way had	
	28"		Guns consolidated gains day	

WAR DIARY
or
INTELLIGENCE SUMMARY

(Erase heading not required.)

Army Form C. 2118.

R.H. & R.A. Record Office
8 - MAR 1919
WOOLWICH

Place	Date	Hour	Summary of Events and Information	Remarks and references to Appendices
	29th		56th Bde relieved 62th Bde. RAHQ 23rd Bde relieved RAHQ 40th Bde. HQ 4.C. HQRA to WORMHOUDT 240 & 241 Bdes remained in station number	
	22nd Bde			
	30th		RAHQ at WORMHOUDT	
	31st		Ditto	

[signature]

WAR DIARY
or
INTELLIGENCE SUMMARY.

(Erase heading not required.)

Army Form C. 2118.

R.H. & R.F.A. 8 - MAR. 1919 WOOLWICH

Place	Date	Hour	Summary of Events and Information	Remarks and references to Appendices
	7 Aug.		HQ 241 returned HQ 240 in MILTOP – 34th Bde BHQ registers from new positions.	
	8 Aug		HQ 166 Bde to DELLE ALLIANCE – one Bhq 168 moved up to new map Lane also C/153. HQ + personnel of 34th Bde relieved HQ + personnel of 174 & 13 Bde (F.G.) with waggon lines.	
	9 Aug		Major TODD & Lt FULLERTON A/240 killed.	
	10 Aug	4.35am	Bombardment by 48 DA-Group in conjunction with operations by II Corps further South. Group commanders conference at R.A. H.Q.	

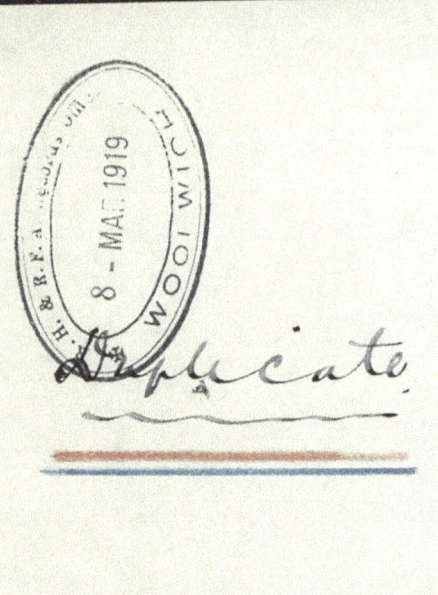

Duplicate

48th Divisional Artillery War Diary

From 1st September, 1917

To 30th September, 1917

L. Lyon. Major R.A.
Brigade Major R.A. 48th Divl Arty

30th Sept 1917.

WAR DIARY
or
INTELLIGENCE SUMMARY

(Erase heading not required.)

Army Form C. 2118.

Instructions regarding War Diaries and Intelligence Summaries are contained in F. S. Regs., Part II. and the Staff Manual respectively. Title Pages will be prepared in manuscript.

Place	Date	Hour	Summary of Events and Information	Remarks and references to Appendices
	1st Sept to 3rd Sept		RAHQ at WORMHOUDT — 23rd & 24th Bdes in action until 2nd Sept. 5th Bde	
	4 Sept		Ditto	
			IN 5th Bde took over from J.H.P.R.A. 23rd Bde — Latter went out to DROOGENTAK for R.	
	5 Sept to 16 Sept		RAHQ at WORMHOUDT	
	17th		RAHQ moved to POLINCOVE	
	18th to 26th		RAHQ moved to LANDRETHUN	
	26		RAHQ moved to BRAKE CAMP G 66	
	27		Relief of 5th Bde by 18th Bde Art began	
	28	10 am	IN 5th Bde & 24 RA took over from 5th Bde 1st HPRA. Relief of 18thBdeArt by 18thBdeArt finished. 5th Bde Art concentrated in wagon lines & marched to C Camp G 66	
			S.C.R.A. accompanies Bde Art 1H RA remained at C Camp G 66	
			1st Lt Bde	

Army Form C. 2118.

WAR DIARY
or
INTELLIGENCE SUMMARY
(Erase heading not required.)

Place	Date	Hour	Summary of Events and Information	Remarks and references to Appendices
	Sept 29		Quiet day - R & L group B4's began to move up near ST JULIAN. 1 sect. per B4y of S.B4y completed by midnight.	
	30"		Moving up of R & L group B4's continued - owed enemy artillery to concentrate battery work	

Signature

8 - MAR 1919
WOOLWICH
R.H. & R.F.A. Records...

48th Divisional Artillery
War Diary.

From 1st October, 1917.

To 31st October, 1917.

VOLUME XXXIX

D.D. Bassett Lt.
Jnr. Major R.A.

Brigade Major R.A. 48th Division

31st October, 1917

Army Form C. 2118.

WAR DIARY
or
INTELLIGENCE SUMMARY
(Erase heading not required.)

Instructions regarding War Diaries and Intelligence Summaries are contained in F.S. Regs., Part II. and the Staff Manual respectively. Title Pages will be prepared in manuscript.

Place	Date	Hour	Summary of Events and Information	Remarks and references to Appendices
	1917 Oct.		Usual counter Bty work by us & enemy - 'Quietish day' - Forward move of Btys continued	
	2 Oct		All Bty's in & amougst ammunition up - rain in night	
	3 Oct		Quiet day. R.F.H.Q. moved up to CANAL BANK H.Q. - weather cloudy 2 NZ Fire 143 Inf Bde relieved 143 Inf Bde	
	4 Oct	6 am	Zero hour. 143 Inf Bde attacked with 5th 6th & 7th Warwick - 2nd Worcesters in reserve. 1st Objective gained up to time 6.41 am Advance proceeded and second objective gained. Exact BURNS H.Q. & VATCHER F.M. at F 38 am. Very high wind + some rain. BURNS H.Q. not taken - ground rough About 200 prisoners taken	
		8—	Total prisoners 333 + 9 MGs & 2 anti tank guns	
	5 Oct	6	Some new Btys began to move up. Our D.A. relieved the 9th D.A. in the line, under 3rd Aust Div 2nd ANZAC CORPS	
	6 Oct		Quiet day, rear battery positions continue to move up	
	7 Oct	"	" Very wet.	
	8 Oct	"	"	

WAR DIARY
~~INTELLIGENCE SUMMARY~~
(Erase heading not required.)

Army Form C. 2118.

Hour, Date, Place	Summary of Events and Information	Remarks and references to Appendices
1917		
9th Oct 5.20am	Zeestraat. 144th Bde attacked the gun line.	
10"	Nothing to Rept. 50th Bde relieves the 82nd Bde	
11" 10am	48th hand over to 9th Div at CANAL BANK, 48th Div move to "X" Camp AIBCSS	
12"	Nothing to report.	
13"	48th Div HQ & two artillery bdes by rail to PERNES to 1st Corps area	
	Our guns withdraw to wagon lines + come under orders from CRA 48th Div on the night	
	B 13"/14".	
14"	48th Div Arty now to EECKE AREA –	
15"	" " " " – MORBECQUE.	
16"	" " " " – BETHUNE AREA.	
17"	" " " " – Wagon Lines ABLAINES-ST-NAZAIRES – CRA's HQ to FORT GEORGE, near front St ELOI.	
18"	48th Div bde artillery taking over from the 2nd Canadian Div in the line. (South of LENS)	
	Three batteries 2nd Canadian D.A. night 18/19" remaining section	

WAR DIARY or INTELLIGENCE SUMMARY

Army Form C. 2118

(Erase heading not required.)

Instructions regarding War Diaries and Intelligence Summaries are contained in F.S. Regs., Part II. and the Staff Manual respectively. Title Pages will be prepared in manuscript.

Place	Date	Hour	Summary of Events and Information	Remarks and references to Appendices
	Oct 19"		on the night 19"/20"	
	Oct 20"	10am	48" D.A. take over from 2nd Canadian D.A. 8" C.F.A. Bde left under Command of CRA 48 Divn on taking in the line with each Bde - remainder at wagon Lines. Quiet day. relief completed satisfactorily.	
	Oct 21st		Light firing carried out as per programme. Hostile artillery very quiet and little movement observed.	
	Oct 22"		Light firing carried out - very quiet day.	
	Oct 23"		R.A.H.Q. move back to VILLERS - aust Bdes to join the Divisions - DAC moved to new wagon Lines at LA TARGETTE + 2+0 Bde moved to wagon Lines L-A7L and 54.1 Bde to A.1.b. G.O.C's Conference at Fort GEORGE.	
	Oct 24"		H.Q 2 32" Army F.A. Bde - Relieves the 8" Can F.A. Bde - who proceed to the Can Corps.	
	Oct 25"		232" A.F.A Bde H.Q. ST ELOY - and batteries in wagon Lines at A7a.	

1875 Wt. W593/826 1,000,000 4/15 J.B.C. & A. A.D.S.S./Forms/C. 2118.

Army Form C. 2118.

WAR DIARY
or
INTELLIGENCE SUMMARY.
(Erase heading not required.)

Instructions regarding War Diaries and Intelligence Summaries are contained in F.S. Regs., Part II. and the Staff Manual respectively. Title pages will be prepared in manuscript.

Hour, Date, Place	Summary of Events and Information	Remarks and references to Appendices
Oct 26"	Slight firing carried out - front very quiet.	
" 27"	Enemy trolling him a sniping section prevent.	
" 28"	Very quiet - some night firing - ants movement Egypt.	"
" 29"	" " " " "	"
" 30"	Very Quiet.	"
" 31"	" nothing to report.	"

RBunge Lt

DUPLICATE
WAR DIARY

48TH DIVISIONAL ARTILLERY

From 1st October 1917

To 31st October 1917

WAR DIARY
or
INTELLIGENCE SUMMARY.
(Erase heading not required.)

1917 Hour, Date, Place	Summary of Events and Information	Remarks and references to Appendices
1st Oct	Wind [?] R.H. work by us to [?] — [?] flag [?] [?]	
	of 13th continues	
2nd Oct	All B#ys in & amust ammunition up — 2cm in right	
3rd Oct	Quiet day. R.A.H.Q. moved up to CANAL BANK H.Q.	weather cloudy
	2nd pm 143 Inf Bde relieved 145 Inf Bde	
4th Oct 6 am	Zero hour. 143rd Inf Bde attacked with 5" 6" 7" Wounds	
	in support. 1st objective gained up to time 6.41am. Casualties protected and	for Onwards
	2nd Objective gained. Except BURNS Ho. & VACHER FM at 6.38 am	
	About 200 prisoners taken. Very high words & some rain. BURNS Ho not taken - Quiet night	
5pm	Total prisoners 333 + 9 MGs + 2 anti-tank guns.	
5th &	Own D.A. [?] B#ys begin to move up.	
6th Oct	Own D.A. relieves the 9th D.A. in the line. Ammunition from 3rd Anti-tank Div	2" Anzac Corps
	Quiet day. New battery positions continued to move up	
7th Oct	,, Very wet.	
8th Oct	,, ,,	

WAR DIARY
or
INTELLIGENCE SUMMARY
(Erase heading not required.)

Place	Date	Hour	Summary of Events and Information	Remarks and references to Appendices
	1917			
	9th Oct	5.20 am	Zeppelin 104th Bde attacked the front line	
	10"		Nothing to Rpt. [30th Bde relieved the 82nd Bde	
	10"	10 am	48th Recd over to 9th Div at CINNAH BANK. 48th Div move to "X" Camp AIRCES	
	11"			
	12"		Nothing to report	
	13"		48" Div Hd Qrs Artillery moves by rail to PERNES 1st Corps area	
			Own Guns withdraws to wagon lines & come in the orders from CRA 48" Div on the right	
		8.15/14"		
	14"		48" Div HQrs move to ECKRE AREA –	
	15"		" " – MORBECQUE	
	16"		" " – BETHUNE AREA.	
	17"		" " – bugs line MOLINNES - ST. NAZAIRES - ST. ELOI.	
			GEORGE, near hurst St Eloi.	
	18"		48" Div has Artillery letter over from the 2nd Canadian Div on the line	
			(South of LENS) – CRA's HQ to FORT	

WAR DIARY or INTELLIGENCE SUMMARY

(Erase heading not required.)

Army Form C. 2118

Place	Date	Hour	Summary of Events and Information	Remarks and references to Appendices
	Oct 19		On the night 19/20	
		10 am	4.3" D.A. take over from 2nd Canadian D.A. 8" C.F.A. Bde left under Command of C.R.A. 4th Divn. One Battery in the line with each Bde. Remainder at Wagon lines.	
	Oct 20		Quiet day. Relief completed satisfactorily.	
	Oct 21st		Light firing. Carried out as per programme. Hostile artillery very quiet and little movement observed.	
	Oct 22		Light firing carried out - very quiet day	
	Oct 23		R.H.Q. moved back to VILLERS-aux-BOIS to join the Division. D.A.C. moved to new wagon lines at LA TARGETTE and 240 Bde moved wagon lines to A.7.b. and 24.1 Bde to A.1.b. C.O.'s Conference at Fort GEORGE	
	Oct 24		The 232 "Army" F.A. Bde - relieves the 5" Can. F.A. Bde - who proceed to 1st Cav. Corps.	
	Oct 25		232 a F.A. Bde HQ ST ELOY. and batteries in wagon lines at 197a	

Army Form C. 2118.

WAR DIARY
or
INTELLIGENCE SUMMARY.
(Erase heading not required)

Instructions regarding War Diaries and Intelligence Summaries are contained in F. S. Regs., Part II. and the Staff Manual respectively. Title pages will be prepared in manuscript.

Place	Date	Hour	Summary of Events and Information	Remarks and references to Appendices
Oct	26"		hostile forces cannot not - front very quiet	
"	27"		Enemy trying him a bombing section forward	
"	28"		very quiet - some night firing - and movement tps	
"	29"		" "	
"	30"		very quiet -	
"	31"		nothing to report.	

R.R.Bennett